MCSD
Architectures

Donald R. Brandt

MCSD Architectures Exam Cram
© 1999 The Coriolis Group. All Rights Reserved.

Limits Of Liability And Disclaimer Of Warranty

Trademarks

The Coriolis Group, LLC
14455 N. Hayden Road, Suite 220
Scottsdale, Arizona 85260

480/483-0192
FAX 480/483-0193
http://www.coriolis.com

Library of Congress Cataloging-in-Publication Data
Brandt, Donald
    MCSD architectures exam cram / Donald Brandt.
      p. cm.
    ISBN 1-57610-378-1
    1. Electronic data processing personnel--Certification. 2. Microsoft software--Examinations study guides. 3. Computer architecture I. Title.
QA76.3.B73 1999
004.2'2--dc21   99-23865
                                                          CIP

Printed in the United States of America
10 9 8 7 6 5 4 3 2 1

President, CEO
Keith Weiskamp

Publisher
Steve Sayre

Acquisitions Editor
Shari Jo Hehr

Marketing Specialist
Cynthia Caldwell

Project Editor
Michelle Stroup

Technical Reviewer
Tom Sandberg

Production Coordinator
Jon Gabriel

Cover Design
Jesse Dunn

Layout Design
April Nielsen

Coriolis: The Training And Certification Destination ™

Thank you for purchasing one of our innovative certification study guides, just one of the many members of the Coriolis family of certification products.

Certification Insider Press™ has long believed that achieving your IT certification is more of a road trip than anything else. This is why most of our readers consider us their *Training And Certification Destination*. By providing a one-stop shop for the most innovative and unique training materials, our readers know we are the first place to look when it comes to achieving their certification. As one reader put it, "I plan on using your books for all of the exams I take."

To help you reach your goals, we've listened to others like you, and we've designed our entire product line around you and the way you like to study, learn, and master challenging subjects. Our approach is *The Smartest Way To Get Certified™*.

In addition to our highly popular *Exam Cram* and *Exam Prep* guides, we have a number of new products. We recently launched Exam Cram Live!, two-day seminars based on *Exam Cram* material. We've also developed a new series of books and study aides—*Practice Tests Exam Crams* and *Exam Cram Flash Cards*—designed to make your studying fun as well as productive.

Our commitment to being the *Training And Certification Destination* does not stop there. We just introduced *Exam Cram Insider*, a biweekly newsletter containing the latest in certification news, study tips, and announcements from Certification Insider Press. (To subscribe, send an email to **eci@coriolis.com** and type "subscribe insider" in the body of the email.) We also recently announced the launch of the Certified Crammer Society and the Coriolis Help Center—two new additions to the Certification Insider Press family.

We'd like to hear from you. Help us continue to provide the very best certification study materials possible. Write us or email us at **cipq@coriolis.com** and let us know how our books have helped you study, or tell us about new features that you'd like us to add. If you send us a story about how we've helped you, and we use it in one of our books, we'll send you an official Coriolis shirt for your efforts.

Good luck with your certification exam and your career. Thank you for allowing us to help you achieve your goals.

Keith Weiskamp
President and CEO

When I first told my family I was writing a book, my children Megan and Kristopher thought it sounded like a really good idea. I don't think any of us realized the time and energy that would eventually be required, except for Jan, my wife, who just seems to know these things, and stuck by me. I would like to dedicate this book to them for supporting my effort to write it.

About The Author

Donald R. Brandt is the founder and principal consultant of Donald R. Brandt Software Consulting, where he specializes in solution architectures and database systems design and integration. Donald spends most of his consulting hours developing software and helping his clients design and implement business solutions that utilize the newer Internet and software development technologies. He has been a software engineering professional for more than thirty years and developed his first computer programs using punched cards and a keypunch.

Before starting his own company in 1994, Donald was a senior systems and software consultant for Digital Equipment Corporation where he provided technical sales support to the western region of the United States. He specialized in consulting with customers building mission-critical information processing systems. Prior to that, he was a principal engineer and manager in the Software Engineering organization at Digital Equipment Corporation, where he participated in the development of software products.

In addition to software consulting activities, Donald has recently taught courses for Microsoft Solution Developer Certification as well as courses in computer science. He has also developed several MCSD course-related guides on Visual Basic and the Microsoft Windows Architecture. He is a Microsoft Certified Professional Solution Developer, a member of the Independent Computer Consultants Association, and holds an MS degree in computer science and a BS degree in electrical engineering, both from the University of Arizona. Donald is a married father of two children, whom he supports along with numerous pets. He enjoys hiking and model trains.

Acknowledgments

Although I am the author listed for this book, a number of individuals have contributed to its development and deserve credit for making this book a reality. I would like to thank them for their assistance and support throughout this project. Although I have never met any of these people in person, I know a few by name, because they have worked directly with me.

I first met Shari Jo Hehr, the Acquisitions Editor, who discussed with me the idea of writing this book. She has supported me throughout the entire project, and was especially helpful when I needed to reorganize the project schedule.

Michelle Stroup, the Project Editor, provided the assistance I needed to get started. She explained the various editing styles and conventions and was always available when I got stuck. Michelle went out of her way to make my job of reviewing corrections as easy as possible, remaining positive throughout the project even though the end sometimes seemed to drift out of sight.

When I produced the first manuscript pages, Bonnie Smith, the Copyeditor, provided many helpful suggestions, but she was especially instrumental in showing me more creative alternatives for using the English language to express an idea. Later, Bart Reed also assisted with some of the copyediting.

Thomas Sandberg, the Technical Reviewer, provided many useful suggestions for refining some of my ideas, clarifying points where I was ambiguous and correcting places where I was simply wrong. Thomas was very helpful in providing supplemental information.

I would also like to thank those I didn't work directly with, but were instrumental in the completion of this book: Jon Gabriel, Production Coordinator; Jesse Dunn, Cover Designer; and April Nielsen, Interior Designer. Finally, I would also like to express a special thanks to those whose names I don't know. These are the managers, graphic artists, and others who worked behind the scenes at The Coriolis Group to bring this book to publication.

Contents At A Glance

Table Of Contents

Introduction

Welcome to *MCSD Architectures Exam Cram*! This book aims to help you get ready to take—and pass—the Microsoft certification test numbered 70-100, "Analyzing Requirements and Defining Solution Architectures." This Introduction explains Microsoft's certification programs in general and talks about how the *Exam Cram* series can help you prepare for Microsoft's certification exams.

Exam Cram books help you understand and appreciate the subjects and materials you need to pass Microsoft certification exams. *Exam Cram* books are aimed strictly at test preparation and review. They do not teach you everything you need to know about a topic (such as all the nitty-gritty details involved in actually developing an application). Instead, I present and dissect the questions and problems that you're likely to encounter on a test. I've worked from Microsoft's own training materials, preparation guides, and tests, as well as from a battery of third-party test preparation tools. My aim is to bring together as much information as possible about Microsoft certification exams.

Nevertheless, to completely prepare yourself for any Microsoft test, I recommend that you begin by taking the Self-Assessment included in this book immediately following this Introduction. This tool will help you evaluate your knowledge base against the requirements for an MCSD under both ideal and real circumstances.

Based on what you learn from that exercise, you might decide to begin your studies with some classroom training or to pick up and read one of the many study guides available. I also strongly recommend that you install, configure, and fool around with the software or environment that you'll be tested on, because nothing beats hands-on experience and familiarity when it comes to understanding the questions you're likely to encounter on a certification test. Book learning is essential, but hands-on experience is the best teacher of all.

The Microsoft Certified Professional (MCP) Program

The MCP program currently includes eight separate tracks, each of which boasts its own special acronym (as a would-be certificant, you need to have a high tolerance for alphabet soup of all kinds):

➤ **MCP (Microsoft Certified Professional)** This is the least prestigious of all the certification tracks from Microsoft. Passing any of the major Microsoft exams (except the Networking Essentials exam) qualifies an individual for MCP credentials. Individuals can demonstrate proficiency with additional Microsoft products by passing additional certification exams.

➤ **MCP+Internet (Microsoft Certified Professional + Internet)** This midlevel certification is attained by completing three core exams: "Windows NT Server 4," "TCP/IP," and "Internet Information Server" (3 or 4).

➤ **MCP+Site Building (Microsoft Certified Professional + Site Building)** This certification program is designed for individuals who are planning, building, managing, and maintaining Web sites. Individuals with the MCP+Site Building credential will have demonstrated the ability to develop Web sites that include multimedia and searchable content and Web sites that connect to and communicate with a back-end database. It requires passing two of the following three exams: "Designing and Implementing Commerce Solutions with Microsoft Site Server 3.0, Commerce Edition," "Designing and Implementing Web Sites with Microsoft FrontPage 98," and "Designing and Implementing Web Solutions with Microsoft Visual InterDev 6.0."

➤ **MCSD (Microsoft Certified Solution Developer)** The MCSD credential reflects the skills required to create multitier, distributed, and COM-based solutions, in addition to desktop and Internet applications, using new technologies. To obtain an MCSD, an individual must demonstrate the ability to analyze and interpret user requirements, select and integrate products, platforms, tools, and technologies, design and implement code and customize applications, and perform necessary software tests and quality-assurance operations.

To become an MCSD, you must pass a total of four exams: three core exams (available sometime in 1999) and one elective exam. The required core exam is "Analyzing Requirements and Defining Solution Architectures." Each candidate must also choose one of two desktop application exams—"Designing and Implementing Desktop Applications with

Microsoft Visual C++ 6.0" or "Designing and Implementing Desktop Applications with Visual Basic 6.0"—plus one of two distributed application exams—"Designing and Implementing Distributed Applications with Microsoft Visual C++ 6.0" or "Designing and Implementing Distributed Applications with Microsoft Visual Basic 6.0."

Elective exams cover specific Microsoft applications and languages, including Visual Basic, C++, the Microsoft Foundation Classes, Access, SQL Server, Visual InterDev, and more. If you're on your way to becoming an MCSD and have already taken some exams, visit www.microsoft.com/train_cert/ for information about how to proceed with your MCSD certification under this new track. Table 1 shows the requirements for the MCSD certification.

➤ **MCDBA (Microsoft Certified Database Administrator)** The MCDBA credential reflects the skills required to implement and administer Microsoft SQL Server databases. To obtain an MCDBA, an individual must demonstrate the ability to derive physical database designs, develop logical data models, create physical databases, create data services by using Transact-SQL, manage and maintain databases, configure and manage security, monitor and optimize databases, and install and configure Microsoft SQL Server.

To become an MCDBA, you must pass a total of five exams: four core exams and one elective exam. The required core exams are "Administering Microsoft SQL Server 7.0," "Designing and Implementing Databases with Microsoft SQL Server 7.0," "Implementing and Supporting Microsoft Windows NT Server 4.0," and "Implementing and Supporting Microsoft Windows NT Server 4.0 in the Enterprise."

The elective exams you can choose from cover specific uses of SQL Server and include "Designing and Implementing Distributed Applications with Visual Basic 6.0," "Designing and Implementing Distributed Applications with Visual C++ 6.0," "Designing and Implementing Data Warehouses with Microsoft SQL Server 7.0 and Microsoft Decision Support Services 1.0," and two exams that relate to NT: "Internetworking with Microsoft TCP/IP on Microsoft Windows NT 4.0" and "Implementing and Supporting Microsoft Internet Information Server 4.0."

➤ **MCSE (Microsoft Certified Systems Engineer)** Anyone who has a current MCSE is warranted to possess a high level of expertise with Windows NT (version 3.51 or 4) and other Microsoft operating systems and products. This credential is designed to prepare individuals to plan, implement, maintain, and support information systems and networks built around Microsoft Windows NT and its BackOffice family of products.

Table 1   MCSD Requirements*

Core

Choose 1 from the desktop applications development group	
Exam 70-016	Designing and Implementing Desktop Applications with Microsoft Visual C++ 6.0
Exam 70-176	Designing and Implementing Desktop Applications with Microsoft Visual Basic 6.0
Choose 1 from the distributed applications development group	
Exam 70-015	Designing and Implementing Distributed Applications with Microsoft Visual C++ 6.0
Exam 70-175	Designing and Implementing Distributed Applications with Microsoft Visual Basic 6.0
This solution architecture exam is required	
Exam 70-100	Analyzing Requirements and Defining Solution Architectures

Elective

Choose 1 from this group	
Exam 70-015	Designing and Implementing Distributed Applications with Microsoft Visual C++ 6.0
Exam 70-016	Designing and Implementing Desktop Applications with Microsoft Visual C++ 6.0
Exam 70-029	Designing and Implementing Databases with Microsoft SQL Server 7.0
Exam 70-024	Developing Applications with C++ Using the Microsoft Foundation Class Library
Exam 70-025	Implementing OLE in Microsoft Foundation Class Applications
Exam 70-055	Designing and Implementing Web Sites with Microsoft FrontPage 98
Exam 70-057	Designing and Implementing Commerce Solutions with Microsoft Site Server 3.0, Commerce Edition
Exam 70-165	Developing Applications with Microsoft Visual Basic 5.0
	OR
Exam 70-175	Designing and Implementing Distributed Applications with Microsoft Visual Basic 6.0
	OR
Exam 70-176	Designing and Implementing Desktop Applications with Microsoft Visual Basic 6.0
Exam 70-069	Application Development with Microsoft Access for Windows 95 and the Microsoft Access Developer's Toolkit
Exam 70-091	Designing and Implementing Solutions with Microsoft Office 2000 and Microsoft Visual Basic for Applications
Exam 70-152	Designing and Implementing Web Solutions with Microsoft Visual InterDev 6.0

* This is not a complete listing—you can still be tested on some earlier versions of these products. However, we have tried to include the most recent versions so that you may test on these versions and thus be certified longer. We have not included any tests that are scheduled to be retired.

The MCSD program is being expanded to include FoxPro and Visual J++. However, these tests are not yet available and no test numbers have been assigned.

Core exams that can also be used as elective exams can be counted only once toward certification. The same test cannot be used as both a core and elective exam.

To obtain an MCSE, an individual must pass four core operating system exams, plus two elective exams. The operating system exams require individuals to demonstrate competence with desktop and server operating systems and with networking components.

You must pass at least two Windows NT-related exams to obtain an MCSE: "Implementing and Supporting Microsoft Windows NT Server" (version 3.51 or 4) and "Implementing and Supporting Microsoft Windows NT Server in the Enterprise" (version 3.51 or 4). These tests are intended to indicate an individual's knowledge of Windows NT in smaller, simpler networks and in larger, more complex, and heterogeneous networks, respectively.

You must pass two additional tests as well. These tests relate to networking and desktop operating systems. At present, the networking requirement can be satisfied only by passing the Networking Essentials test. The desktop operating system test can be satisfied by passing a Windows 95, Windows NT Workstation (the version must match whichever core NT curriculum you're pursuing), or Windows 98 test.

The two remaining exams are elective exams. An elective exam may fall in any number of subject or product areas, primarily BackOffice components. These include tests on Internet Explorer 4, SQL Server, IIS, SNA Server, Exchange Server, Systems Management Server, and the like. However, it's also possible to test out on electives by taking advanced networking tests such as "Internetworking with Microsoft TCP/IP on Microsoft Windows NT" (but here again, the version of Windows NT involved must match the version for the core requirements taken).

Whatever mix of tests is completed toward MCSE certification, individuals must pass six tests to meet the MCSE requirements. It's not uncommon for the entire process to take a year or so, and many individuals find that they must take a test more than once to pass. The primary goal with the *Exam Cram* series is to make it possible, given proper study and preparation, to pass all Microsoft certification tests on the first try.

➤ **MCSE+Internet (Microsoft Certified Systems Engineer + Internet)**
This is a newer Microsoft certification. It focuses not just on Microsoft operating systems but also on Microsoft's Internet servers and TCP/IP.

To obtain this certification, an individual must pass seven core exams, plus two elective exams. The core exams include not only the server operating systems (NT Server and Server in the Enterprise) and a desktop operating system (Windows 95, Windows 98, or Windows NT

Workstation) but also Networking Essentials, TCP/IP, Internet Information Server, and the Internet Explorer Administration Kit (IEAK).

The two remaining exams are electives. These elective exams can be in any of four product areas: SQL Server, SNA Server, Exchange Server, and Proxy Server.

➤ **MCT (Microsoft Certified Trainer)** Microsoft Certified Trainers are individuals deemed able to deliver elements of the official Microsoft curriculum based on technical knowledge and instructional ability. Therefore, it's necessary for an individual seeking MCT credentials (which are granted on a course-by-course basis) to pass the related certification exam for a course and to take the official Microsoft training on the subject, as well as to demonstrate an ability to teach.

This latter criterion may be satisfied by proving that one has already attained training certification from Novell, Banyan, Lotus, the Santa Cruz Operation, or Cisco, or by taking a Microsoft-sanctioned workshop on instruction. Microsoft makes it clear that MCTs are important cogs in the Microsoft training channels. Instructors must be MCTs before Microsoft will allow them to teach in any of its official training channels, including Microsoft's affiliated Authorized Technical Education Centers (ATECs), Authorized Academic Training Programs (AATPs), and the Microsoft Online Institute (MOLI).

Certification is an ongoing activity. Once a Microsoft product becomes obsolete, MCPs typically have 12 to 18 months in which to recertify on current product versions. (If individuals do not recertify within the specified time period, their certifications become invalid.) Because technology keeps changing and new products continually supplant old ones, this should come as no surprise.

The best place to keep tabs on the MCP program and its various certifications is on the Microsoft Web site. The current root URL for the MCP program is at www.microsoft.com/mcp/. However, Microsoft's Web site changes frequently, so if this URL doesn't work, try using the search tool on Microsoft's site with either "MCP" or the quoted phrase "Microsoft Certified Professional program" as the search string. This will help you find the latest and most accurate information about the company's certification programs.

Taking A Certification Exam

Alas, testing is not free. Each computer-based MCP exam costs $100, and if you do not pass, you may retest for an additional $100 for each additional try. In the United States and Canada, tests are administered by Sylvan Prometric and Virtual University Enterprises (VUE). Here's how you can contact them:

➤ **Sylvan Prometric** You can sign up for a test through the company's Web site at www.slspro.com. You can also register by phone at 800-755-3926 (within the United States and Canada) or at 410-843-8000 (outside the United States and Canada).

➤ **Virtual University Enterprises** You can sign up for a test or get the phone numbers for local testing centers through the Web page at www.microsoft.com/train_cert/mcp/vue_info.htm.

To sign up for a test, you must possess a valid credit card or contact either company for mailing instructions to sending a check (in the United States). Only when payment is verified, or a check has cleared, can you actually register for a test.

To schedule an exam, call Sylvan or VUE, or sign up online at least one day in advance. To cancel or reschedule an exam, you must call by 7 P.M. (Pacific time) the day before the scheduled test (otherwise, you may be charged, even if you don't appear to take the test). When you want to schedule a test, have the following information ready:

➤ Your name, organization, and mailing address.

➤ Your Microsoft test ID. (Inside the United States, this is your Social Security number; citizens of other nations should call ahead to find out what type of identification number is required to register for a test.)

➤ The name and number of the exam you wish to take.

➤ A method of payment. (As we've already mentioned, a credit card is the most convenient method, but alternate means can be arranged in advance, if necessary.)

Once you sign up for a test, you'll be informed as to when and where the test is scheduled. Try to arrive at least 15 minutes early. You must supply two forms of identification to be admitted into the testing room—one of which must be a photo ID.

All exams are completely "closed book." In fact, you won't be permitted to take anything with you into the testing area. However, you will be furnished with a blank sheet of paper and a pen. We suggest that you immediately write down on that sheet of paper all the information you've memorized for the test.

In *Exam Cram* books, this information appears on The Cram Sheet inside the front of each book. You'll have some time to compose yourself, record this information, and even take a sample orientation exam before you must begin the real thing. I suggest you take the orientation test before taking your first exam, but because they're all more or less identical in layout, behavior, and controls, you probably won't need to do this more than once.

When you complete a Microsoft certification exam, the software will tell you whether you've passed or failed. Results are broken into several topic areas. Even if you fail, we suggest you ask for—and keep—the detailed report that the test administrator should print for you. You can use this report to help you prepare for another go-around, if needed.

If you need to retake an exam, you'll have to call Sylvan Prometric or VUE, schedule a new test date, and pay another $100. Microsoft has the following policy regarding failed tests: The first time you fail a test, you are able to retake the test the next day. However, if you fail a second time, you must wait 14 days before retaking that test.

Tracking MCP Status

As soon as you pass any Microsoft exam (other than Networking Essentials), you'll attain Microsoft Certified Professional (MCP) status. Microsoft also generates transcripts that indicate which exams you have passed and your corresponding test scores. You can order a transcript by email at any time by writing to mcp@msprograms.com. You can also obtain a copy of your transcript by downloading the latest version of the MCT guide from the Web site and consulting the section titled "Key Contacts" for a list of telephone numbers and related contacts.

Once you pass the necessary set of exams (one for MCP or four for MCSD), you'll be certified. Official certification normally takes anywhere from four to six weeks, so don't expect to get your credentials overnight. When the package for a qualified certification arrives, it includes a Welcome Kit that contains a number of elements:

➤ An MCP or MCSD certificate, suitable for framing, along with a Professional Program Membership card and lapel pin.

➤ A license to use the MCP logo, thereby allowing you to use the logo in advertisements, promotions, and documents, as well as on letterhead, business cards, and so on. Along with the license comes an MCP logo sheet, which includes camera-ready artwork. (Note that before using any of the artwork, individuals must sign and return a licensing agreement that indicates they'll abide by its terms and conditions.)

➤ A subscription to *Microsoft Certified Professional Magazine*, which provides ongoing data about testing and certification activities, requirements, and changes to the program.

➤ A one-year subscription to the Microsoft Beta Evaluation program. This subscription will get you all beta products from Microsoft for the next year. (This does not include developer products. You must join the MSDN program or become an MCSD to qualify for developer beta products. To join the MSDN program, go to http://msdn.microsoft.com/developer/join/.)

Many people believe that the benefits of MCP certification go well beyond the perks that Microsoft provides to newly anointed members of this elite group. We're starting to see more job listings that request or require applicants to have an MCP, MCP+Site Building, MCSD, and so on, and many individuals who complete the program can qualify for increases in pay and/or responsibility. As an official recognition of hard work and broad knowledge, one of the MCP credentials is a badge of honor in many IT organizations.

How To Prepare For An Exam

Preparing for any Microsoft product-related test (including "Analyzing Requirements and Defining Solution Architectures") requires that you obtain and study materials designed to provide comprehensive information about the products and their capabilities that will appear on the specific exam for which you're preparing. The following list of materials will help you study and prepare:

➤ The CD-ROMs for the Microsoft development tools, including Visual Studio, Visual Basic, and Visual C++, contain comprehensive online documentation, application examples, and related materials; one of these CD-ROMs should be a primary resource when you're preparing for the test.

➤ Microsoft Press offers titles on solution architecture and application design. Visit http://mspress.microsoft.com/findabook/list/subject_MF.htm for a complete list of its offerings.

➤ The Microsoft Developer Network Library (MSDN) CD-ROM contains a vast amount of technical programming information for developers, including sample code, documentation, technical articles, the Microsoft Developer Knowledge Base, and anything else you might need to develop solutions that implement Microsoft technology. It's available through a subscription and as an online version. Visit http://msdn.microsoft.com for more information.

➤ The Microsoft TechNet CD-ROM delivers numerous electronic titles, including Product Manuals, Product Facts, Technical Notes, Tips and Techniques, and Tools and Utilities, as well as information on how to access the Seminars Online training materials. A subscription to TechNet costs $299 per year but is well worth the price. Visit www.microsoft.com/technet/ and check out the information under the "TechNet Subscription" menu entry for more details.

➤ Find, download, and use the exam prep materials, practice tests, and self-assessment exams on the Microsoft Training And Certification Download page (www.microsoft.com/train_cert/download/downld.htm).

➤ Review the preparation guide for the specific exam you are planning to take. For exam 70-100 you will find this guide at www.microsoft.com/MCP/exam/stat/sp70-100.htm. This preparation guide lists the skills needed for the exam. In addition, it provides a reference to a practice demo exam that will acquaint you with the interactive question formats used on the 70-100 exam. This practice demo is extremely useful, even if you have previously taken a Microsoft certification exam, because exam 70-100 uses new question formats.

In addition, you'll probably find any or all of the following materials useful in your quest for solution architecture expertise:

➤ **Microsoft Training Kits** Although there's no training kit currently available from Microsoft Press for the Analyzing Requirements and Defining Solution Architectures exam, many other topics have such kits. It's worthwhile to check to see if Microsoft has come out with anything by the time you need this information.

➤ **Study Guides** Several publishers—including Certification Insider Press—offer learning materials necessary to pass the tests. The Certification Insider Press series includes:

  ➤ The *Exam Cram* series These books give you information about the material you need to know to pass the tests.

  ➤ The *Exam Prep* series These books provide a greater level of detail than the *Exam Cram* books. *MCSD Architectures Exam Prep* (1-57610-413-3) will be available by The Coriolis Group in the fall of 1999.

➤ **Classroom Training** ATECs, AATPs, MOLI, and unlicensed third-party training companies (such as Wave Technologies, American Research Group, Learning Tree, Data-Tech, and others) all offer classroom training on MCSD topics. Although such training runs upwards of $350 per day in class, most of the individuals lucky enough to partake find them to be quite worthwhile.

➤ **Other Publications** You'll find direct references to other publications and resources in this text, but there's no shortage of materials available about solution architecture and application design. To help you sift through some of the publications out there, we end each chapter with a "Need To Know More?" section that provides pointers to more complete and exhaustive resources covering the chapter's information. This should give you an idea of where we think you should look for further coverage.

By far, this set of required and recommended materials represents a nonpareil collection of sources and resources for "Analyzing Requirements and Defining Solution Architectures" and related topics. I anticipate you'll find this book belongs in this company. In the section that follows, I explain how this book works, and I give you some good reasons why this book counts as a member of the required and recommended materials list.

About This Book

Each topical *Exam Cram* chapter follows a regular structure, along with graphical cues about important or useful information. Here's the structure of a typical chapter:

➤ **Opening Hotlists** Each chapter begins with a list of the terms, tools, and techniques you must learn and understand before you can be fully conversant with that chapter's subject matter. I follow the hotlists with one or two introductory paragraphs to set the stage for the rest of the chapter.

➤ **Topical Coverage** After the opening hotlist, each chapter covers a series of topics related to the chapter's subject title. Throughout this section, I highlight topics or concepts likely to appear on a test using a special Exam Alert layout, like this:

This is what an Exam Alert looks like. Normally, an Exam Alert stresses concepts, terms, software, or activities that are likely to relate to one or more certification test questions. For that reason, I think any information offset in Exam Alert format is worthy of unusual attentiveness on your part. Indeed, most of the information that appears on The Cram Sheet appears as Exam Alerts within the text.

Pay close attention to material flagged as an Exam Alert; although all the information in this book pertains to what you need to know to pass the exam, I flag certain items that are really important. You'll find what appears in the meat of each chapter to be worth knowing, too, when preparing for the test. Because this book's material is very condensed, I recommend that you use this book along with other resources to achieve the maximum benefit.

In addition to the Exam Alerts, I've provided tips that will help you build a better foundation for Solution Architecture knowledge. Although the information may not be on the exam, it's certainly related and will help you become a better test taker.

This is how tips are formatted. Keep your eyes open for these, and you'll become a Solution Architecture guru in no time.

➤ **Practice Questions** Although I talk about test questions and topics throughout each chapter, this section presents a series of mock test questions and explanations of both correct and incorrect answers. I also try to point out especially tricky questions by using a special icon:

Ordinarily, this icon flags the presence of a particularly devious inquiry, if not an outright trick question. Trick questions are calculated to be answered incorrectly if not read more than once—and carefully at that. Although they're not ubiquitous, such questions make regular appearances on the Microsoft exams. That's why I say exam questions are as much about reading comprehension as they are about knowing your material inside out and backwards.

➤ **Details And Resources** Every chapter ends with a section titled "Need To Know More?". These sections provide direct pointers to Microsoft and third-party resources offering more details on the chapter's subject. In addition, these sections try to rank or at least rate the quality and thoroughness of the topic's coverage by each resource. If you find a resource you like in this collection, use it, but don't feel compelled to use all the resources. On the other hand, I recommend only resources I use on a regular basis, so none of our recommendations will be a waste of your time or money (but purchasing them all at once probably represents an expense that many developers and would-be MCSDs might find hard to justify).

The bulk of the book follows this chapter structure slavishly, but there are a few other elements we'd like to point out. Chapter 10 is a sample test that provides a good review of the material presented throughout the book to ensure you're ready for the exam. Chapter 11 is an answer key to the sample test that appears in Chapter 10. Additionally, you'll find a glossary that explains terms and an index that you can use to track down terms as they appear in the text.

Finally, the tear-out Cram Sheet attached next to the inside front cover of this *Exam Cram* book represents a condensed and compiled collection of facts, figures, and tips that I think you should memorize before taking the test. Because you can dump this information out of your head onto a piece of paper before taking the exam, you can master this information by brute force—you need to remember it only long enough to write it down when you walk into the test room. You might even want to look at it in the car or in the lobby of the testing center just before you walk in to take the test.

How To Use This Book

If you're prepping for a first-time test, I've structured the topics in this book to build on one another. Therefore, some topics in later chapters make more sense after you've read earlier chapters. That's why I suggest you read this book from front to back for your initial test preparation. If you need to brush up on a topic or have to bone up for a second try, use the index or table of contents to go straight to the topics and questions you need to study. Beyond helping you prepare for the tests, I think you'll find this book useful as a tightly focused reference to some of the most important aspects of the "Analyzing Requirements and Defining Solution Architectures" exam.

Given all the book's elements and its specialized focus, I've tried to create a tool that will help you prepare for—and pass—Microsoft Exam 70-100, "Analyzing Requirements and Defining Solution Architectures." Please share your feedback on the book with me, especially if you have ideas about how I can improve it for future test takers. We'll consider everything you say carefully, and we'll respond to all suggestions.

Please send your questions or comments to me at drb@azstarnet.com. Please include "MCSD Architectures" in the subject of your message.

Thanks, and enjoy the book!

Self-Assessment

Based on recent statistics from Microsoft, as many as 250,000 individuals are at some stage of the certification process but haven't yet received an MCP or other Microsoft certification. What's more, three or four times that number may be considering whether to obtain a Microsoft certification of some kind. That's a huge audience.

The reason I included a Self-Assessment in this *Exam Cram* book is to help you evaluate your readiness to tackle MCSD certification. It should also help you understand what you need to master the topic of this book—namely, Exam 70-100, "Analyzing Requirements and Defining Solution Architectures." However, before you tackle this Self-Assessment, let's talk about concerns you may face when pursuing an MCSD, and what an ideal MCSD candidate might look like.

MCSDs In The Real World

In the next section, I describe an ideal MCSD candidate, knowing full well that only a few real candidates will meet this ideal. In fact, my description of that ideal candidate might seem downright scary. But take heart: Although the requirements to obtain an MCSD may seem pretty formidable, they are by no means impossible to meet. However, you should be keenly aware that it does take time, requires some expense, and consumes substantial effort to get through the process.

You can get all the real-world motivation you need from knowing that many others have gone before, so you'll be able to follow in their footsteps. If you're willing to tackle the process seriously and do what it takes to obtain the necessary experience and knowledge, you can take—and pass—the four certification tests involved in obtaining an MCSD. In fact, we've designed these *Exam Crams*, and the companion *Exam Preps*, to make it as easy on you as possible to prepare for these exams. But prepare you must!

 MCSD Architectures Exam Prep (1-57610-413-3) will be available by The Coriolis Group in the fall of 1999.

The same, of course, is true for other Microsoft certifications, including these:

➤ MCSE, which is aimed at network engineers and requires four core exams and two electives, for a total of six exams.

➤ MCSE+Internet, which is like the MCSE certification but requires seven core exams and two electives drawn from a specific pool of Internet-related topics, for a total of nine exams.

➤ Other Microsoft certifications whose requirements range from one test (such as MCP and MCT) to many tests (such as MCP+Internet, MCP+Site Building, and MCDBA).

The Ideal MCSD Candidate

Just to give you some idea of what an ideal MCSD candidate is like, here are some relevant statistics about the background and experience such an individual might have. Don't worry if you don't meet these qualifications or even don't come that close—this is a far-from-ideal world, and where you fall short is simply where you'll have more work to do.

➤ Academic or professional training in application design and development as well as relevant database design and usage.

➤ Typically, six years of professional development experience (32 percent of MCSDs have less than four years of experience, 20 percent have five to eight years of experience, and 48 percent have eight plus years of experience). This experience will include development tools such as Visual Basic, Visual C++, and so on. This must include application design, requirements analysis, debugging, distribution, and an understanding of the Microsoft Services Model.

➤ Three-plus years in a relational database environment designing and using database tools such as SQL Server and Access. The ideal MCSD will have performed both logical and physical database designs from entity modeling through normalization and database schema creation.

➤ A thorough understanding of issues involved in the creation and deployment of distributed applications to include knowledge of COM and DCOM, issues involved in the usage of in-process and out-of-process components, and the logical and physical design of those components.

➤ An understanding of both operating system architectures (Windows 9x and NT) and network issues as they relate to application architectures including Internet application architectures. (You won't, of course, be expected to demonstrate the level of knowledge that a network engineer needs to have. Instead, you want to be familiar with the issues that networks—particularly the Internet—raise in client/server applications.)

Fundamentally, this boils down to a bachelor's degree in computer science, plus at least three to four years of development experience in a networked environment, involving relational database design and usage as well as application architecture design, development, and deployment. Given the relative newness of the technologies involved, there are probably few certification candidates that meet these requirements. Particularly in the area of multitiered applications, most meet less than half of these requirements—at least, when they begin the certification process. However, because those who have already achieved their MCSD certification have survived this ordeal, you can survive it, too—especially if you heed what this Self-Assessment can tell you about what you already know and what you need to learn.

Put Yourself To The Test

The following series of questions and observations is designed to help you figure out how much work you must do to pursue Microsoft certification and what kinds of resources you may consult on your quest. Be absolutely honest in your answers, or you'll end up wasting money on exams you're not yet ready to take. There are no right or wrong answers, only steps along the path to certification. Only you can decide where you really belong in the broad spectrum of aspiring candidates.

Two things should be clear from the outset:

➤ Even a modest background in applications development will be helpful.

➤ Hands-on experience with Microsoft development products and technologies is an essential ingredient to certification success.

Educational Background

1. Have you ever taken any computer-programming classes? [Yes or No]

   If Yes, proceed to Question 2; if No, proceed to Question 5.

2. Have you taken any classes on applications design? [Yes or No]

   If Yes, you'll probably be able to handle Microsoft's architecture and system component discussions. You'll be expected, in most of the exams, to demonstrate core COM concepts. This will include an understanding of the implications of in-process and out-of-process components, cross-process procedure calls, and so forth.

If No, consider some basic reading in this area. The "Component Tools Guide" in the Visual Basic documentation is actually quite good and covers the core concepts. Third-party COM books can also be helpful.

Designing Component-Based Applications, by Mary Kirtland (Microsoft Press, 1999, ISBN 0-7356-0523-8), is a relatively new publication that describes, in detail, the technologies for building distributed, multitiered applications.

3. Have you taken any classes oriented specifically toward Visual Basic or C++? [Yes or No]

   If Yes, you'll probably be able to handle the programming-related concepts and terms in the "Desktop Applications" and "Distributed Applications" portions of the MCSD track. Each section allows you to choose between a Visual Basic or a Visual C++ exam. If you feel rusty, brush up on your VB or VC++ terminology by going through the Glossary in this book and the product documentation.

   If No, and if you don't have a good deal of on-the-job experience, you might want to read one or two books in this topic area. *Visual Basic 6 Black Book*, by Steven Holzner (The Coriolis Group, 1998, ISBN 1-57610-283-1), is worth considering and is at an appropriate level.

4. Have you taken any database design classes? [Yes or No]

   If Yes, you'll probably be able to handle questions related to general data access techniques. If you do not have experience specific to Microsoft Access or Microsoft SQL Server, you'll want to touch up on concepts specific to either of these two products.

   If No, you'll want to look over the exams that you can take from the "Elective Exams" portion of the MCSD. These include a wide variety of topics, such as SQL Server and Access. You may have expertise in one of these areas and should, therefore, aim to take one of these exams. All in all, whether you take the SQL Server (or Access) exam, you should consider reading a book or two on the subject. For example, *Microsoft SQL Server 6.5 Unleashed*, by David Solomon and Ray Rankins (Sams Publishing, 1998, ISBN 0-672-31190-9), covers design concepts as well as some of the issues appropriate to a DBA.

5. Have you done any reading on application design and development? [Yes or No]

   If Yes, proceed to the next section, "Hands-On Experience."

If No, be particularly alert to the questions asked in the next section, "Hands-On Experience." Frequently, a little experience goes a long way. For any areas where you may be weak, consider doing extra reading, as outlined in Questions 2, 3, and 4. Carefully review the glossary in this book and take unfamiliar terms as cues to areas you need to brush up on. Look at the "Terms You'll Need To Know" and "Techniques You'll Need To Master" lists at the front of each chapter. Again, for any terms or techniques that are unfamiliar, consider boning up in those areas.

Hands-On Experience

The most important key to success on all the Microsoft tests is hands-on experience, especially with the core tool on which you're testing (Visual Basic or Visual C++), as well as an understanding of COM and ADO. If I leave you with only one realization after taking this Self-Assessment, it should be that there's no substitute for time spent developing real-world applications. The development experience should range from both logical and physical design, to the creation of remote COM services, to database programming. The recurring theme through nearly all the tests will be COM and database techniques.

Hands-on experience is especially important for Exam 70-100, "Analyzing Requirements and Defining Solution Architectures." This exam makes extensive use of case studies. If you have real-world experience, you may find similarities between the situations presented in the case studies and your own experiences.

However, if your own real-world experience is limited, you can always read about other's. There are numerous case studies and success stories available on the Microsoft Web site. You should definitely check these out to see how Microsoft technologies are being effectively utilized to solve business problems.

6. Have you created COM components?

   If Yes, you'll probably be prepared for Exam 70-100. This satisfies the "Solutions Architecture" section of the MCSD requirements. Go to Question 7.

   If No, you need to bone up on COM concepts as outlined in Question 2.

7. Have you done database programming?

   If Yes, go to Question 8.

   If No, you'll be in a weak position on all the tests. You need to consult a book such as the one recommended in Question 3.

8. Have you done ADO development?

   If Yes, go to Question 9.

   If No, you need to consult an ADO reference. Use the MSDN library on your product's (Visual Basic, Visual C++, or Visual Studio) CD-ROM and review the ADO articles. Additionally, check out a book such as the one recommended in Question 4.

9. Have you developed with Visual Basic?

   If Yes, you should be prepared to take Exam 70-176, "Designing and Implementing Desktop Applications with Microsoft Visual Basic 6.0." This will satisfy the Desktop Applications Development requirement. Go to Question 10.

   If No, go to Question 10.

10. Have you developed with Visual C++?

    If Yes, you should be prepared to take Exam 70-016, "Designing and Implementing Desktop Applications with Microsoft Visual C++ 6.0." If you also answered Yes to Question 9, you can use Exam 70-016 as your elective requirement (see Question 12). Go to Question 11.

    If No and if you also answered No to Question 9, you probably should consider getting some real-world experience with either Visual Basic or Visual C++. (If you answered Yes to Question 9 and No to this question, you'll want to take Exam 70-176.)

11. Have you developed distributed applications with either Visual Basic or Visual C++?

    If Yes, you should be prepared to take either Exam 70-175, "Designing and Implementing Distributed Applications with Microsoft Visual Basic 6.0" or Exam 70-015, "Designing and Implementing Distributed Applications with Microsoft Visual C++ 6.0." Either exam will satisfy the Distributed Applications requirement of the MCSD. Go to Question 12.

    If No, consult the books recommended in Questions 2 and 3.

12. Have you used one of the products listed in the "Elective Exams" section of the MCSD?

    If Yes, go ahead and take that exam after consulting the Microsoft Web site for a list of the MCSD requirements (see Chapter 1).

    If No, consider boning up on Microsoft Access or Microsoft SQL Server, as outlined in Question 4, and taking one of those exams. If you're qualified in both Visual Basic and Visual C++, consider taking Exam 70-016 (Visual C++ Desktop) for the Desktop Applications Development section and Exam 70-176 (Visual Basic Desktop) as your elective.

Testing Your Exam Readiness

Whether you attend a formal class on a specific topic to get ready for an exam or use written materials to study on your own, some preparation for the Microsoft certification exams is essential. At $100 a try, pass or fail, you want to do everything you can to pass on your first try. That's where studying comes in.

We've included practice questions at the end of each chapter. If you do well, take the practice exam in Chapter 10 to see how you do.

For any given subject, consider taking a class if you've tackled self-study materials, taken the test, and failed anyway. The opportunity to interact with an instructor and fellow students can make all the difference in the world, if you can afford that privilege. For information about Microsoft classes, visit the Training and Certification page at www.microsoft.com/train_cert/ (use the "Find a Course" link).

If you can't afford to take a class, visit the Training And Certification page anyway, because it also includes pointers to free practice exams. Even if you can't afford to spend much at all, you should still invest in some low-cost practice exams from commercial vendors, because they can help you assess your readiness to pass a test better than any other tool. The following links may be of interest to you in locating practice exams:

➤ **Self Test Software (www.stsware.com)** At the time of this writing, the cost for the first test ordered was $79, although the "Analyzing Requirements and Defining Solution Architectures" exam was not yet ready.

➤ **Transcender (www.transcender.com)** At the time of this writing, MCSD tests averaged around $149. The Analyzing Requirements and Defining Solution Architectures exam was not yet ready.

➤ **MeasureUp (www.measureup.com)** At the time of this writing, tests cost $99. The Analyzing Requirements and Defining Solution Architectures exam was not yet ready.

13. Have you taken a practice exam on your chosen test subject? [Yes or No]

   If Yes and you scored 70 percent or better, you're probably ready to tackle the real thing. If your score isn't above that crucial threshold, keep at it until you break that barrier. (If you scored above 80, you should feel pretty confident.)

If No, obtain all the free and low-budget practice tests you can find (see the preceding list) and get to work. Keep at it until you can break the passing threshold comfortably.

 When it comes to assessing your test readiness, there's no better way than to take a good-quality practice exam and pass with a score of 70 percent or better. If you pass an exam at 80 percent or better, you're probably in great shape.

Assessing Readiness For Exam 70-100

In addition to the general exam-readiness information in the previous section, there are several things you can do to prepare for the "Analyzing Requirements and Defining Solution Architectures" exam. As you're getting ready for Exam 70-100, you should cruise the Web looking for "braindumps" (recollections of test topics and experiences recorded by others) to help you anticipate topics you're likely to encounter on the test.

A good place to start is the Microsoft Certified Professional Magazine Web site (www.mcpmag.com). Here you'll find discussion forums on many of the exams, including Exam 70-100. Another Web site to check is Durham Software's Web site (www.durhamsoftware.com/cert).

 When using any braindump, it's OK to pay attention to information about questions. However, you can't always be sure that a braindump's author will also be able to provide correct answers. Therefore, use the questions to guide your studies, but don't rely on the answers in a braindump to lead you to the truth. Double-check everything you find in any braindump.

While on the Web, also check out the Exam 70-100 Preparation Guide maintained by Microsoft. Go to the Training and Certification page at www.microsoft.com/train_cert/ and use the "Find an Exam" link. On the Preparation Guide page, you'll also find a link to a practice test that you can download.

Microsoft exam mavens also recommend checking the Microsoft Knowledge Base (available on its own CD as part of the TechNet collection as well as on the Microsoft Web site at http://support.microsoft.com/support/) for "meaningful technical support issues" that relate to your exam's topics. Although I'm not sure exactly what the quoted phrase means, I have noticed some overlap between technical support questions on particular products and troubleshooting questions on the exams for those products.

In a nutshell, to prepare for Exam 70-100 you can do the following:

➤ Read and study this *Exam Cram* book, which covers the course objective topics.

➤ Obtain and read one or more of the supplemental texts listed in the previous questions to obtain more in-depth information.

➤ Use the developer software products (Visual Studio, Visual Basic, and Visual C++) for some hands-on development practice.

➤ Review technical articles and other relevant publications available in the MSDN Library.

➤ Try some practice tests.

➤ Get some real-world experience and practice analyzing case studies of business problems.

One last note: The MCSD exams are increasingly being designed to pose real-world problems. For these types of questions, book learning simply can't replace having actually "done it."

Onward, Through The Fog!

Once you've assessed your readiness, undertaken the right background studies, obtained the hands-on experience that will help you understand the products and technologies at work, and reviewed the many sources of information to help you prepare for a test, you'll be ready to take a round of practice tests. When your scores come back positive enough to get you through the exam, you're ready to go after the real thing. If you follow my assessment regime, not only will you know what you need to study, you'll also know when you're ready to make a test date at Sylvan or VUE. Good luck!

Microsoft Certification Exams

Terms and concepts you'll need to understand:

√ Radio button

√ Checkbox

√ Exhibit

√ Multiple-choice question formats

√ Drop-and-connect question formats

√ Build-list-and-reorder question formats

√ Create-a-tree question formats

√ Careful reading

√ Process of elimination

√ Adaptive tests

√ Fixed-length tests

√ Simulations

Techniques you'll need to master:

√ Assessing your exam-readiness

√ Preparing to take a certification exam

√ Practicing (to make perfect)

√ Making the best use of the testing software

√ Budgeting your time

√ Saving the hardest questions until last

√ Guessing (as a last resort)

1

Exam taking isn't something most people anticipate eagerly, no matter how well prepared they may be. In most cases, familiarity helps offset test anxiety. In plain English, this means you probably won't be as nervous when you take your fourth or fifth Microsoft certification exam as you'll be when you take your first one.

Whether it's your first exam or your tenth, understanding the details of exam taking (how much time to spend on questions, the environment you'll be in, and so on) and the exam software will help you concentrate on the material rather than on the setting. Likewise, mastering a few basic exam-taking skills should help you recognize—and perhaps even outfox—some of the tricks and snares you're bound to find in some of the exam questions.

This chapter, besides explaining the exam environment and software, describes some proven exam-taking strategies you should be able to use to your advantage.

Assessing Exam-Readiness

Before you take any more Microsoft exams, we strongly recommend that you read through and take the Self-Assessment included with this book (it appears just before this chapter, in fact). This will help you compare your knowledge base to the requirements for obtaining an MCSD, and it will also help you identify parts of your background or experience that may be in need of improvement, enhancement, or further learning. If you get the right set of basics under your belt, obtaining Microsoft certification will be that much easier.

Once you've gone through the Self-Assessment, you can remedy those topical areas where your background or experience may not measure up to an ideal certification candidate. What's more, you can tackle subject matter for individual tests at the same time, so you can continue making progress while you're catching up in some areas.

Once you've worked through an *Exam Cram*, have read the supplementary materials, and have taken the practice test, you'll have a pretty clear idea of when you should be ready to take the real exam. We strongly recommend that you keep practicing until your scores top the 70 percent mark; 75 percent would be a good goal to give yourself some margin for error in a real exam situation (where stress will play more of a role than when you practice). Once you hit that point, you should be ready to go. However, if you get through the practice exam in this book without attaining that score, you should keep taking practice tests and studying the materials until you get there. You'll find more information about other practice test vendors in the Self-Assessment, along with even more pointers on how to study and prepare. But now, on to the exam!

The Exam Situation

When you arrive at the testing center where you scheduled your exam, you'll need to sign in with an exam coordinator. He or she will ask you to show two forms of identification, one of which must be a photo ID. After you've signed in and your time slot arrives, you'll be asked to deposit any books, bags, or other items you brought with you. Then, you'll be escorted into a closed room. Typically, the room will be furnished with anywhere from one to half a dozen computers, and each workstation will be separated from the others by dividers designed to keep you from seeing what's happening on someone else's computer.

You'll be furnished with a pen or pencil and a blank sheet of paper, or, in some cases, an erasable plastic sheet and an erasable pen. You're allowed to write down anything you want on both sides of this sheet. Before the exam, you should memorize as much of the material that appears on The Cram Sheet (in the front of this book) as you can, so you can write that information on the blank sheet as soon as you're seated in front of the computer. You can refer to your rendition of The Cram Sheet anytime you like during the test, but you'll have to surrender the sheet when you leave the room.

Most test rooms feature a wall with a large picture window. This permits the exam coordinator to monitor the room, to prevent exam-takers from talking to one another, and to observe anything out of the ordinary that might go on. The exam coordinator will have preloaded the appropriate Microsoft certification exam—for this book, that's Exam 70-100—and you'll be permitted to start as soon as you're seated in front of the computer.

Most exams include a small practice exam that you can take before you get started on the actual exam. This is a good way to relax and get the feel of the exam computer.

All Microsoft certification exams allow a certain maximum amount of time in which to complete your work (this time is indicated on the exam by an onscreen counter/clock, so you can check the time remaining whenever you like). The Analyzing Requirements and Defining Solution Architectures exam is divided into five or six sections called "testlets." There is a fixed amount of time allowed for completing each testlet. Once you complete a testlet, you cannot return to it to change any answers. Overall, there are approximately 20 questions on the exam and approximately 165 minutes are allowed for the entire exam.

All Microsoft certification exams are computer generated, and many questions use a multiple-choice format. Although this may sound quite simple, the questions are constructed not only to check your mastery of Analyzing Requirements and Defining Solution Architectures, but they also require you to evaluate one or more sets of circumstances or requirements. Often, you'll be asked to give more than one answer to a question. Likewise, you might be asked to select the best or most effective solution to a problem from a range of choices, all of which technically are correct. In addition to the multiple-choice format, Microsoft has introduced three new question formats for the 70-100 exam. These are described later in this chapter. Taking an exam is quite an adventure, and it involves real thinking. This book shows you what to expect and how to deal with the potential problems, puzzles, and predicaments.

Some Microsoft exams employ more advanced testing capabilities than might immediately meet the eye. Although the questions that appear are still multiple choice, the logic that drives them is more complex than older Microsoft tests, which use a fixed sequence of questions (called a *fixed-length* computerized exam). Other exams employ a sophisticated user interface (which Microsoft calls a *simulation*) to test your knowledge of the software and systems under consideration in a more or less "live" environment that behaves just like the original.

For upcoming exams, Microsoft is turning to a well-known technique, called *adaptive testing*, to establish a test-taker's level of knowledge and product competence. These exams look the same as fixed-length exams, but adaptive exams discover the level of difficulty at and below which an individual test-taker can correctly answer questions. At the same time, Microsoft is in the process of converting all its older fixed-length exams into adaptive exams as well.

Test-takers with differing levels of knowledge or ability therefore see different sets of questions; individuals with high levels of knowledge or ability are presented with a smaller set of more difficult questions, whereas individuals with lower levels of knowledge are presented with a larger set of easier questions. Both individuals may answer the same percentage of questions correctly, but the test-taker with a higher knowledge or ability level will score higher because his or her questions are worth more.

Also, the lower-level test-taker will probably answer more questions than his or her more knowledgeable colleague. This explains why adaptive tests use ranges of values to define the number of questions and the amount of time it takes to complete the test.

Adaptive tests work by evaluating the test-taker's most recent answer. A correct answer leads to a more difficult question (and the test software's estimate of the test-taker's knowledge and ability level is raised). An incorrect answer leads to a less difficult question (and the test software's estimate of the test-taker's knowledge and ability level is lowered). This process continues until the test targets the test-taker's true ability level. The exam ends when the test-taker's level of accuracy meets a statistically acceptable value (in other words, when his or her performance demonstrates an acceptable level of knowledge and ability) or when the maximum number of items has been presented (in which case, the test-taker is almost certain to fail).

Microsoft tests come in one form or the other—either they're fixed-length tests or they're adaptive tests. Therefore, you must take the test in whichever form it appears—you can't choose one form over another. However, if anything, it pays off even more to prepare thoroughly for an adaptive exam than for a fixed-length one: The penalties for answering incorrectly are built into the test itself on an adaptive exam, whereas the layout remains the same for a fixed-length test, no matter how many questions you answer incorrectly.

> The biggest difference between an adaptive test and a fixed-length test is that, on a fixed-length test, you can revisit questions after you've read them over one or more times. On an adaptive test, you must answer the question when it's presented, and you'll have no opportunities to revisit that question thereafter. As of this writing, the Analyzing Requirements and Defining Solution Architectures exam is a fixed-length exam, but this can change at any time. Therefore, you must prepare for the test as if it were an adaptive exam to ensure the best possible results.

In the section that follows, you'll learn more about what Microsoft test questions look like and how they must be answered.

Exam Layout And Design

Exam 70-100, "Analyzing Requirements and Defining Solution Architectures," introduces a new exam format based on case studies. The exam consists of a series of case studies or "testlets." Each case study presents a problem that you must read and analyze. Following the case study is a set of questions related to the case study. Careful attention to details provided in the case study is the key to success. Be prepared to toggle frequently between the case study and the question as you work. Chapter 2 of this book presents more details on the case studies.

Once you complete a case study, you can review all the questions and your answers. However, once you move on to the next case study, you can't return to the previous case study and make any changes.

Exam 70-100 also introduces some new questions formats. Four types of questions formats are used:

➤ Multiple choice

➤ Build list and reorder

➤ Create a tree

➤ Drop and connect

Multiple-Choice Question Format

Some exam questions require you to select a single answer, whereas others ask you to select multiple correct answers. The following multiple-choice question requires you to select a single correct answer. Following the question is a brief summary of each potential answer and why it is either right or wrong.

Question 1

> Which of the following statements best describes the computing environment found in today's business environment?
>
> ○ a. No computing facilities
>
> ○ b. A single mainframe computer
>
> ○ c. A single high-end desktop system
>
> ○ d. A distributed network of computers

Answer d is correct. Today's business environment usually consists of multiple desktop systems integrated with servers and other legacy systems on a network. The network often provides access to the Internet as well.

This sample question format corresponds closely to the Microsoft certification exam format—the only difference on the exam is that questions are not followed by answer keys. To select an answer, position the cursor over the radio button next to the answer. Then, click the mouse button to select the answer.

Let's examine a question that requires choosing multiple answers. This type of question provides checkboxes rather than radio buttons for marking all appropriate selections.

Question 2

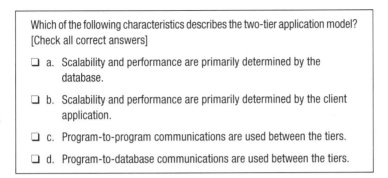

Which of the following characteristics describes the two-tier application model? [Check all correct answers]

❑ a. Scalability and performance are primarily determined by the database.

❑ b. Scalability and performance are primarily determined by the client application.

❑ c. Program-to-program communications are used between the tiers.

❑ d. Program-to-database communications are used between the tiers.

Answers a and d are correct. The database and the server limit performance and scalability. In the two-tier application model, program-to-database communications (for example, ODBC) are used between the tiers.

For this type of question, more than one answer may be required. As far as this author can tell (and Microsoft won't comment), such questions are scored as wrong unless all the required selections are chosen. In other words, a partially correct answer does not result in partial credit when the test is scored. For Question 2, you have to check the boxes next to answers a and d to obtain credit for a correct answer. Notice that picking the right answers also means knowing why the other answers are wrong.

Build-List-And-Reorder Question Format

Questions in the build-list-and-reorder format present two lists of items—one on the left and one on the right. To answer the question, you must move items from the list on the right to the list on the left. The final list must then be reordered into a specific order.

These questions can best be characterized as "From the following list of choices, pick the choices that answer the question. Arrange the list in a certain order." To give you practice with this type of question, some questions of this type are included in this book. Here's an example.

Question 3

> From the following list of famous people, pick those that have been elected President of the United States. Arrange the list in the order that they served.
>
> Thomas Jefferson
>
> Ben Franklin
>
> Abe Lincoln
>
> George Washington
>
> Andrew Jackson
>
> Paul Revere

The correct answer is:

George Washington

Thomas Jefferson

Andrew Jackson

Abe Lincoln

On an actual exam, the entire list of famous people would initially appear in the list on the right. You would move the four correct answers to the list on the left, and then reorder the list on the left. Notice that the answer to the question did not include all items from the initial list. However, this may not always be the case.

Create-A-Tree Question Format

Questions in the create-a-tree format also present two lists—one on the left side of the screen and one on the right side of the screen. The list on the right consists of individual items, and the list on the left consists of nodes in a tree. To answer the question, you must move items from the list on the right to the appropriate node in the tree.

These questions can best be characterized as simply a matching exercise. Items from the list on the right are placed under the appropriate category in the list on the left. Here's an example.

Question 4

> The calendar year is divided into four seasons:
>
>   Winter
>
>   Spring
>
>   Summer
>
>   Fall
>
> Identify the season when each of the following holidays occurs:
>
>   Christmas
>
>   Fourth of July
>
>   Labor Day
>
>   Flag Day
>
>   Memorial Day
>
>   Washington's Birthday
>
>   Thanksgiving
>
>   Easter

The correct answer is:

Winter

   Christmas

   Washington's Birthday

Summer

   Fourth of July

   Labor Day

Spring

   Flag Day

   Memorial Day

   Easter

Fall

   Thanksgiving

In this case, all the items in the list were used. However, this may not always be the case.

Drop-And-Connect Question Format

Questions in the drop-and-connect format present a group of objects and a list of "connections." To answer the question, you must move the appropriate connections between the objects.

This type of question is best described using graphics. Here's an example.

Question 5

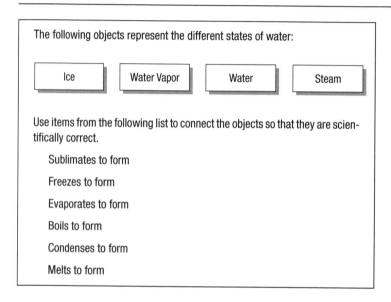

The correct answer is:

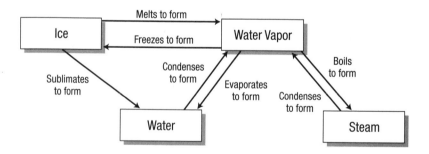

For this type of question, it's not necessary to use every object, and each connection can be used multiple times.

Recognizing Your Test Type: Fixed Length Or Adaptive

When you begin your exam, the software will tell you the test is adaptive if in fact the version you're taking is presented as an adaptive test. If your introductory materials fail to mention this, you're probably taking a fixed-length test. However, when you look at your first question, you'll be able to tell for sure: If it includes a checkbox that lets you mark the question (for later return and review), you'll know you're taking a fixed-length test, because adaptive test questions can only be visited (and answered) once, and they include no such checkboxes.

The Fixed-Length Test-Taking Strategy

A well-known principle when taking fixed-length exams is to first read over the entire exam from start to finish while answering only those questions you feel absolutely sure of. On subsequent passes, you can dive into more complex questions more deeply, knowing how many such questions you have left. On adaptive tests, you get only one shot at the question, which is why preparation is so crucial for such tests.

Fortunately, the Microsoft exam software for fixed-length tests makes the multiple-visit approach easy to implement. At the top-left corner of each question is a checkbox that permits you to mark that question for a later visit. (Note that marking questions makes review easier, but you can return to any question if you're willing to click the Forward or Back button repeatedly.) As you read each question, if you answer only those you're sure of and mark for review those that you're not sure of, you can keep working through a decreasing list of questions as you answer the trickier ones in order.

 For Exam 70-100, each case study can be regarded as a mini fixed-length exam. Before reading the actual case study, you might consider scanning the questions to determine what is covered. Then, when you read the case study, you can be on the lookout for certain types of information. Remember, too, that once you complete a case study, you can't return to it to change any answers.

Here are some question-handling strategies that apply only to fixed-length tests. Use them if you have the chance:

➤ When returning to a question after your initial read-through, read every word again—otherwise, your mind can fall quickly into a rut. Sometimes, revisiting a question after turning your attention elsewhere lets you see something you missed, but the strong tendency is to see what you've seen before. Try to avoid that tendency at all costs.

➤ If you return to a question more than twice, try to articulate to yourself what you don't understand about the question, why the answers don't appear to make sense, or what appears to be missing. If you chew on the subject for awhile, your subconscious might provide the details that are lacking, or you might notice a "trick" that will point to the right answer.

As you work your way through the exam, another counter that Microsoft thankfully provides will come in handy—the number of questions completed and questions outstanding. For fixed-length tests, it's wise to budget your time by making sure that you've completed one-quarter of the questions one-quarter of the way through the exam period and three-quarters of the questions three-quarters of the way through.

If you're not finished when only five minutes remain, use these last five minutes to guess your way through the remaining questions. Remember, guessing is potentially more valuable than not answering, because blank answers are always wrong, but a guess may turn out to be right. If you don't have a clue about any of the remaining questions, pick answers at random or choose all a's, b's, and so on. The important thing is to submit an exam for scoring that has an answer for every question.

 At the very end of your exam period, you're better off guessing than leaving questions unanswered.

The Adaptive Test-Taking Strategy

If there's one principle that applies to taking an adaptive test, it could be summed up as "Get it right the first time." You cannot elect to skip a question and move on to the next one when taking an adaptive test, because the testing software uses your answer to the current question to select whatever question it plans to present to you next. Also, you cannot return to a question once you've moved on, because the software only gives you one chance to answer the question.

When you answer a question correctly, you're presented with a more difficult question next to help the software gauge your level of skill and ability. When you answer a question incorrectly, you're presented with a less difficult question, and the software lowers its current estimate of your skill and ability. This continues until the program settles into a reasonably accurate estimate of what you know and can do, and it takes you through somewhere between 25 and 35 questions, on average, as you complete the test.

The good news is that if you know your stuff, you'll probably finish most adaptive tests in 30 minutes or so. The bad news is that you must really, really know your stuff to do your best on an adaptive test. That's because some questions are so convoluted, complex, or hard to follow that you're bound to miss one or two, at a minimum, even if you do know your stuff. Therefore, the more you know, the better you'll do on an adaptive test, even accounting for the occasionally weird or unfathomable question that appears on these exams.

As of this writing, Microsoft has not advertised which tests are strictly adaptive. You'll be best served by preparing for the exam as if it were adaptive. That way, you should be prepared to pass no matter what kind of test you take (that is, fixed length or adaptive). If you do end up taking a fixed-length test, remember the tips from the preceding section. They should help you improve on what you could do on an adaptive test.

If you encounter a question on an adaptive test that you can't answer, you must guess an answer. Because of the way the software works, you may have to suffer for your guess on the next question if you guess right, because you'll get a more difficult question next.

Exam-Taking Basics

The most important advice about taking any exam is this: Read each question carefully. Some questions are deliberately ambiguous, some use double negatives, and others use terminology in incredibly precise ways.

Here are some suggestions on how to check the tendency to jump to an answer too quickly:

➤ Make sure you read every word in the question. If you find yourself jumping ahead impatiently, go back and start over.

➤ As you read, try to restate the question in your own terms. If you can do this, you should be able to pick the correct answer(s) much more easily.

Above all, try to deal with each question by thinking through what you know about analyzing business requirements and designing solution architectures—the characteristics, behaviors, facts, and figures involved. By reviewing what you know (and what you've written down on your information sheet), you'll often recall or understand things sufficiently to determine the answer to the question.

Question-Handling Strategies

Based on exams we've taken, some interesting trends have become apparent. For those questions that take only a single answer, usually two or three of the answers will be obviously incorrect, and two of the answers will be plausible; of course, only one can be correct. Unless the answer leaps out at you (if it does, reread the question to look for a trick; sometimes those are the ones you're most likely to get wrong), begin the process of answering by eliminating those answers that are most obviously wrong.

Things to look for in obviously wrong answers include spurious menu choices or utility names, nonexistent software options, and terminology you've never seen. If you've done your homework for an exam, no valid information should be completely new to you. In that case, unfamiliar or bizarre terminology probably indicates a totally bogus answer.

Numerous questions assume that the default behavior of a particular utility is in effect. If you know the defaults and understand what they mean, this knowledge will help you cut through many Gordian knots.

Mastering The Inner Game

In the final analysis, knowledge breeds confidence, and confidence breeds success. If you study the materials in this book carefully and review all the practice questions at the end of each chapter, you should become aware of those areas where additional learning and study are required.

Next, follow up by reading some or all of the materials recommended in the "Need To Know More?" section at the end of each chapter. The idea is to become familiar enough with the concepts and situations you find in the sample questions that you can reason your way through similar situations on a real exam. If you know the material, you have every right to be confident you can pass the exam.

After you've worked your way through the book, take the practice exam in Chapter 10. This will provide a reality check and help you identify areas to study further. Make sure you follow up and review materials related to questions you miss on the practice exam before scheduling a real exam. Only when you've covered all the ground and feel comfortable with the whole scope of the practice exam should you take a real one.

If you take the practice exam and don't score at least 75 percent correct, you'll want to practice further. Though one is not available for Exam 70-100 yet, Microsoft usually provides free Personal Exam Prep (PEP) exams and the self-assessment exams from the Microsoft Certified Professional Web site's download page (its location appears in the next section). If you're more ambitious or better funded, you might want to purchase a practice exam from a third-party vendor.

As of this writing, although a true practice exam for Analyzing Requirements and Defining Solution Architectures is not available on the Microsoft download page, a demo exam showing the new question types is available. It's definitely worth spending some practice time with this demo.

Armed with the information in this book and with the determination to augment your knowledge, you should be able to pass the certification exam. However, you need to work at it; otherwise, you'll spend the exam fee more than once before you finally pass. If you prepare seriously, you should do well. Good luck!

Additional Resources

A good source of information about Microsoft certification exams comes from Microsoft itself. Because its products and technologies—and the exams that go with them—change frequently, the best place to go for exam-related information is online.

If you haven't already visited the Microsoft Certified Professional site, do so right now. The MCP home page resides at www.microsoft.com/mcp (see Figure 1.1).

Note: This page might not be there by the time you read this, or it might have been replaced by something new and different, because things change regularly on the Microsoft site. Should this happen, please read the section titled "Coping With Change On The Web."

The menu options in the left column of this site point to the most important sources of information in the MCP pages. Here's what to check out:

➤ **Certifications**   Use this menu entry to pick whichever certification program you want to read about.

➤ **Find Exam**   Use this menu entry to pull up a search tool that lets you list all Microsoft exams and locate all exams relevant to any Microsoft certification (MCP, MCP+SB, MCSD, and so on) or those exams that cover a particular product. This tool is quite useful not only to examine the options but also to obtain specific exam preparation information, because each exam has its own associated preparation guide.

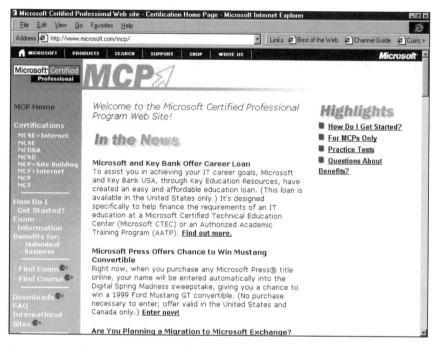

Figure 1.1 The Microsoft Certified Professional Web site.

➤ **Downloads**   Use this menu entry to find a list of the files and practice exams that Microsoft makes available to the public. These include several items worth downloading, especially the Certification Update, the Personal Exam Prep (PEP) exams, various assessment exams, and a general exam study guide. Try to make time to peruse these materials before taking your first exam.

These are just the high points of what's available in the Microsoft Certified Professional pages. As you browse through them—and we strongly recommend that you do—you'll probably find other informational tidbits mentioned that are every bit as interesting and compelling.

Coping With Change On The Web

Sooner or later, all the information we've shared with you about the Microsoft Certified Professional pages and the other Web-based resources mentioned throughout the rest of this book will go stale or be replaced by newer information. In some cases, the URLs you find here might lead you to their replacements; in other cases, the URLs will go nowhere, leaving you with the dreaded "404 File not found" error message. When that happens, don't give up.

You can always find what you want on the Web if you're willing to invest some time and energy. Most large or complex Web sites—and Microsoft's qualifies on both counts—offer a search engine. On all of Microsoft's Web pages, a Search button appears along the top edge of the page. As long as you can get to Microsoft's site (it should stay at www.microsoft.com for a long time), use this tool to help you find what you need.

The more focused you can make a search request, the more likely the results will include information you want. For example, search for the string "training and certification" to produce a lot of data about the subject in general, but if you're looking for a preparation guide for Exam 70-100, "Analyzing Requirements and Defining Solution Architectures," you'll be more likely to get there quickly if you use a search string similar to the following:

```
"Exam 70-100" AND "preparation guide"
```

Likewise, if you want to find the Training and Certification downloads, try a search string such as this:

```
"training and certification" AND "download page"
```

Finally, feel free to use general search tools—such as www.search.com, www.altavista.com, and www.excite.com—to look for related information. Although Microsoft offers great information about its certification exams online, there are plenty of third-party sources of information and assistance that need not follow Microsoft's party line. Therefore, if you can't find something where the book says it lives, start looking around. If worst comes to worst, you can email me at drb@azstarnet.com. Please include "MCSD Architectures" in the subject of your message.

Overview
Of Solutions
Development

Terms you'll need to understand:

√ Case study

√ Legacy system

√ Mainframe

√ Distributed application

√ Client/server

√ Business process

√ Business rules

√ Data model

Techniques you'll need to master:

√ Identifying the major steps for developing an information systems solution

√ Differentiating between a two-tier and three-tier application model

√ Analyzing a case study to gather relevant information

√ Describing the conceptual, logical, and physical designs of an application

√ Describing a user interface

√ Describing a data model

For most businesses today, information systems play an integral part in determining the success of the business. With the advent of desktop computing, computer systems and applications have proliferated throughout most business organizations. These newer systems, along with the existing legacy systems, provide the facilities for storing, organizing, accessing, and reporting information that's critical to the business operation. Potentially, these systems can provide access to the detailed information needed to generate better business decisions, and furthermore, they can be instrumental in enabling management to respond quickly to changes in the marketplace. And perhaps most important, the systems can help the business create a better return on its investments and become more profitable.

For the most part, today's information systems are distributed; that is, they're made up of multiple pieces typically working together across a network. One of the contributing factors leading to distributed systems is that no single system will have all the data or capabilities needed for all the computing requirements. Distributing the systems, and including redundant capabilities, also provides a recovery mechanism for dealing with failures in other parts of the system.

Different terms are used to describe the characteristics of these information systems. Because businesses today are continually changing, a major characteristic of the computing systems supporting the business is that the systems must be able to adapt to these changes as well. In addition to being extensible, these systems may also be robust, mission critical, fault tolerant, scalable, flexible, and available.

This book delves into the processes for developing the architecture of such systems and the technology used to build them. However, building these systems is more than simply exploiting the latest technology; it also involves understanding the business processes for which the system will be used. In particular, an information system won't be successful if it doesn't help the business solve its problems and achieve its goals.

Evolution Of Information Systems

By the 1960s, the use of computer technology had expanded from the scientific and military environments into the business environment. These early systems were *centralized*; that is, the hardware, software, and data were all located in one place. By today's standards, these mainframe systems were very large and very expensive, and most companies probably had only one of these computers in the organization. Thus, all the computing took place on a single system. The applications developed for these early systems were *monolithic* in that a single large application running on a single computer performed all the processing needed to solve a specific problem or accomplish a specific task.

Punched cards, paper tapes, and magnetic tapes were the primary means of entering data into these computers. The cards and tapes were physically brought to the location where the computer hardware was located, and the computer could then process the data. This type of processing is commonly referred to as *batch processing*. Later, *interactive processing* allowed users to access these systems using computer terminals that could be used to enter data.

Although the centralized computing model was inconvenient for end users who had to go to the computer to use it, maintaining the system was simplified, because everything was located in one place.

In the 1970s, time-sharing was introduced, but time-sharing systems were still centralized systems. Access to these systems was provided using a computer terminal, and multiple users accessed and used the system simultaneously. By definition, a time-sharing system provided the user perception that each user was the only user on the system. In addition to local terminals, time-sharing systems also provided remote access using telecommunication lines. These lines connected the remote terminals with the computer, and although the computing was still centralized, it was no longer necessary for the users to be at the same site as the computer.

By the 1980s, smaller minicomputer systems were replacing or augmenting the mainframe and time-sharing systems. Minicomputer systems were typically networked together; that is, a telecommunications link connected multiple systems together. The network links were limited in features and capacity and usually restricted to the same kinds of computers. However, the network connections did make it possible for one system to access the files on another system. With networking, it was no longer required that the hardware, applications, and data all reside in a central location. Thus, the technology began evolving from a centralized model to a *distributed model*. These smaller systems were less costly than the large mainframe systems, so companies could purchase multiple systems and deploy them throughout various departments. Monolithic applications could be broken down, or *modularized*, into several smaller applications that could run on different systems. Furthermore, the use of computers in business became more widespread because many smaller businesses that could not afford a large mainframe could purchase a minicomputer.

However, the smaller, distributed systems also introduced a problem that hadn't existed in the centralized environment. Maintaining and managing multiple systems that were geographically distributed was much more complex than managing a single centralized system.

In the 1990s, businesses began utilizing personal desktop workstations and high-end servers to provide a major source of computing resources. Some of the tasks previously relegated to a mainframe or minicomputer were migrated to these systems. The computing model also began shifting from distributed systems to *distributed applications*. In a distributed application, a problem is solved or a task is accomplished by multiple applications running separately and working together. Distributed applications communicate with one another using *interprocess communication (IPC)* mechanisms. When applications are distributed across different computer systems, the resources of multiple computers can be utilized.

A good example of a distributed application is the *two-tier client/server* model that became very popular for implementing applications requiring access to a database. In this model, an application running on each desktop (the client) accesses the data in a centralized database on a backend system (the server), which supports numerous distributed clients. Although the client/server model enables the sharing of computer resources and also provides a centralized database, management of the client applications is still more complex than the centralized systems of the past.

 Many distributed applications are implemented as client/server applications in which a requestor (the client) requests services from a provider (the server). Client/server applications are usually implemented as separate applications running on separate systems; however, this isn't a requirement. The different applications can also run on the same computer system. The interaction between the two applications, in which one requests services that the other provides, determines the nature of a client/server application.

An enhancement to the two-tier client/server model is the *three-tier client/ server* model that draws on the strengths of the centralized and distributed models used in the past. In the three-tier model, applications are partitioned into three distinct, self-contained functional areas: user services, business services, and database services. Many new development projects are utilizing this model, and from the development perspective, it enables multiple development teams to simultaneously work on the application, with each team focusing on a specific functional area.

From the deployment perspective, the different services might be implemented on a single system or distributed across multiple systems, depending on the application requirements. A typical three-tier application may utilize centralized business and database services with distributed user business services. This way, the application services, which contain the bulk of the business logic, can be easily modified to adapt to changing business conditions. Another important feature of this three-tier model is that a variety of different user service clients can access the same business and database services.

Although the technology has advanced significantly from the mainframe days, understanding the evolution of information processing systems is important because remnants of some of these earlier systems still exist today in many businesses. Some legacy systems still provide processing that's critical to the survival of the business. Furthermore, processes and procedures that were imposed on organizations by the earlier systems may still be in place. A key part of developing a new system will be integrating it successfully with the systems and processes that are already in place.

The Internet

A limitation of the first distributed systems was that only similar systems could participate in the network. True *interoperability* among different computers also required a translation of data between the systems.

During the late 1960s, several research agencies working with the Department of Defense needed a way of networking their systems together so they could exchange data with each other. However, this wasn't possible because the different agencies were using different types of systems. Although each agency could network its own systems together, it wasn't possible to communicate across the different networks. The Advanced Research Projects Agency of the Department of Defense provided the funding for producing additional networking technologies that enabled this internetworking communication. The first implementation, known as ARPAnet, has since evolved into what we now call the Internet.

Developing Solutions To Business Problems

Developing a solution that solves a business problem is more than simply writing a slick software application utilizing the latest technologies. In particular, the application must address the business requirements that are driving the application development. And, once developed, the application must be accepted by the end users and must be useful to them for solving their day-to-day problems. In other words, the application must be tailored to the particular processes that drive the business and incorporate the business rules into the software.

To accomplish this, a series of steps are used to determine a viable solution. The first question to be answered is: What do we want? Answering the next question—How can we build it?—may, in fact, constrain the original wish list. But once the requirements are refined and a viable solution appears feasible, the high-level abstractions can provide the information needed to produce the detailed designs that will be the basis for the actual implementation. These steps are depicted in Figure 2.1. The steps include:

➤ Analyzing business requirements

➤ Defining technical architecture

➤ Developing data models

➤ Developing applications

➤ Deploying

➤ Maintaining

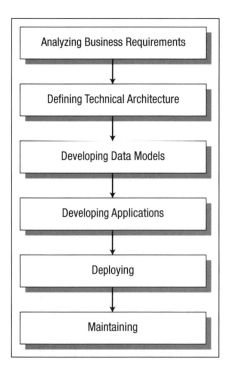

Figure 2.1   The processes for developing a business-oriented information system.

Analyzing Business Requirements

Solution development begins by analyzing the business's requirements. This is a high-level process of gathering information from key players about what needs to be done, why it needs to be done, and what the outcome is expected to produce. Business requirements can then be summarized and documented. A complete *business requirements analysis* will provide information on:

➤ Project scope

➤ Business needs

➤ Security

➤ Performance

➤ Maintainability

➤ Extensibility

➤ Availability

➤ Scalability

➤ Human factors

➤ Integration with the existing environment

➤ Methodologies

Chapter 4 provides information on analyzing business requirements and discusses these topics in more detail.

Defining Solution Architectures

Once the business requirements have been identified, the capabilities and constraints of the enabling technologies can be evaluated to begin formulating a technical architecture that's appropriate for the solution.

The first consideration is: What is the scope of the solution? Perhaps the solution is best implemented as a single-user desktop application. A two-tier solution might be appropriate for a small number of users. Or perhaps an Internet solution is required that supports tens of thousands of users.

The next consideration is: What technologies are appropriate? Are there any standards in place that should be followed? Will the solution require any proprietary technologies? Answers to these questions will have an impact on the integration of the solution into the company environment.

In addition to the technology issues, the technical architecture must also address data-related issues:

➤ How is the data going to be stored?

➤ How much data is there?

➤ How many users will need access to the data?

➤ Will users only need to read the data or will they also require write access to the data?

➤ What reports will be produced from the data?

Developing a technical architecture also involves determining how to verify the feasibility of implementing this particular solution. Will the solution satisfy all the requirements given the technology and environmental constraints?

And lastly, the technical architecture should outline a strategy that can be used to deploy the solution once it's been developed. Chapter 5 provides information on defining that technical architecture and discusses these topics in more detail.

Developing Data Models

The technical architecture provides the data requirements needed for the solution, but the technical architecture itself doesn't specify any information about actual data items and how they're organized. This information is defined in the data model, which, in turn, defines the *metadata*; that is, the data about the data.

The data model will identify all the data elements, *entities*, and define the characteristics, *attributes*, for each element, so an important consideration of the data model is specifying how the numerous entities will be organized. *Data normalization rules* are used to provide the guidelines for organizing the data. In addition, the data model will specify how entities are *related* to each other, and it will also specify any special rules, *constraints*, that will be used to enforce the *integrity* of the data.

Chapter 6 provides information on developing data models and discusses these topics in more detail.

Developing Applications

After the technical architecture and data models are developed, the next task is to start identifying and designing the applications you'll need. Developing applications involves three different activities:

➤ Developing a conceptual and logical application design

➤ Designing the user interface and user services

➤ Deriving the physical design

Most people assume that the key activities for developing applications are writing and debugging code. Though these are essential development activities, they really can't begin until the conceptual, logical, and physical designs have been determined.

Developing The Conceptual And Logical Design

Application design begins with a conceptual design that's based on the business requirements and typically includes scenarios, workflow process models, and task sequence models.

The logical design, which is later derived from the conceptual design, describes the application system on a high level of abstraction. The logical model breaks the application into functional modules that represent the business components for an application. The logical design defines the *application services* that will be provided by the application.

Using the models produced by the conceptual and logical designs makes it possible to view the application in terms of business components and software architectures.

Six key factors are usually used to evaluate the logical design. The exact evaluation criteria will be determined by the particular solution; however, *performance*, *maintainability*, *extensibility*, *availability*, *scalability*, and *security* usually present the most difficult constraints that must be addressed by the logical design.

Chapter 7 provides information on developing the conceptual and logical design of an application and discusses these topics in more detail.

Designing The User Interface And User Services

The user interface typically provides the presentation services for the application. That means it provides facilities for:

➤ Navigation

➤ Data input

➤ Data output

➤ User assistance

Depending on the physical implementation, the user interface may simply be part of an application or it could be a separate client application. It could even be a set of scripted Web pages that are displayed in a browser.

Chapter 8 provides information on designing the user interface and services and discusses these topics in more detail.

The "user" of an application usually refers to the person using the application, so the user interface refers to the forms, controls, reports and other objects that are provided so that the end user can interact with the application. But the "user" of an application doesn't necessarily have to be a person; another application can also be considered the user. In this case, the user interface is the program-to-program communication facility that's provided for the applications to work together.

Deriving The Physical Design

After the data models are designed, the conceptual and logical models are determined, the user interface is designed, and the application services are identified, it's almost time to start building the application. That is, as soon as all considerations regarding the physical design are incorporated into the solution. These activities involve:

➤ Evaluating the physical design

➤ Designing the components

➤ Developing a database access strategy

The physical design specifies how the actual application is going to be implemented, and it identifies specific technologies that will be utilized. A number of options are usually available, and a series of tradeoff decisions will be required to determine a viable physical design. The same six key factors used to evaluate the logical design are now used to evaluate the physical design. Here again, the exact evaluation criteria will be determined by the particular solution; however, *performance, maintainability, extensibility, availability, scalability,* and *security* usually present the most difficult constraints that must be addressed by the physical design.

Two specific areas require special attention at this time—*component design* and *database access.* The design of these pieces can greatly affect the overall operation of the application.

Chapter 9 provides information on deriving the physical design and discusses these topics in more detail.

Deploying And Maintaining Solutions

Once the applications have been implemented and tested, the system is deployed. And as soon as the system is deployed, it must be maintained. Both deployment and maintenance are important to the overall acceptance and success of the solution. However, in this book, these topics are discussed only in the context of other solution planning and development processes. In particular, separate chapters aren't devoted to these topics. This is done to maintain focus on the stated exam objectives, not because these activities are any less important in the solution development process.

Case Studies

Throughout this book, case studies will be used to provide practical applicability to the topics being discussed. These case studies present typical types of information processing problems that businesses are encountering today. Each case study will first provide a little background information about the business, then the case study will introduce the problem and some of the players.

You won't be asked to develop a solution to the problem for the case studies used here. Instead, a solution will be provided. You'll then have the opportunity to evaluate certain aspects of the solution. For example, you may be asked questions about how the solution works, and to answer this, it may be helpful to create a data flow diagram. Or you may be asked about certain implications of the data model being used. For instances like this, it may be helpful to create an entity relationship diagram.

It's important to understand how these case studies work.

The following strategy is useful for effectively working with case studies:

1. Determine what is going on; get a full picture of the background of the problem.

2. Determine who the players are and how each perceives the problem and solution.

3. Determine the current environment.

4. Analyze the solution architecture.

For the certification exam, case studies are presented using tabbed dialog boxes. Each tab presents a particular aspect of the case study. The All tab allows you to view the entire case study as a single document.

Because the case studies can be somewhat detailed, review the questions before reading the case study. This will help you focus on the relevant details when you read the case study.

What's Going On?

The background information will lay the groundwork to help you determine what's going on. Here you can find out key information about the company, including the type of business the company is involved in, and some of the problems the company is experiencing.

Who Are The Players?

A number of key players will have a vested interest in the problem that's being discussed, and it's important to remember that each player has a unique perception of:

➤ What the problem actually is

➤ What the key requirements are for the solution

➤ What the ultimate solution should provide

In particular, each player will reflect on how the problem affects him or his department. For example, the data entry supervisor may know that to enter the weekly timecard data for all of the company employees into the current system, the data entry clerks are working overtime. The auditor may know that there's an unacceptable level of inaccurate charges being made to customers for hours that are incorrect. And the CIO may know that there's a high error rate of the time being reported against various projects. The vice president simply wants to reduce operational expenses.

By understanding each player's perception of the problem and what needs to be done, you'll be able to determine how the problem is impacting the business and how to start prioritizing the various solution requirements.

Determine The Current Environment

In today's business environment, new systems are rarely rolled into production while the existing systems are being unplugged. Rather than a revolution, an evolution usually takes place as the new solution is integrated into the old environment. Likewise, in the case studies, the current environment is usually not being totally abandoned. Therefore, understanding the current environment is important to the solution design process.

Analyze The Solution Architecture

The new system will most likely be based on an architecture that consists of new components integrated with the older legacy systems. It's important to be able to understand and evaluate how the new solution addresses the requirements. Performance, scalability, security, and extensibility are a few of the key aspects to examine to see if the requirements are being met.

Practice Questions

Question 1

Which of the following statements best describes the computing environment found in today's business environment?

○ a. No computing facilities

○ b. A single mainframe computer

○ c. A single high-end desktop system

○ d. A distributed network of computers

Answer d is correct. Today's business environment usually consists of multiple desktop systems integrated with servers and other legacy systems on a network, which often provides access to the Internet as well.

Question 2

Which of the following statements is a business rule?

○ a. Orders are only accepted for valid customers.

○ b. The overtime rate is 1.5 times the base pay rate.

○ c. Deleting an order must delete all associated order line items as well.

○ d. All of the above.

Answer d is correct. All of the responses represent examples of business rules that might be implemented in an application.

Question 3

> Which of the following statements best describes a distributed application?
>
> ○ a. Application software that is shipped for installation on a number of end-user systems
>
> ○ b. Software that solves a specific problem but utilizes the computing resources of multiple systems
>
> ○ c. The software layer that provides the infrastructure for connecting various application pieces
>
> ○ d. Application software that is produced for a mainframe system

Answer b is correct. Distributed applications consist of multiple applications distributed across different computing resources, all working together to solve a specific problem. It's often easier to develop such applications using a software layer that provides the infrastructure for the entire application as described in choice c. Microsoft Transaction Server is an example of software that provides this type of infrastructure.

Question 4

> Reorder the following steps into the sequence recommended for developing business information systems.
>
> Deploying the solution
>
> Analyzing business requirements
>
> Maintaining the solution
>
> Developing the applications for the solution
>
> Developing data models for the solution
>
> Defining the technical architecture for the solution

The correct order is:

Analyzing business requirements

Defining the technical architecture for the solution

Developing data models for the solution

Developing the applications for the solution

Deploying the solution

Maintaining the solution

Question 5

The following types of designs are used for developing an application:

Conceptual

Logical

Physical

Identify the appropriate design in which each of the following might be found:

A data flow diagram showing the workflow

The specific systems in the network in which the software will run

A list of services the application will provide

The indexes used on a database table

The organization of data into database tables

The sequence of tasks that will be performed to compute the answer

The correct answer is

Conceptual

A data flow diagram showing the workflow

The sequence of tasks that will be performed to compute the answer

Logical

A list of services the application will provide

The organization of data into database tables

Physical

The specific systems in the network in which the software will run

The indexes used on a database table

Question 6

What are the three services provided by a three-tier client/server model?

- ○ a. Interactive, batch, and remote
- ○ b. User, business, and data
- ○ c. Hardware, software, and middleware
- ○ d. Business, network, and data

Answer b is correct. User, business, and data are the three types of services provided in the three-tier client/server model.

Question 7

Which of the following pieces are not required for building a distributed application? [Check all correct answers]

- ❑ a. Network components
- ❑ b. Database access components
- ❑ c. Infrastructure or middleware components
- ❑ d. Microsoft Transaction Server

Answers b and d are correct. Notice that the question asks for pieces that are not required. A distributed application, an application that runs on multiple computing resources, would definitely require networking components. Likewise, an infrastructure is needed to tie all the pieces together. Although Microsoft Transaction Server can be used to provide this infrastructure, distributed applications can be built without it. And though many applications do require access to a database, many do not. Therefore, database access components may not be required.

Need To Know More?

 The Enterprise Edition of Visual Studio V6 contains an online book titled *Developing for the Enterprise*. This online documentation is also available on the Microsoft Developer Network Library. Part 1, "Enterprise Design and Architecture," discusses application requirements and design methodologies.

 www.microsoft.com/

Many of the product groups at Microsoft publish case studies. Although these studies have a positive marketing spin to them, they do describe how Microsoft technologies and methodologies are being utilized to solve business problems and develop solutions. Many of these case studies provide further insight that's useful for the certification exam.

 www.microsoft.com/data/duwamish.htm

This Web site presents a detailed case study for a fictional company called Duwamish Books. As the company grows, the application requirements and software evolves from a desktop application to a three-tier client/server environment and, finally, to a Web-based retail store. The site provides documentation of the different applications as well as discussions of the issues and strategies involved with the design and migration.

 www.microsoft.com/industry/

This is a good starting point for enterprise application case studies. From this Web page you can search for case studies by specific industry.

Microsoft Solution Framework

Terms you'll need to understand:

√ Microsoft Solution Framework (MSF)

√ Team model

√ Process model

√ Application model

√ Solutions design model

√ User services

√ Business services

√ Data services

√ Conceptual design

√ Logical design

√ Physical design

Techniques you'll need to master:

√ Identifying the roles in the MSF team model

√ Identifying the phases and milestones in the MSF process model

√ Identifying the services in the MSF application model

√ Identifying the perspectives in the MSF solutions design model

MSF provides a set of models and measurable milestones that can provide essential guidelines as well as a roadmap for planning, building, and managing Information Technology projects. Microsoft created this framework by collecting and analyzing the experiences of its internal product development organizations, its customers, and its business partners. The best practices with repeatable success factors were then incorporated into MSF.

The solution framework utilizes these valuable models:

➤ **Team Model**   This model, one of the core MSF models, shows you how to organize people in building high-performance teams.

➤ **Process Model**   This standard guides you in organizing project activities, so you can make better development tradeoffs. It, too, is one of the core MSF models.

➤ **Application Model**   The application archetype provides a blueprint for designing modular applications to include the flexibility needed for scaling, performance, enhancement, and distribution.

➤ **Solutions Design Model**   The solutions design guideline shows you how to design applications from a user and business perspective for anticipating users' needs.

➤ **Enterprise Architecture Model**   This example provides guidelines for making key decisions regarding the information, applications, and technology needed to support the business as it grows and evolves.

➤ **Total Cost of Ownership Model**   This model provides a process for assessing, improving, and managing information technology costs to minimize costs and maximize value.

The rest of this chapter will describe these various models in greater detail.

A key aspect of MSF is that it allows everyone to agree on the higher-level aspects of the project, including vision, architecture, and responsibilities. Another key aspect is that the team stays with the project, driving it to completion, rather than working in one narrow specialty discipline and passing the work to another team to complete. Each team has all the skills needed to make the trade-off decisions necessary to release a product, and the entire project is gated by a series of milestones that serve as a useful tool for the team in measuring progress against the original project goals.

Microsoft is continually evaluating its own project methodologies and gathering feedback from others who are using MSF. Based on this information, existing MSF models will be enhanced and new models will be developed. Thus, MSF is dynamically evolving to adapt to new technologies and incorporate the best practices.

Team Model

One of the fundamental success factors for any project is having the right project team. A keystone in MSF is the team model. Six essential and clearly defined roles make up the model. Team members perform overlapping roles and share responsibility for *Program Management, Product Management, Development, Testing, User Education,* and *Logistics Management.* Each project role is responsible for different milestones in the project life cycle.

In particular, the team model doesn't define a management or reporting structure for who reports to whom. In fact, in many cases, the project team includes members from several different organizations, who may report to different managers. Figure 3.1 depicts the roles in the team model.

The team consists of a group of peers who have the skills needed to make the important trade-off decisions that are required to successfully build and release the product. Team members have a well-defined project role and are focused on a specific mission, while the leaders of each team are responsible for the management, guidance, and coordination among the teams. It's the job of everyone on the team to ship the right product at the right time. Working together, team members determine the vision for the product, define the product, define the development process, and schedule milestones; and the team is responsible for tracking team progress and reporting status.

The team model supports empowerment, accountability, identity, consensus, and checks and balances for the team members. These terms are defined as follows:

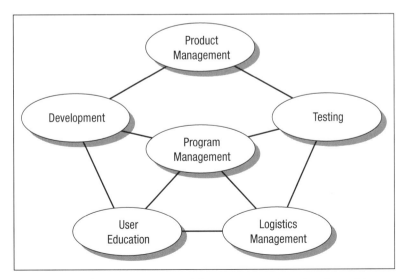

Figure 3.1   The MSF team model isn't a reporting structure; it's a group of peers who perform six clearly defined project roles.

➤ **Empowerment** Team members working on a project are given the authority to make decisions in their areas of expertise. For example, developers may be given substantial control in deciding how to build an application and what technologies to use.

➤ **Accountability** Team members are individually accountable for all aspects of a project, including envisioning, planning, developing, stabilizing, and shipping the product.

➤ **Identity** Team members identify with a higher degree of control and shared responsibility. For example, a team member may view his job as shipping the product by July 12 rather than simply developing the order entry forms.

➤ **Consensus** An atmosphere of openness exists among team members because they identify more with the product than with their individual functional contributions and because they share a mutual accountability for the product.

➤ **Checks and Balances** Team members represent a balance of diverse skill sets, assignments, and viewpoints.

Characteristics Of The MSF Team Model

Each of the six essential and clearly defined roles in the MSF team model has clear goals and objectives. To fulfill these roles, individuals organize into small multidisciplinary teams, with team size varying from three to eight members who work as part of a larger project team. Small teams facilitate the freedom of communication among team members. Teams work in parallel, with frequent synchronization points because in this way, project assignments can be made to a small group of people who share the responsibility for their own fate. Small teams are more effective than larger teams because of lower communication overhead, as well as lower management overhead, and smaller teams usually lead to faster implementation and higher product quality.

The project is driven by a shared vision in which team members have interdependent and overlapping roles and shared responsibilities. This encourages teams to work closely with each other and to share the common responsibility for releasing the right product at the appropriate time. As a result, everyone on the team knows what the group is trying to do, what the finished product will look like, what the basis of the product strategy is, and when the team must deliver the product if the product is to have its intended effect. A harmonious sense of purpose is shared by the team members.

Everyone in the group also participates in the design of the product. Indeed, successful product design requires that the best ideas become the basis for the product.

Team members also have both technology and business knowledge. Team members not only have a deep understanding of technology but also know how to translate this knowledge into applications that solve real business problems.

The project focus is on competency and on releasing the product. Team members concentrate on doing what they do well and on completing the project on time. Completing the project means that the product is available to the users who can start using it and who can benefit from the facilities the product provides.

The team solicits and evaluates end-user feedback throughout the project rather than waiting for feedback after the product is released. In the envisioning phase, the team establishes a shared vision for the product with the end user and begins setting the proper expectations. During the planning phase, user requirements are analyzed and refined. Finally, the end user participates by testing prototypes and prerelease beta versions of the product.

Lastly, reviews are planned at project milestones to learn from current and past projects. Immediately after achieving a milestone, the project teams conduct a review to highlight what has been learned. In particular, the team identifies what practices worked well and what practices might need to be changed in the future.

Roles In The MSF Team Model

The six roles in the Microsoft team model include: Product Management, Program Management, Development, Testing, User Education, and Logistics Management.

Product Management

Product management's main function is to establish and sustain the business case for the project. In addition, this role drives the team to achieve a shared project vision with the customer and sets the customer's expectations. *Satisfied customers* is its key goal.

In summary, product management:

➤ Drives shared project vision/scope.

➤ Manages the definition of customer requirements.

➤ Develops and maintains the business case.

➤ Manages customer expectations.

➤ Drives feature versus schedule trade-off decisions.

➤ Manages marketing, evangelizing, and public relations.

Program Management

Program management's main role is the overall responsibility for the application's functional specification and managing the day-to-day coordination that will ensure a successful product completion. In this capacity the role serves as a critical link between development and product management, and the role is best described as the leader, facilitator, and coordinator of the project, but not the boss. *Delivery within project constraints* is its key goal.

In summary, program management:

➤ Drives the development process.

➤ Manages the product specification.

➤ Facilitates communication and negotiation within the team.

➤ Maintains the project schedule and reports project status.

➤ Drives overall critical trade-off.

Development

Development's role is to create the product for the team; it defines the vision for each feature, then designs, builds, and tests the features. *Delivery to product specifications* is a key goal.

In summary, development:

➤ Specifies the features of the physical design.

➤ Estimates the time and effort needed to complete each feature.

➤ Builds the features.

➤ Prepares the product for distribution.

Testing

The testing role, sometimes referred to as quality assurance, ensures that all issues are known to the team and addressed before releasing the product; an issue is any matter that's in dispute between two or more parties in the project. Testing independently verifies compliance of all project team deliverables. In the MSF, testing is more than simply checking the pieces at project completion because it plays an active role early in the life of a project. *Release after addressing all issues* is a key goal.

In summary, testing:

➤ Ensures that all issues are known.

➤ Develops testing strategy and plans.

User Education

The primary role of user education is to act as the advocate on the team for the end user of the product. *Improved user performance* is the key goal here.

In summary, user education:

➤ Acts as an end-user advocate on the team.

➤ Manages the user requirement definition.

➤ Designs and develops performance support systems, including documentation, online help files, and training.

➤ Drives the trade-off decisions relating to usability and user performance enhancement.

Logistics Management

The logistics management role is the advocate on the team for operations, product support, help desk, and other delivery channel organizations. In this capacity, logistics management ensures that deployment of the product is smooth and that the product is manageable and supportable in the future. The key goal here for team members is *smooth product deployment*.

In summary, logistics management:

➤ Acts as advocate for operations, support, and delivery channels.

➤ Manages procurement.

➤ Manages product deployment.

➤ Drives the trade-off decisions associated with manageability and supportability.

➤ Manages operations, support, and delivery channel relationships.

Sharing Team Roles

Although there are six roles defined by the team model, smaller projects do not necessarily require six separate team members. The team model allows some of the roles to be shared as long as the combination presents no conflicts of interest. For example, it might be possible for the same team member to fulfill the logistics management role as well as the user education role. On the other hand, sharing the roles of development and testing is not recommended. Likewise, because product management is the advocate for the end-user and program management is responsible for project deadlines, these two roles are best filled by different people.

Process Model

Another core model in the Microsoft Solution Framework is the process model, the purpose of which is to provide a framework that will guide the team throughout the development effort and keep the project on track. Organizations have used different process models for years with varying degrees of success, including the traditional System Development Life Cycle model, which is described later in this chapter.

The MSF process model is based on the product life cycle model utilized successfully within the Microsoft development groups. This model consists of four distinct phases, with each phase culminating in a major milestone, and a set of deliverables, produced by the team, is also associated with each milestone. Figure 3.2 graphically illustrates the MSF process model, and the milestones are depicted as points in a cyclical, spiral process. This is done to emphasize that the process is, in fact, iterative and based on successive refinements. Because the MSF process model is iterative rather than linear, it provides flexibility and enables the project team to respond to changing priorities as the project evolves.

The four distinct phases of the MSF process model are *envisioning*, *planning*, *developing*, and *stabilizing*. These four phases identify the critical planning,

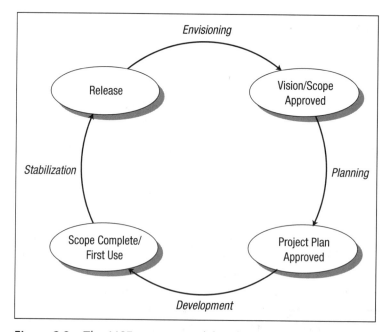

Figure 3.2 The MSF process model is characterized by four major milestones that are part of an iterative cycle.

assessment, and coordination activities between the project team and the key project stakeholders.

Each phase is marked with a single major milestone that represents the successful culmination of all the activities of the phase. In addition to this major event, each phase may also have intermediate milestones leading up to the major milestone.

These events mark the self-regulation points of the process. They're review and synchronization points rather than freeze points. They represent points in time when all team members synchronize their project deliverables, and members of the project team agree they've achieved the objectives of that particular project phase. Milestones allow the team to adjust the project scope to accommodate changing customer requirements or to allow for changes that have developed during the course of the project.

Characteristics Of The MSF Process Model

The MSF process model has the following four characteristics:

➤ **Milestone-Based Approach**   Major milestones, as well as interim milestones, serve as checkpoints for synchronizing project deliverables.

➤ **Clear Ownership and Accountability**   The responsibility for each milestone is clearly identified and associated with a team role.

➤ **Risk-Driven Scheduling**   Project elements with the most risk are identified and addressed as early in the project as possible.

➤ **Versioned Releases**   The concept of dividing large projects into multiple versioned releases having multiple releases throughout the product life cycle enables the team to set more realistic expectations. In addition, new functionality can be planned and managed with a higher probability of meeting release date goals.

Phases Of The MSF Process Model

The MSF Process Model is a *process-oriented model* consisting of four distinct project phases, discussed in greater detail here.

Envisioning Phase

This first phase is the point in time when the project team achieves agreement with the customer on the overall direction to be taken for the project, including what will and will not be included in the product. Both the vision and scope are determined during this phase. Vision describes what is most desirable from a business and user perspective, but isn't limited by the technical details of implementation.

Once a vision is established, the team can develop the project scope, which maps the vision against the reality of what can actually be done to achieve the vision. Scope encompasses factors such as available technologies, costs, schedules, and resources.

The envisioning phase culminates in the vision/scope approved milestone. This event signifies team consensus on:

➤ The overall vision for the product.

➤ Which business requirements need to be addressed first.

➤ The time frame when the functionality is required.

➤ Any risks and assumptions associated with the project.

➤ Any business constraints that may affect the project.

Three intermediate milestones lead up to the final milestone of the envisioning phase. The milestones and deliverables associated with the envisioning phase are shown in Table 3.1.

Planning Phase

This project phase expands on the vision and scope defined during the envisioning phase. The project team, the customer, and the key project stakeholders all agree on what the priorities are, what will be delivered, and when it will be delivered. This is all specified in the project plan, which establishes the structure for completing the project.

The planning phase culminates in the project plan approved milestone, which means that the team agrees to the total solution and that the project should proceed to the next phase.

Table 3.1 Envisioning phase milestones and deliverables.		
Phase	**Milestones**	**Deliverables**
Envisioning	Team formation complete	Vision/scope document
	Draft vision/scope	Risk management plan
	Final vision/scope	Project structure document
	Vision/scope approved	Next phase estimate
		Issues and bug database

In fact, the entire team may not agree on every single issue. It's possible to agree to disagree on certain aspects of the project and still achieve the level of consensus necessary to proceed with the project.

Three intermediate milestones lead up to the final milestone of the planning phase. These and the deliverables associated with the planning phase are shown in Table 3.2.

The combined content of the conceptual design document and the design specification encompasses the information found in a functional specification.

Development Phase

During this phase, plans are converted into actions; in particular, a production-ready solution is developed. This implies that all features have been completed and the product is ready for external testing and stabilization. The completion of this phase marks the opportunity for all to evaluate the product, allowing any remaining issues to be identified and addressed before the product is released.

Table 3.2   Planning phase milestones and deliverables.

Phase	Milestones	Deliverables
Planning	Conceptual design complete	Conceptual design document
	Design specification complete	Design specification
	Master project plan complete	Security plan
	Project plan approved	Test plan
		User education plan
		Logistics plan
		Updated risk management plan
		Master project schedule
		Master project plan

The developing phase culminates in the scope complete/first use milestone, which means that the team agrees that the solution is ready to be deployed. Furthermore, it means that any additional facilities for support and training are also ready to be deployed.

Three intermediate milestones lead up to the final milestone of the development phase, which with the deliverables associated with that phase are shown in Table 3.3.

Stabilization Phase

During this project phase, the focus is on testing and quality assurance. Although these activities have also taken place during the development phase, they're now performed concurrently with further code refinements.

The stabilization phase culminates in the release milestone, which means that the team agrees the solution is fully deployed as defined by the scope of the project and the performance of the solution is consistent with the project objectives. Releasing the product could mark the beginning of full-scale customer shipments, or it might mean that the product is ready to be placed in service. In either case, the project team officially hands the product off to another group and is no longer involved with problem escalation.

Four intermediate milestones lead up to the final event of the stabilization phase; these and the deliverables associated with the phase are shown in Table 3.4.

Table 3.3 Development phase milestones and deliverables.		
Phase	**Milestones**	**Deliverables**
Development	Lab testing complete	Pilot plan
	Proof of concept complete	Training plan
	Pilot complete	Capacity plan
	Scope complete/ first use	Business continuation plan
		Rollout plan
		Updated risk management plan
		Documentation
		Versioned functional specification
		Updated schedule

Table 3.4 Stabilization phase milestones and deliverables.		
Phase	Milestones	Deliverables
Stabilization	Rollout begins	Project binaries
	Training complete	Release notes
	Rollout complete	Versioned source
	Stabilization complete	Training manuals
	Release	Documentation
		Updated Risk Management Plan
		Facility and platform installation
		Software/data setup/conversion

Traditional Process Models

Traditional process models are usually based on the Systems Development Life Cycle (SDLC). The SDLC is a *task-oriented model* consisting of distinct phases that usually include the following stages:

➤ Definition

➤ Analysis

➤ Design

➤ Construction

➤ Test

➤ Transition and Migration

➤ Production

Each phase consists of a set of tasks that must be completed before the next phase can begin. Usually, different teams are responsible for each phase of the project. For example, system analysts may gather the requirements and develop the specifications that will be used by programmers to generate the software.

One of the characteristics of the SDLC model is that each phase must be heavily documented before another group can proceed with the next phase. This tends to finalize many aspects early in the project; it's then often difficult to adapt to changing priorities as the project evolves. The SDLC is sometimes referred to as a waterfall model because each project phase is analogous to the steps in a waterfall.

Although the MSF process model also consists of distinct phases, it differs from the SDLC model because it's a *process-oriented model* with high-level milestones rather than a task-oriented model.

Application Model

An application model describes in conceptual terms what an application is, and it establishes definitions, rules, and relationships that form the structure of an application. Although the application model doesn't describe how an application will be implemented, it does provide a starting point for discussing form and function. Using an application model makes it possible to exchange ideas about how the logical design of an application might be structured, and it also makes it easy to exchange ideas about how the physical design of an application might be implemented. Thus, the model helps determine how applications will eventually be built, so understanding the application model is essential if the project team is to effectively develop applications that will be successful in the organization.

Using Microsoft's definition, an application is constructed from a logical network of *consumers* and *suppliers* of services. These services can be distributed across both physical and functional boundaries to support the needs of many different applications. A service is a unit of application logic that implements operations, functions, or transformations that are applied to objects, and they can enforce business rules, perform calculations, manipulate data, and provide facilities for entering, retrieving, viewing, or modifying information.

The MSF application model defines three categories of services: user, business, and data. These promote an n-tiered logical model for distributed applications, which is why the MSF application model is the recommended approach for designing such applications.

Using a model based on clearly defined categories of services directly supports the concept of modularization. Modular applications have many advantages over the single monolithic applications built in the past. Furthermore, the Component Object Model (COM) is an enabling technology that can be used for implementing such modular applications based on this model.

 With the evolution of Internet technologies, the application model has become very attractive because it allows the same set of business services and data services to be accessed from a Web page, as well as from user service components in a client application.

User Services

User services are the units of application logic that provide an application with its interface. The user of an application could be a person or another application; therefore, user services could be a graphical user interface or a programmatic interface.

For example, each of the Microsoft Office products has an extensive graphical user interface. In addition to the user interface, each of these products also provides a set of programmatic interfaces offering the same features and functionality in the form of automation. The two types of interfaces—graphical user and programmatic—are both considered user services.

An application's user services are responsible for managing all aspects of the interaction between the user and the application. Achieving this requires an understanding of the users, the activities that they will need to perform, and the interaction styles that are best suited to the different combinations of user and activity.

 Typical user service components could include code to manipulate forms or perform some application-specific functions. However, it's highly unlikely that user service components would include code such as structured query language (SQL) statements that are used to directly access data. These SQL statements would be found in the business or data services.

Business Services

Business services are the units of application logic that control the enforcement of business rules and ensure the transactional integrity of the operations that they perform. Using the appropriate application of business rules, business services map raw data into information for the user.

The goal of a properly designed business service is to isolate business rule enforcement and data transformation logic from consumers of the service. For example, a user service or another business service won't be aware of what specific operations are being performed. Similarly, the underlying data services, which are the providers to a business service, will also be isolated from the business service. Isolating the business services logic from the user and data services yields the following advantages:

➤ Flexibility in deploying the business services components. For example, business services can be implemented on a separate application server, as stored procedures in a database management system, or as procedures on the client system.

➤ The ability to place different user interface logic in front of a standard set of business services. For example, a set of business services for performing operations on a customer is implemented as a single component running on an application server. The services that the component provides could be used in any of the following client scenarios: as macros running inside Microsoft Office, from a custom application developed with Microsoft Visual Basic, or from Web pages being displayed by Microsoft Internet Explorer.

➤ Greater ease in maintaining business rules and logic by isolating changes from the application's user and data services.

Data Services

Data services are the units of application logic that provide the low-level facilities used for manipulating data. An important concept of the application model is that data services control and provide access to data in such a way that the data service consumers don't need to know where the data is located or how it's accessed. This allows total isolation of details regarding the physical implementation of the data store.

Although it's possible to identify discrete user and business services, such as services that relate to a customer, services at the data service level tend to be more general. For example, a system might contain service components for customers, employees, and vendors. At the business service level, each service component would have a unique set of attributes, services, and rules. However, at the data service level, a data service component named Account Information might be implemented to provide create, read, update, delete, and rollback services for employees, vendors, and customers.

Data services implement data storage and provide the abstraction that relates the schema within business services onto the target data store. Data services aren't restricted to permanent, nonvolatile or structured data; they can handle any situation in which a defined interface can access and manipulate the data.

 The separation of services into three distinct and isolated levels provides several advantages to the development team. Someone experienced in graphical user interface (GUI) design but having little expertise on relational databases can create a user interface without getting bogged down with the details of which database tables and fields are affected. Likewise, the database designer can tune and restructure the database without breaking forms that are bound to a specific field in a table.

Solutions Design Model

The solutions design model provides a step-by-step strategy for designing business-oriented solutions driven by a specific business need. The objective is to align the solution with the goals of the business. The design process is evolutionary and presents three perspectives of the solution:

➤ Conceptual

➤ Logical

➤ Physical

An analogy of the process of designing a building is often used to understand the software design process. A building design starts with the architect's sketches that provide a view of the building for the client. They may contain floor plans and diagrams showing how the building fits in with the surroundings. In designing a software solution, the conceptual design for the project corresponds to the architect's sketches. It all starts with understanding what the user really needs to do and creating one or more easily communicated models that demonstrate this understanding.

The architect's sketches are followed by architectural plans that show the building from the architect's perspective. This second phase in the architectural process combines the client's view with the architect's view and knowledge. From the sketches comes a set of detailed drawings that enable communication with contractors and other parties. This phase corresponds to the logical design phase of the project in which the logical elements and communication paths between them are identified.

Finally, the contractor's plans are drawn up for the builder. At this point, detail is added to the architect's plans to make adjustments for the physical environment of the site as well as the materials that are available to construct the building. This view directs all construction activities. It contains sufficient detail for individual subcontractors to construct their pieces. Similarly, the physical design for an application applies the real-world constraints of technology, as well as implementation and performance considerations to the logical model, enabling developers to build the software.

Conceptual Design

Conceptual design is the process of acquiring, documenting, and validating user and business perspectives of a problem and its solution. The goal is to understand what users do and to identify business needs. The output is scenarios.

Logical Design

Logical design is a view of the solution from the project team's perspective that defines the solution as a set of cooperating objects and their services. These services are grouped into the categories of user, business and data services according to the MSF application model.

The goal of logical design is to describe the structure of the solution and the communication among its elements. The output is a set of objects and services, a high-level user interface design, and a logical database design.

Physical Design

Physical design is a view of the solution from the developer's perspective that defines the components, services, and technologies for the solution. The goal is to apply real-world technology constraints to the logical model, including implementation and performance considerations. The outputs are components, a specific user interface design for a particular platform, and a physical database design.

Practice Questions

Question 1

> Which of the following isn't a role defined by the MSF team model?
>
> ○ a. Development
>
> ○ b. Testing
>
> ○ c. Marketing
>
> ○ d. User education

Answer c is correct. Marketing isn't one of the six major team roles identified in the MSF team model. The marketing function is covered under the role of product manager. Other roles include development, testing, user education, logistics management, and program management.

Question 2

> Which of the following characteristics describe the MSF process model? [Check all correct answers]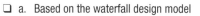
>
> ❏ a. Based on the waterfall design model
>
> ❏ b. Uses the concept of versioned releases
>
> ❏ c. Based on four distinct project phases including envisioning, planning, development, and release
>
> ❏ d. Uses project milestones to synchronize and gate project processes

Answers b and d are correct. The waterfall design model is the basis of the System Development Life Cycle model. The SDLC is different from the MFS process model. Answer c is incorrect because the fourth project phase is stabilization. Release is the major milestone that marks the culmination of the stabilization phase.

Question 3

> Which of the following statements best describes the MSF application model?
>
> ○ a. Provides a set of guidelines for developing C++ component objects
>
> ○ b. Conceptually partitions applications into user, business, and data services
>
> ○ c. Requires a one-to-one mapping between logical and physical components
>
> ○ d. Uses the concept of versioned software releases

Answer b is correct. Answer a is incorrect because the application model isn't tied to any particular implementation language. Answer c is incorrect because the application model doesn't impose any restrictions on the logical or physical design. Although the application will most likely be implemented using versioned releases, this isn't a characteristic of the application model. Versioned releases is a characteristic of the MSF process model.

Question 4

> Which of the following statements best describes the MSF solutions design model?
>
> ○ a. Encompasses concepts from other MSF models
>
> ○ b. Provides an architecture that aligns the solution with the business
>
> ○ c. Uses conceptual, logical, and physical designs to describe a software system
>
> ○ d. All of the above

Answer d is correct.

Question 5

The MSF Team Model defines six major roles. These are:

Product management

Program management

Development

Testing

User education

Logistics management

Identify the appropriate role for each of the following project responsibilities.

Builds the features.

Designs and develops performance support systems (documentation, online help files, training).

Manages operations, support, and delivery channel relationships.

Manages customer expectations.

Drives the development process.

Acts as end-user advocate on the team.

Drives shared project vision/scope.

Manages product deployment.

Manages the product specification.

Drives feature versus schedule trade-off decisions.

Facilitates communication and negotiation within the team.

Maintains the project schedule and reports project status.

Manages the definition of customer requirements.

Specifies the features of the physical design.

Manages marketing, evangelizing, and public relations.

Estimates the time and effort needed to complete each feature.

Acts as advocate for operations, support, and delivery channels.

Develops testing strategy and plans.

Manages the user requirement definition.

Develops and maintains the business case.

Drives the trade-off decisions relating to usability and user performance enhancement.

(continued)

Question 5 (continued)

> Ensures that all issues are known.
>
> Manages procurement.
>
> Drives overall critical trade-off.
>
> Prepares the product for distribution.
>
> Drives the trade-off decisions associated with manageability and supportability.

The correct answers are:

Product management

> Drives shared project vision/scope.
>
> Manages the definition of customer requirements.
>
> Develops and maintains the business case.
>
> Manages customer expectations.
>
> Drives feature versus schedule trade-off decisions.
>
> Manages marketing, evangelizing, and public relations.

Program management

> Drives the development process.
>
> Manages the product specification.
>
> Facilitates communication and negotiation within the team.
>
> Maintains the project schedule and reports project status.
>
> Drives overall critical trade-off.

Development

> Specifies the features of the physical design.
>
> Estimates the time and effort needed to complete each feature.
>
> Builds the features.
>
> Prepares the product for distribution.

Testing

Ensures that all issues are known.

Develops testing strategy and plans.

User education

Acts as end-user advocate on the team.

Manages the user requirement definition.

Designs and develops performance support systems (documentation, online help files, training).

Drives the trade-off decisions relating to usability and user performance enhancement.

Logistics management

Acts as advocate for operations, support, and delivery channels.

Manages procurement.

Manages product deployment.

Drives the trade-off decisions associated with manageability and supportability.

Manages operations, support, and delivery channel relationships.

Question 6

The MSF application model defines three application services. These are:

User services

Business services

Data services

Identify the appropriate service for providing each of the following functions:

Retrieving an invoice record

Creating a monthly customer statement

Providing a graphical user interface

Deleting a particular customer data record

Providing an automation interface

Ensuring that each order item had a corresponding valid order number

Creating a new order for three items

The correct answers are:

User services

Providing a graphical user interface

Providing an automation interface

Business services

Creating a new order for three items

Creating a monthly customer statement

Data services

Retrieving an invoice record

Deleting a particular customer data record

Ensuring that each order item had a corresponding valid order number

Question 7

The MSF process model defines four project phases. These are:

Envisioning

Planning

Development

Stabilization

Identify the appropriate project phase where each of the following project activities would occur:

Selected end users begin evaluating the product.

Appropriate members are selected for the project team.

The project team examines the requirements and agrees on a high-level vision for the product.

Developers write the code.

Detailed project plans and specifications are written.

The product is documented.

The product is prepared to move into production.

A master project schedule is prepared.

The product is tested.

Release notes are prepared.

The correct answers are:

Envisioning

Appropriate members are selected for the project team.

The project team examines the requirements and agrees on a high-level vision for the product.

Planning

A master project schedule is prepared.

Detailed project plans and specifications are written.

Development

> Developers write the code.
>
> The product is documented.
>
> The product is tested.

Stabilization

> Selected end users begin evaluating the product.
>
> The product is tested.
>
> Release notes are prepared.
>
> The product is prepared to move into production.

Need To Know More?

 Smith, Will. "Managing Infrastructure Deployment Projects." Paper presented at TechEd 97. This paper, available on the Microsoft Developer Network Library, describes different aspects of the MSF models and how they apply to a project. Details are provided on many of the team roles during the different project phases, as well as details on the phase deliverables.

 The Microsoft Developer Network Library

This contains numerous technical articles and white papers on the Microsoft Solution Framework, on the enabling technologies like Component Object Model (COM) that are used to develop solutions, and on software development in general. Search the library using keywords like "Architecture," "MSF," "Team Model," "Process Model," and "Application Model."

 www.microsoft.com/enterprise/

This Microsoft Web site provides information on developing solutions for the enterprise. Further information on many of the issues presented in this chapter can be found here along with links to other sites may provide related information.

 www.microsoft.com/enterprise/support/support/consult/c_msfOverview.htm

This Microsoft Web site provides a complete overview of the MSF.

Analyzing Business Requirements

4

. . . .

Terms you'll need to understand:

√ Project scope

√ Business needs

√ Security

√ Performance

√ Transaction

√ Bandwidth

√ Capacity

√ Maintainability

√ Extensibility

√ Availability

√ Fault tolerance

√ Scalability

√ Human factors

√ Accessibility

√ Localization

√ Integration

√ Methodologies

Techniques you'll need to master:

√ Analyzing the scope of a project

√ Analyzing security requirements

√ Analyzing performance requirements

√ Describing the difference between real performance and perceived performance

√ Describing the difference between peak and average performance

√ Analyzing maintainability requirements

√ Analyzing availability requirements

√ Analyzing extensibility requirements

√ Analyzing scalability requirements

√ Analyzing human factors requirements

√ Analyzing integration requirements

Requirements analysis is the first step, and a crucial step, in developing any business solution. This is a high-level process of gathering information, so you can clearly define what the problem really is and what a viable strategy is for solving it. Conducting a detailed requirements analysis involves gathering and analyzing data from many areas. It also involves documenting your findings in one or more specification documents so there's a common understanding among everyone of what the end results will be.

One of the most common reasons cited for the failure of a new system is that the design didn't deliver what the customer really wanted. This often happens because the customer didn't know what he or she wanted until it was *not* delivered. The purpose of requirements analysis is to help ensure that the right system is designed.

This chapter identifies and discusses each of the areas you'll want to include in a requirements analysis for a business. To better understand the process of gathering requirements, a case study is presented that describes Action Aerospace, a fictitious engineering design and manufacturing company that's experiencing a serious problem. This study is referred to throughout the chapter as the various requirements are analyzed.

CASE STUDY: Action Aerospace

The Situation

Action Aerospace is a large organization with over 2,000 employees located in four different facilities. The company is organized into 10 major departments, and each department is further organized into groups of approximately 20 employees each. The company bids on projects to design customized aircraft instrumentation. The main function of Action Aerospace is to design the systems. Once the design has been completed, another company that works closely with Action Aerospace handles the manufacturing process. Business has been good for Action Aerospace, and the company is presently in the process of actively recruiting additional employees.

At any one time, the company will be involved in a number of different projects. The accounting of resources on each project is important not only for resource management but also for auditing purposes. Most of the clients require detailed monthly reports showing the hours spent on project activities. Some of the contracts are with private industry; however, a large number of contracts are sponsored by government agencies. These contracts require additional details for accounting of resources.

To accurately track the time spent on each project, company employees fill out a time card on a daily basis. Theoretically, the time card is filled out at the end of each day. The employee enters an activity code, the time spent doing that activity, and a project code for the activity. Employees are authorized to work only on certain projects, so, consequently, they can only enter a project code on the time card for one of their approved projects.

On Friday afternoon, each employee turns the time card into his supervisor. The supervisor then reviews the time card; they're allowed to make some minor corrections, including the addition of sick time. However, supervisors can't make any new entries on the time card for work-related activities. If this type of correction is required, the supervisor returns the time card to the employee who then makes the necessary changes.

The supervisor then approves the time card by signing it. By noon on Monday, each supervisor submits the signed time cards from the previous week to the Data Entry group. The Data Entry group enters the data into the system for processing Tuesday night.

Unfortunately, getting accurate data entered into the system is a cumbersome process. Many of the time card entries entered into the system get rejected. Error rates frequently run as high as 40 percent. When an error occurs, a report is generated for each supervisor. Supervisors examine these reports, identify the time cards with the errors, and proceed to get them corrected. Reports are generated Tuesday night, and supervisors need to get all errors resolved before the Wednesday night payroll run.

Errors come from three main causes:

➤ Data entry errors

➤ Illegible entries on the time card

➤ Use of unauthorized project codes

After an intense brainstorming session, a specially appointed management team concluded that an online time card system for the employees might reduce the error rate as well as cut the turnaround time on error resolution. The vice president of Operations funded a pilot project that has been underway for the last three months.

For this project, the Information Technology (IT) staff modified several of the data entry applications, so an individual employee could enter his own time card data directly into the system. This eliminates the process of having the Data Entry group do this task. Having each employee enter his own time card data could conceivably reduce the errors from all three of the identified categories.

The Engineering Design group has been participating in the pilot project for the last three months. Each employee in the Engineering Design group has been entering all of his or her own time card data online. The use of paper time cards has been abandoned. Although the error rate has been reduced, there are still significant obstacles to rolling out the pilot project to all departments.

The Environment

Each employee at Action Aerospace has a desktop workstation that's running the Windows 95 operating system. Until recently, only employees engaged in engineering activities had access to workstations; however, as of last month, all employees now have access to a desktop system. The systems are networked together, and each department has an NT Server complete with Back Office and SNA Server software. At this point in time, however, the workstations are used primarily for standalone applications and most departments haven't utilized any of the capabilities of the NT Server.

A single IBM mainframe computer tracks all the company projects. The technology utilized in the current system consists of a number of Common Business-Oriented Language (COBOL) applications operating under Customer Information Control System (CICS). Most data, including all the time card data, is stored in DataBase 2 (DB2) relational databases on the mainframe system. These applications have been developed over a period of years and have evolved with the business. One of the applications in this system is the reporting application, which produces over 100 different reports. This application has been repeatedly enhanced to produce the various reports required by different clients.

Figure 4.1 depicts the current Action Aerospace computing environment.

The IT Department maintains all of these applications. Although the staff is quite knowledgeable in the mainframe environment, they have little experience with the desktop systems and have no experience developing applications that might be distributed between a desktop and a server.

To expedite the pilot deployment, as well as limit the development of new software, some of the existing COBOL applications were modified for the pilot. By running a terminal emulation program in the desktop environment, users can access these applications on the mainframe.

This approach had minimal impact on the existing environment. Although the data entry procedures have been modified, the rest of the mainframe applications have remained untouched, and processing has remained the same.

On a daily basis, each member of the Engineering Design group logs into the mainframe environment, using the terminal emulation software, and runs the

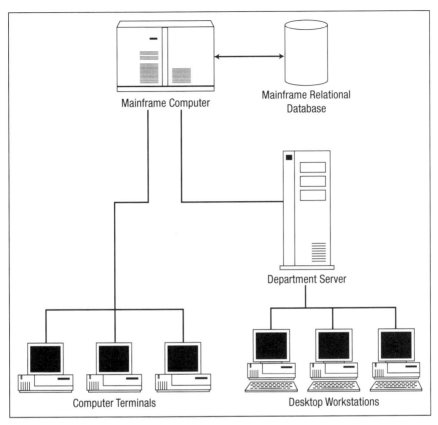

Figure 4.1 The computing environment at Action Aerospace.

Time Card Application, which executes remotely on the mainframe computer. The application features a series of forms and menus that are nearly identical to the original ones used by the Data Entry group.

The Players

The chief information officer (CIO) is pleased with the results of the pilot project. "We have cut the error rate down to less than 10 percent for the Design Engineering group. Previously, we would average around 35 percent for this same group of employees. I really like the idea of an online system, and that's the direction I would like to go. But the end users are complaining a lot about the system interface. It's unlikely we could use the same software from the pilot for everyone else. I think that the nontechnical employees will have a difficult time logging into the mainframe and using the current application. There also seems to be some performance limitations on the mainframe, and, frankly, I don't want to invest new hardware dollars on upgrading the mainframe. Our long-term strategy is to get off the mainframe system."

The design engineers participating in the pilot program like the idea of entering their own time card data directly from the desktop. Although most of the design engineers use graphical users interface (GUI) applications in the Windows 95 environment, they've had difficulty using a mainframe-based application. Jill, one of the engineers, describes the situation this way: "This is certainly preferable to using the paper time card system. However, most of the other engineers and I have found the user interface to be very frustrating. We are not mainframe users and don't know the mainframe commands. It's difficult to remember the special keystrokes used to navigate the entry forms. What's worse, once you get stuck, there's no online help."

The development manager for the IT group has stated that given the priority of other projects, her group has very little time to devote to system enhancements. "We were able to create the pilot application, because it required minimal impact to our current system and did not require substantial programming effort. It's unfortunate that the users are having difficulty using the terminal emulation program. However, my group does not have the expertise or time to develop a GUI front end."

The system manager for the IBM mainframe computer has expressed another concern. "I am not sure that the mainframe can handle the load if we let each employee manage his own time card online. We might have hundreds of employees all trying to log onto the system at one time. Our system was never intended to support that kind of a load. We would certainly have to upgrade the hardware."

The Plan

The CIO of Action Aerospace has hired you to help them analyze the situation and determine the best course of action. One option is to begin deploying the pilot project to other departments. However, you take another approach: first, you analyze the requirements, then you determine an appropriate solution. You refer to your project as the Employee Time Card System.

Business Requirements

Business requirements analysis is a high-level assessment for the entire project that addresses the *what*, *where*, *when*, *why*, *who*, and *how* for the project. You must consider a number of factors in order to clearly identify the problem and propose a viable solution. These factors include:

➤ Project scope

➤ Business needs

➤ Security

➤ Performance

➤ Maintainability

➤ Extensibility

➤ Availability

➤ Scalability

➤ Human factors

➤ Integration

➤ Methodologies

As data is gathered and analyzed for each of these areas, the results are documented. Following the Microsoft Solution Framework models, three primary documents are generally used for this purpose: the vision/scope document, the risk management plan, and the project structure document.

Project Scope

All projects start out as a vision. *Project scope* maps this vision against the reality of what can actually be done toward achieving this vision. In particular, a number of constraints, including technology, resources, budget, and schedule, will all influence the actual project scope. The existing environment and how it will be impacted by the project will greatly determine the project scope.

Project scope analysis encompasses several key considerations including:

➤ Existing applications

➤ Anticipated changes to the current environment

➤ Expected lifetime of the solution

➤ Time, cost, budget, and benefit trade-offs

When the project scope has been determined, the features, functionality, and high-level schedule can be identified and documented in the vision/scope document for the project.

Existing Applications

Most development projects aren't simply new applications that will be used in isolation. On the contrary, most development projects consist of enhancements to existing applications or to new applications that must be integrated to operate with those already in production.

Even in the situations where replacement applications are being developed, the existing application will still influence the design and/or deployment of the new application. Therefore, the constraints that existing applications place on the environment are a key component of the requirements analysis.

Consider the following characteristics of existing applications to determine if they'll impact your solution:

➤ **Hardware or software platforms**   Is the new solution expected to use existing hardware and software systems?

➤ **Network protocols**   Are network protocols being utilized that the new solution will have to support?

➤ **Data formats**   Will the new solution need to process data files created by the existing applications?

➤ **Developer skill sets**   Is the skill set available to build the new solution? If not, can outside resources be acquired, or must the solution be constrained by the existing skill set?

➤ **End-user training**   Will the solution require extensive end-user training? Maybe it will need to conform to existing user interfaces to minimize any training requirements.

These items represent only a small number of ways existing applications might affect the solution design.

At Action Aerospace, existing databases and applications on the mainframe will influence any new application design for the Employee Time Card System. A network infrastructure is already in place consisting of desktop systems, department servers, and the network itself. Therefore, these will also influence the design. Because minimal IT resources are available to modify the existing applications and database, any new work must try to accommodate the existing applications. And, finally, the IT staff has little or no experience with client/server application development.

Anticipated Changes In Environment

You'll also want to factor in any anticipated environment changes. For example, most businesses have steadily been replacing desktop terminals with desktop workstations. Understanding the overall business strategy and direction can benefit your solution design in two ways. Your solution won't depend on resources being phased out, and you may be able to utilize new technology that's planned but not currently in place.

At Action Aerospace, the environment has been changing. Departments have been replacing computer terminals with personal workstations on the desktops. Although the terminals are still in place for heavy mainframe users like the Data Entry group, each employee has access to a personal workstation. You'll want to factor this into your planning.

Expected Lifetime Of The Solution

The expected solution lifetime is another important consideration that's established during the requirements analysis. This will affect how much time should be spent on requirements analysis and on design and how much time and money can be spent on the eventual development and deployment.

The expected solution lifetime can directly affect the technology that might be chosen for the solution. For example, the development team at Action Aerospace chose terminal emulation software as the primary supporting technology for the time card pilot project. This option required very little investment in new software, and also allowed them to quickly produce a working prototype.

Time, Cost, Budget, And Benefit Trade-Offs

Early in the requirements analysis you'll need to start asking some questions: How fast must the project be delivered? How expensive can it be to deploy? What level of investment will provide the best financial return?

Having the answers to these questions is critical to any project, because the design will depend on many decisions. And each of these decisions will require knowing the cost, considering the time frame, evaluating the benefits, and determining the trade-offs. Therefore, time, cost, and budget are important items to factor into the requirements analysis.

I Want It Good, Fast, And Cheap!

The customer told the project manager there were only three requirements for the new application. He needed it to be good, fast, and cheap.

"Naturally, the solution needs to be *good*," he said. "That is, it must be maintainable, well documented, optimally coded, and, of course, fully tested and bug free. And, time is of the essence here. Every day the company does not have this application running, we are losing business, so the solution is needed *fast*. Finally, we can't spend a fortune on this project. Our budget is very limited, so the solution must be *cheap*."

The project manager thought about the requirements and told the customer it would be possible to satisfy only two of the three requirements. The good news, however, was the customer could choose which two.

"We can build you something quickly, and it can be fairly cheap, but it won't be very good. On the other hand, we can make it good, but in order to keep it cheap, you won't get if very quickly. And, of course, we can make it good, and we can do it pretty quickly. But it won't be cheap."

The three major trade-off options are graphically shown in Figure 4.2.

Business Needs

Business solutions are developed to solve *business needs*. Therefore, the business needs will heavily influence the final solution design and will provide the primary impetus driving the entire project. It's essential that you can clearly demonstrate, at any point during the project, how the proposed solution will satisfy the business needs.

In order to satisfy the business needs of a company, the solution must support the enterprise architecture, facilitate communications and the exchange of information, and facilitate the attainment of business objectives.

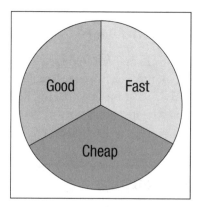

Figure 4.2   Good, Fast, and Cheap. Pick only two. Determining business requirements involves making many trade-offs.

To thoroughly determine what the business needs are and to analyze the extent of the business requirements, you'll need to consider factors in a number of areas. In particular, you'll need to:

➤ Establish the type of problem, such as a messaging problem or a communication problem

➤ Establish and define customer quality requirements

➤ Minimize Total Cost of Ownership (TCO)

➤ Increase Return on Investment (ROI) of the solution

➤ Analyze the current platform and infrastructure

➤ Incorporate planned platform and infrastructure into solution

➤ Analyze impact of technology migration

➤ Plan physical requirements, such as infrastructure

➤ Establish the application environment, such as hardware platform, support, and operating system

➤ Identify organizational constraints, such as financial situation, company politics, technical acceptance level, and training needs

➤ Establish schedule for implementation of solution

➤ Identify audience

Action Aerospace has a database-related problem. The objective is to accurately maintain project data, so it can reliably be used for planning and reporting. The project is being driven by quality standards. Currently, the business process has poor quality with an error rate near 40 percent.

Many pieces that could be utilized by the solution are already in place. The mainframe system, the existing applications, the mainframe database, the desktop systems, and the department servers could all play a part in the Employee Time Card System. Incorporating these could help lower the total cost of ownership and increase the return on investment.

It's unlikely the solution will involve new mainframe applications. The expense needed to upgrade the mainframe system would be prohibitive, and the company has a strategy to gradually migrate applications off the mainframe system.

Another important factor at Action Aerospace is the skill level of the IT staff. Although the staff members are familiar with the mainframe environment, they aren't familiar with developing and maintaining applications using client/ server technology.

Security

You'll need to determine the security requirements for the solution you're planning. Security is important for any application, but it's critical for distributed applications. Applications that involve the Internet may have additional security requirements, and planning the security for distributed and Internet applications can also be more complex than single desktop applications.

Some general guidelines for determining the security requirements are to:

➤ Analyze security requirements

➤ Identify roles of administrator, groups, guests, and clients

➤ Identify impact on existing environment

➤ Establish fault tolerance

➤ Plan for maintainability

➤ Plan distribution of security database

➤ Establish security context

➤ Plan for auditing

➤ Identify levels of security needed

➤ Analyze existing mechanisms for security policies

Analyze Security Requirements

Security requirements vary considerably. For example:

➤ You might need to maintain accounts and passwords for access to the system, applications, and data.

➤ You might need to pass sensitive data between applications or components running on different machines, requiring data encryption and verification procedures.

➤ You might need to maintain the entire computing environment within a physically secure structure.

➤ You might need to ensure that the system continues to operate in case of a power outage or unexpected system failure.

All of these items represent examples of the different aspects of security, and during the analysis requirements, you'll identify those that are appropriate for your solution.

Identify Roles Of Administrator, Groups, Guests, And Clients

It's very likely your solution will have constraints on who is authorized to perform particular operations. You'll want to document which operations require authorization and the types of users who can be authorized to perform these operations.

At Action Aerospace, each user will need to have full access to his own time card, but he can't access the time card of another employee. Furthermore, an employee can't be allowed to put a supervisor approval on his own time card; and once the time card has been approved, the employee can't modify it. Each supervisor will need to be able to read his employees' time cards, but he can't access the time cards of any employee that isn't under his supervision. And there are restrictions on the kinds of changes the supervisor can make to an individual time card.

On Windows NT, all security is user based. That is, all objects including processes, threads, and files have a user as an owner. To make administration and assignments of access rights somewhat easier, Windows NT allows the assignment of users to groups. When a user is assigned to a group, the user is considered a member of the group.

When access rights are assigned to an object, they can be assigned to an individual user or a group. When assigned to a group, the rights apply to all members of the group. Thus, it's possible to set up an object, allowing or denying access to an entire group instead of identifying each member individually.

When a process is invoked, that process is usually executing in the context of a user who has an account on the machine. That user will be able to access any resource that she has been granted access to. The user may have been granted access *explicitly* or *implicitly* because she is a member of a specific group.

Two Windows NT built-in accounts have special uses. The Administrator account is a privileged account and can be used to perform system administration activities. Because this is a powerful account, its use should be restricted to system administration activities. You'll need to maintain strict security policies for this account, and you might consider renaming this account to a less obvious name. The Guest account can be used to provide limited access for casual users. If the system is for public use, consider providing public logons via this account.

Identify Impact On Existing Environment And Mechanisms For Security Policies

As you analyze the security requirements, remember to factor in any existing policies and mechanisms that may already be in place. Also, determine what impact the existing environment may have on the security you're planning. For example, some of the existing platforms may not support the security you plan to implement.

Establish Fault Tolerance

Although security is often associated with "access" and "permissions", security is also closely related to *availability*. That is, can the system continue to operate, or operate at a reduced level, in case of power outage or other system failure?

Therefore, the security requirements won't only consist of requirements for protecting the system from illegal access. Security requirements also consist of requirements for protecting the system from hardware and environmental failures.

Almost all systems rely on power supply protection and on a regular system backup procedure. The general topic of availability is discussed in more detail later in this chapter.

Plan For Maintainability

Security requirements will also address the maintainability needs. Ideally, a distributed system can be maintained from a single site. This is referred to as *remote administration*. Even though servers within an organization may be spread throughout the world, it's possible to design applications to administer remote services running on remote servers.

Plan Distribution Of Security Database

In a distributed environment, it's essential the data needed to administer system security be available where it's needed. In the Windows NT environment, the primary domain controllers (PDCs) and backup domain controllers (BDCs) maintain the security database, which is used to manage user accounts and other network-related services.

The location of the security database directly affects the performance of the login process. And if the security database is not available because the system is down or a data link is broken, users may not even be able to log on.

Establish Security Context

Some operating systems allow one process to take on the security attributes of another process to perform an operation. In this case, the operation is executed on behalf of the other process using the *security context* of the other process. Windows NT allows this through a technique called *impersonation*, which is often used in distributed applications when requests are passed between computer systems.

For example, assume a client makes a request to an application server. The application server must access a database server system to complete the request. The application server impersonates client security context and makes the request to the database server on behalf of the client. The database server uses the original client's security context, rather than the security identity of the application server, to determine whether to complete the task.

Plan For Auditing

Auditing allows you to track when certain events occur. In theory, auditing can inform you of actions that could pose a security risk and also identify the user accounts from which audited actions were taken. Of course, if password security has been breached, someone other than the user assigned to an account could have performed the action.

When you identify the events you want to audit, you'll also want to factor in the resources that will be required. Auditing will require disk space as well as CPU resources. Therefore, you'll need to balance the trade-off between auditing capabilities and the resources that are dedicated to auditing. Some of the common events that are audited include failed logon attempts, attempts to access-sensitive data, and changes to security settings.

Identify Level Of Security Needed

You'll want to identify the *level of security* needed for the solution. At one extreme this might be no security or a fairly relaxed level of security. Low levels of security are easier to maintain and don't burden the users with some of the added responsibilities necessitated by a secure environment. Although this might be acceptable for the development environment, it probably is inadequate for the production environment.

At the other extreme, many government agencies will specify a security level requirement that represents the minimum acceptable level. The National Computer Security Center (NCSC), the U.S. government agency responsible for performing software product security evaluations, has published a set of requirements for different security levels. This book, commonly referred to as the "Orange Book" is officially titled *Department of Defense Trusted Computer System Evaluation Criteria* (The Office of Standards and Products, National Computer Security Center, Fort Meade, MD; 1987).

Windows NT has been successfully evaluated by the NCSC at the C2 level.

Performance

In general, *performance* refers to how fast the system runs or how quickly it can complete a requested task. Many different metrics are used to measure performance, and a number of factors determine performance, including workload, hardware configuration, and database activity. However, the solution design will play a major factor in the system performance.

 Workload, hardware configuration options like memory and the CPU, database activity, and application design are all key factors that will affect system performance.

When the time comes to design and implement the solution, you may have a variety of alternatives. For example, you may decide to use a strategy that optimizes performance in one particular area at the expense of degrading performance in another area. To make these decisions, you'll need to understand the performance expectations, which, ideally, will be determined during the business requirements analysis.

When dealing with performance, keep in mind that there are two types of performance: *real performance* and *perceived performance*. Real performance is the true, measurable performance of a system and is based on *quantitative* data metrics that can be gathered, processed, and analyzed. Perceived performance is a *qualitative* metric, and it's largely determined by how the users perceive that the system is performing. Anytime the user is waiting for the system to respond, he might perceive that the system performance is inadequate.

Benchmarks are often used to establish performance requirement guidelines as well as verify system performance.

When you analyze performance requirements, you'll need to consider:

➤ Transactions per time slice

➤ Bandwidth

➤ Capacity

➤ Interoperability with existing standards

➤ Peak versus average requirements

➤ Response time expectations

➤ Existing response time characteristics

➤ Barriers to performance

This chapter focuses on performance from the perspective of gathering requirements. Performance will be discussed again when the logical and physical designs are developed.

Transactions Per Time Slice

A *transaction* is a task or unit of work that either succeeds or fails in its entirety. Transactions have a beginning and an ending, and all the processing that occurs in between makes up the transaction. A transaction has one of two outcomes. If it succeeds, all the changes that occurred during the transaction are committed and become permanent. If the transaction fails, all the changes that occurred are rolled back and everything is left in the same state as it was before the transaction started. In particular, part of a transaction doesn't succeed while other parts fail.

Transactions provide a framework for ensuring reliability in a system. Online transaction processing (OLTP) systems are designed for performing transaction-oriented tasks. For example, a banking system that's designed to transfer funds between a checking account and a savings account is a transaction processing system. Both the debit from the checking account and the credit to the savings account must complete or fail together. If the system allowed only one of the operations to complete, the data records for the bank would quickly become useless.

OLTP systems typically have a large number of simultaneous users all performing the same kinds of operations on a shared database. System performance of these systems is usually specified using the metric of *transactions per second*, or TPS.

Online systems usually have transactions of very short duration, so the TPS metric is appropriate. However, transaction-oriented operations can also be complex and lengthy. For these systems, another unit of time such as minute or hour is more appropriate for specifying system performance.

The Time Card Application for Action Aerospace is an online transaction processing system. Many users will be simultaneously entering time card data into the system. Consequently, during the requirements analysis, you'll need to anticipate the processing load and identify this as a performance requirement for the system.

The ACID Test

An operation qualifies as a transaction if it passes the ACID test. The ACID test is an acronym for Atomicity, Consistency, Isolation, and Durability, and by definition, these characterize a transaction.

Atomicity refers to the "all or nothing" characteristic of a transaction. All of the actions complete or none of the actions complete. Atomicity ensures that all updates performed under a specific transaction are committed (and made durable) or that all are aborted and rolled back to their previous state.

Consistency means that, at the end of a transaction, data updates haven't violated any of the constraints on the data. All of the data integrity rules are still enforced.

Isolation ensures that concurrent transactions don't interfere with each other. One transaction can't read the partial and uncommitted results of another transaction, which might create inconsistencies.

Durability means that committed updates made during the transaction, such as a change to a database, remain permanent even if the system experiences a failure, including communication failures, process failures, and disk system failures.

Bandwidth

Bandwidth refers to the rate at which data is transferred over a telecommunications link. Typically, it's expressed as the amount of data that can be transferred over the link in a specified time period. Usually this is the number of data bits that can be transferred in one second or bits per second (bps). Often the bandwidth will be measured in larger units such as kilobits per second (Kbps), where one kilobit per second is equal to 1,024 bits per second, or megabits per second (Mbps), where one megabit per second is equal to 1,024 kilobits per second.

Bandwidth might also be expressed in other forms. For example, it might be a measure of the rate of transferring data packets for a particular network protocol, or it could be a measure of the number of files that can be transferred in a given time period.

Applications like the Time Card Application probably won't require a large bandwidth, because the amount of data being transferred is relatively small. However, applications that transfer hundreds of records at a time can easily consume the available bandwidth and perform poorly.

Bandwidth is an important factor for determining overall performance, because it represents a potential bottleneck for the entire system. Bandwidth is also important because of the recent trend to use telecommunications links for transferring more types of data (for example, video and sound) as well as larger amounts of data.

Capacity

Capacity is another metric for measuring the ability of the communication link to carry network traffic and support multiple resources. The capacity metric usually includes the server and is measured, in part, by the number of connections established and maintained by the server.

Interoperability With Existing Standards

When gathering the requirements, it's important to keep in mind any of the standards that must be adhered to in any new implementation. These standards could have an impact on performance in one of two ways. Technical requirements for the business may require the use of a standard that prohibits the use of a faster-performing alternative. To adhere to a standard, additional processing may be required to convert data from one standard to another.

Peak Vs. Average Requirements

When dealing with performance, it's important to differentiate between the peak-versus-average requirements. Average requirements represent an amount of work that's performed during a specified amount of time. Peak requirements take into account that the actual demand at a given moment might be higher than the average. For example, you may be told that the online system you're designing will process around 50,000 queries a day. Assuming that this occurs over an eight-hour period, the average load is 6,250 queries per hour or about 1.7 queries per second. A system designed to handle two queries per second should perform well.

However, these calculations assume that the load is evenly distributed throughout the day. This is depicted in Figure 4.3. Two queries per second represents an *average* workload. If the queries aren't evenly distributed, a system designed for two queries per second might not be adequate. Figure 4.4 shows the same number of queries, but the majority of the processing occurs late in the afternoon. For this case, the system needs to be capable of handling five queries per second, which represents a *peak* workload.

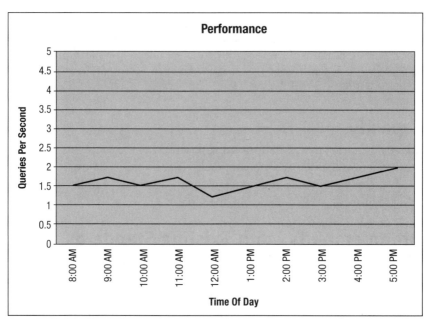

Figure 4.3 Performance requirements for 50,000 queries evenly distributed throughout the workday.

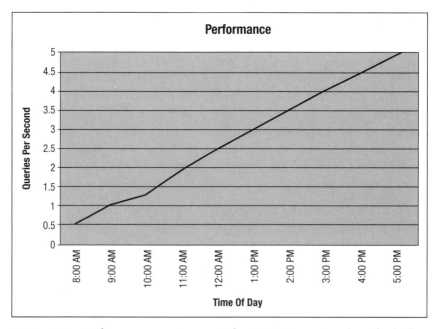

Figure 4.4 Performance requirements for 50,000 queries when the bulk of the load occurs in the late afternoon.

Response Time Expectations

Response time refers to the interval of time between making a request for data and actually receiving the data. For example, your application may issue a query to a database on a server located on a network. The response time will depend on the time spent sending the request across the network from the client to the server, the time spent receiving the request and processing the request on the server, the time spent returning the results across the network from the server to the client, and the time spent on the client processing the results and displaying them.

Different measurements are used to specify response time, so when you gather the requirements, you'll want to make certain that the definitions you use are clearly specified. For example, one method of specifying response time measures the time from requesting the data until the first result is displayed on the screen. Another method measures the time from requesting the data until the entire results have been displayed.

Existing Response Time Characteristics

Existing response time characteristics will strongly influence the perceived performance of any new applications. A new system that has a response time of several seconds might be perceived as "fast" in an environment where no online access was previously available. However, if the new system has a response time of two seconds, it might still be perceived as slow if the response time of an existing system averages around one second.

Barriers To Performance

Performance limitations almost always can be found in one or more of the following key areas:

➤ Hardware, including CPU, disk, and memory

➤ Software

➤ Application design

➤ Data access

➤ Network

➤ Number of users

Maintainability

Maintainability refers to the capability of being able to keep the application in working order. First the software must be installed, then when deficiencies are discovered, they'll have to be corrected. And when new version releases are ready, the software will need to be upgraded.

You'll need to consider these factors to analyze maintainability requirements:

➤ Breadth of application distribution

➤ Method of distribution

➤ Maintenance expectations

➤ Location and knowledge level of maintenance staff

➤ Impact of third-party maintenance agreements

Application Distribution

Application distribution plays an important part in maintaining the application. A single application running on a mainframe computer represents a centralized environment. Contrast the effort of upgrading an application in a centralized environment with an application that is distributed across 2,000 desktops, each of which needs to be updated.

Breadth Of Distribution

The *breadth of distribution* refers to how widely distributed the application is and to geographic distribution, as well as to the number of sites involved. Applications with a broad breadth of distribution are maintainable, but this factor needs to be considered in the planning.

Method Of Distribution

You'll also want to consider the distribution methods available. Often, distributed applications can be maintained and distributed from a central location. This is especially true if the distributed applications are connected by a network infrastructure. It might also be possible for each user to connect to a central site and download the software. In some situations, upgrades can get automatically downloaded across a network and installed when they're needed without any user intervention.

On the other hand, traditional distribution methods using media such as a CD might be appropriate if the amount of data can't easily be transferred across a network link.

One advantage to Web-based applications is they can be easier to maintain than traditional distributed applications. In a Web-based application where processing is centralized on the back end, the only client software required is usually the browser. Thus, the application can be maintained at one location with minimal impact on the clients.

Maintenance Expectations

It's important to determine the maintenance expectations as part of the project planning. Knowing whether the solution is low maintenance, requiring little or no maintenance, or high maintenance with planned maintenance versions could influence the choice of solution architecture.

Location And Knowledge Level Of Maintenance Staff

Another important factor in maintenance planning is determining what skills are required for the maintainer and where the maintenance activities will be performed. In a centralized environment, maintenance is usually required at one site. Most likely, the staff having the required knowledge level for performing the maintenance is at that same site. However, in a distributed environment this is less likely.

It might be possible for each user to perform the required maintenance. Automated procedures can be developed to install the software as well as upgrade the software with maintenance releases. This eliminates the need for additional staff doing the work, but it also raises two other considerations. Did the software and maintenance releases get installed correctly, and is everyone running the same version of the software?

Extensibility

Extensibility is the capacity to extend or enhance a solution beyond its original capabilities. In fact, the entire model of a multiversioned release cycle is based on the concept of extensibility. As business needs evolve and grow, it's important that business systems evolve with them. The solution must be able to handle the growth of functionality.

The Visionary document that gives the overall project vision will provide a good guide to enhancements that are planned for the future. Although the technology may not support implementing these facilities now, the solution design should allow for their future incorporation.

During the requirements analysis, you'll be identifying and prioritizing the capabilities that are to be built into the solution. Every project has a wish list of future capabilities. The ease of implementing these facilities in the future may very well be determined by the initial solution design.

Extensibility not only refers to the enhancements that are incorporated into an application as part of a version release, it also refers to custom enhancements that might be incorporated into an application through the use of a special interface. Many applications support the use of "add-ins" or "plug-ins." Your requirements analysis should also determine if this type of facility is needed.

Availability

Availability is a measurement that specifies how much uptime the system must provide and how much downtime can be tolerated. Reliability of the system depends on the system meeting the availability requirements.

System downtime is often categorized as either planned or unplanned. Planned downtime is time that's scheduled in advance, and it's commonly used for making system backups, installing new software, or reconfiguring computer hardware. Unplanned downtime occurs when a failure, either hardware or software, makes the system unavailable. Planned downtime is far more desirable than unplanned downtime.

Availability is a ratio of the uptime to the total time and is usually expressed as a percentage. One hundred percent availability means that the system is *always* available and will never be down. This is a difficult goal to achieve.

Table 4.1 lists some system downtimes and the corresponding system availability.

From the table, it's possible to see that allowing one hour of downtime per day still results in a fairly high level of availability (greater than 95 percent). This may be acceptable in many situations; however, many mission-critical systems will demand a higher level.

Table 4.1 System availability.	
Down Time	**System Availability**
1 hour every day	95.83%
1 hour every week	99.40%
1 hour every month	99.86%
1 hour every year	99.99%

A general guideline to keep in mind is that the higher the level of availability, the more expensive the system will be. To achieve a high level of availability, redundancy of components is almost always required.

To determine realistic availability requirements, you'll need to consider the hours of operation, the level of availability, the geographic scope, and the impact of downtime.

Fault Tolerance

Fault-tolerant systems represent systems with the highest level of availability. One of the criteria for these systems is that there's no single point for failure within the system. To accomplish this, a true fault-tolerant system will usually have total redundancy of hardware and software components, as well as data. Fault-tolerant systems provide near instantaneous recovery when a fault occurs; however, they can become very expensive.

It's often possible to identify certain areas of the solution architecture where fault tolerance is absolutely required. Other areas of the architecture may still require high availability but not necessarily true fault tolerance. This strategy helps lower the cost by providing a nearly fault-tolerant system.

Clustering is another means of providing high availability. Clustering allows multiple systems to be connected together and appear as a single, highly available server to network clients. Although clustering isn't true fault tolerance, clustered systems do provide a cost-effective alternative.

This chapter focuses on availability from the perspective of gathering requirements. Availability will be discussed again when the logical and physical designs are developed.

Hours Of Operation

Hours of operation refer to the time that the system must usually be available. Although there are exceptions, most businesses require the system to be available during the regular business hours of operation. Determining the required hours of operation is important, because it's usually a key factor behind availability levels.

Level Of Availability

When analyzing the availability requirements, it's also important to determine the level of availability that's needed. For example, distributed systems consist of multiple applications, and it's very possible that all of these applications don't have the same availability requirements. Furthermore, the availability levels may vary, depending on the time of day.

It's often possible for a system to operate with a degraded availability level and still satisfy the business requirements. For example, consider a system that enters orders into a database. Even though the database becomes unavailable, the entire system doesn't necessarily have to stop. It's possible for the application to place the orders into a *queue* as they're entered. Later, when the database is available, orders placed in the queue can be entered into the database. From the business perspective, no time was lost, and no orders were lost, even though the database itself wasn't available 100 percent of the time.

Replicated databases are often used to increase system availability. Thus, if the primary database is unavailable, one of the replicated databases can be used instead.

Geographic Scope

It's common to find a database in one location supporting global operations. Although the business may operate only eight hours at any one site, the database must be available 24 hours a day to support the global operations. When you determine the hours of operation, remember to consider the geographic location of the users as well.

Impact Of Downtime

For you to realistically determine the availability requirements, you'll need to ascertain, and perhaps even quantify, the impact of downtime. That is, what are the business consequences when the system is unavailable? The impact of downtime will greatly influence and justify the effort and the investment required to achieve a high level of availability.

Human Factors

Ideally, the solution that's ultimately produced will be easy to use, so for this to become a reality, you'll need to ensure that it's, in fact, usable by the end users. Therefore, part of requirements analysis is determining who the end users will be, how they'll use the system, and what special requirements they have. These are referred to as the *human factors* requirements.

To determine the human factors requirements, you'll need to consider:

➤ Target users

➤ Localization

➤ Accessibility

➤ Roaming users

➤ Help

➤ Training requirements

➤ Physical environment constraints

➤ Special needs

This section focuses on human factors from the perspective of gathering requirements. Human factors will be discussed from the implementation perspective in Chapter 8 when the design of the user interface is also discussed.

Target Users

Accurately identifying the target users for a system is an essential part of determining the human factors requirements. The type of users, and their skill set, will help in the planning of the user interface.

The Time Card Application pilot project at Action Aerospace used terminal emulation to access an application on the mainframe. However, most of the users weren't familiar with the use of a mainframe terminal, so the solution wasn't readily accepted.

Localization

Localization refers to individual customizations that may be required for the solution. For example, if the solution is to be deployed internationally, it may need to support multiple languages.

Localization could involve translating the user interface, resizing dialog boxes, customizing features, and testing results.

On a smaller scale, localization might also apply to an enterprise solution. For example, each department might have its own department-specific localization of an application. The same techniques used for building international applications can also be applied on a much smaller scale.

Localization can affect the design as well as the implementation. Therefore, it's important to identify these requirements initially in the project.

Accessibility

Accessibility means making computers accessible to a wider range of users than would otherwise be the case. Although there are features in the Windows operating systems that can compensate for many types of disabilities, the application software must exploit these features to produce the most usable software.

For example, customizable colors and good keyboard access are conveniences for many users, but they can represent critical requirements for users with disabilities. To ensure accessibility, applications won't only need to utilize the facilities provided by the operating system, but they'll need to be compatible with any of the additional utilities that can be used to enhance accessibility. To assist people who are blind, an application might utilize speech or Braille output systems or voice recognition products.

The application design must allow for the use of these special features or utilities. Therefore, it's important to identify any special accessibility requirements that may affect the design.

Roaming Users

Roaming users are users that don't always access the system from the same desktop. Often, roaming users access the system remotely via a modem and dial-up connection, and sometimes connections are established using wireless technology. Roaming users often use a computer, such as a laptop, that's isolated from the rest of the system, and at some point in time, they usually want to synchronize the data in their system with the data in the main database. This can involve both uploading data from the remote system as well as downloading data from the main system.

 Roaming users might use *database replication* to keep a database on a laptop computer synchronized with a corporate database on another system. Microsoft Access supports replication using the briefcase, the replication manager, and data access objects (DAO) programming.

Help

A user-friendly solution will have an online Help facility. Most Windows-based applications provide online help information in a variety of forms, ranging from conceptual help that explains the purpose of an application's features to pop-up help windows that provide quick definitions of individual elements in the application's user interface. There are usually a variety of ways to request access to this information.

Part of the human factors requirements analysis will be determining the level of help and types of help facilities that need to be provided.

Training Requirements

Online help alone might not be sufficient for users to learn how to use a new system. Depending on the experience of the target users and the complexity of the applications, end-user training may be required for the solution you are planning.

Training requirements aren't limited to only the end users. System managers may also require training. And the staff that will maintain the system may also need training to do their job effectively.

Integration With The Existing Environment

Business systems rarely consist of a single application. Most are a series of applications that must be smoothly integrated to work together.

Furthermore, many mission-critical systems in use today aren't new applications. They're applications developed years ago, usually written in COBOL, and most have evolved with the business as it grew. These are *legacy applications*, and they aren't going away in the near future. In fact, the Gartner Group estimates that 80 percent of today's legacy applications will still be in use in the year 2000.

Another important aspect to consider when you analyze the solution requirements is determining the requirements for integrating the solution with existing applications. Considerations include:

➤ Legacy applications

➤ Format and location of existing data

➤ Connectivity to existing applications

➤ Data conversion

➤ Data enhancement requirements

Legacy Applications

Replacing legacy applications isn't widely viewed as a cost-effective strategy. Similarly, incorporating new, improved technology into legacy applications also isn't considered a viable strategy.

Therefore, companies are looking for ways to maximize the strengths of the existing legacy systems and still allow use of more efficient development languages, operating environments, and methodologies for new applications. At the same time, companies want to minimize the impact of older technology or poor design decisions that were made in the past.

Integration is the best strategy for leveraging mainframe-based solutions with new technologies. The reality is that legacy systems won't be disappearing in the near future. In fact, legacy systems, in one form or another, still provide most online transaction processing for many large organizations.

This is certainly the case at Action Aerospace where a single mainframe computer still hosts all the applications used to run the business.

Format And Location Of Existing Data

When planning the integration of new systems with the existing environment, you'll need to consider the data that already exists. Where the data resides and what format is used to store the data are important facts, because it's almost certain that at some point the new application will need to access this data.

There are basically two options for accessing the data. Access the data directly from the source, or access the data through an existing application. Both of these choices have their trade-offs.

Many data interfaces, such as open database connectivity (ODBC), allow accessing data directly from the source. However, the downside to this approach is that any processing performed on the data by the existing application is circumvented. For example, the application might map the data values into another value before printing them in a report. Or the application might verify the values before allowing them to be written to the database. When you access the data directly, you would skip this processing. This method is depicted in Figure 4.5.

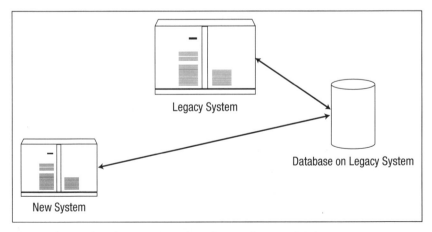

Legacy System

Database on Legacy System

New System

Figure 4.5   Directly accessing data from a legacy database.

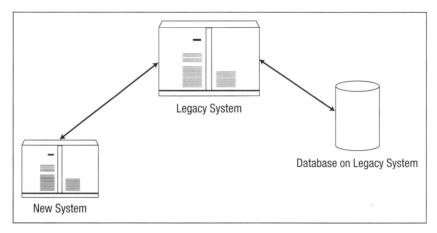

Figure 4.6   Accessing data from a legacy database through the existing
application.

Accessing the data through the application (as shown in Figure 4.6) ensures
that any processing provided by the application will be performed on the data.
However, interfacing with the application is usually a more difficult task.

Connectivity To Existing Applications

Several different methods are used to connect to existing applications. These
include:

➤ Terminal emulation

➤ Scripting languages

➤ Screen scraping

➤ Object interfaces

➤ Program-to-program interfaces

 Terminal emulation software is often a cost-effective way of
accessing legacy applications from a desktop workstation. No
application development is required for the desktop, and the
existing legacy application requires no changes. However, one
of the disadvantages of terminal emulation software is that the
user interface may not provide all the graphical features that
the user is expecting. Most legacy applications use a command
line, or terminal, interface rather than a GUI interface. To access
the application using terminal emulation software, you'll need
to use the command line interface of the application.

Data Conversion

Often, when data is transferred between applications, data conversion or *mapping* must be done. Sometimes this is required, because the new application uses a different set of values for the same data items. For example, a legacy application might use a two-character job code to classify each employee. A newer application might use a three-character code based on an industry standard to represent job codes. To successfully integrate these applications, the data values for the job codes would need to be converted to a common value.

Data conversion considerations include:

➤ Character set used for the data

➤ Data types

➤ Data formats

➤ Values used by the application

Data Enhancement Requirements

The data conversion issues just discussed are rather low-level and relate to how the data is actually stored. Sometimes the stored data must be enhanced before it can be used by the application. New data elements that the application needs are derived from the stored values.

For example, the Time Card Application uses a three-character code for project activities, and all activity records in the database are stored using this code. However, several of the vendors require reports using a different set of codes for representing project activities, so the codes stored in the database must be mapped into the corresponding report code before it's displayed on the report. In summary, data can't always be retrieved directly from the data source and used as is.

Methodologies

Methodologies refer to the processes used to accomplish tasks. From the software development perspective, methodologies refer to the processes and tools that can be used to design, implement, debug, maintain, and deploy a solution. These will influence and impact the solution.

When you analyze the business requirements for a solution, you must examine business methodologies as well as software-related methodologies.

When analyzing existing methodologies and limitations of a business, considerations include:

➤ Legal issues

➤ Current business practices

➤ Organization structure

➤ Process engineering

➤ Budget

➤ Implementation and training methodologies

➤ Quality control requirements

➤ Customer's needs

Scalability

Scalability refers to the ability of the system to respond to growth. As with many other system characteristics, alternative architectures can be utilized to handle different scaling requirements. Therefore, it's essential to gather sufficient background information on projected growth so the appropriate architecture can be deployed.

Growth usually occurs in one of four ways: growth of audience, growth of organization, growth of data, or growth in cycle of use.

At Action Aerospace, scalability is a major factor. Although the pilot project presented no major problems, eventually the solution must support the entire company of 2,000 employees. The current configuration of the mainframe system won't support this number of online users. Furthermore, Action Aerospace is growing, and the company is presently in the process of actively recruiting additional employees. The ultimate solution will need to address these scalability requirements.

This chapter focuses on scalability from the perspective of gathering requirements. Scalability will be discussed again when the logical and physical designs are developed.

Growth Of Audience

The audience refers to the number of users. Initially, of course, you'll know the number of users on the system. However, it's also important to know if this is expected to change, how it will change, and how often it will change. Often, it's best to start with a small number of users, anticipating that the audience will "ramp up" as the business grows. Identifying this information will allow a design that can adjust for the increased load and handle the change.

Growth Of Organization

Ramping up isn't the only factor that will cause the user base of a system to grow. Generally, an organization grows gradually, but sudden growth can also occur, for example, through mergers. Identifying the types of anticipated growth and designing an architecture that will scale accordingly will help ensure a smooth transition when the growth occurs.

Growth Of Data

Another key scalability factor is the amount of data, and how this data will change. In particular, how is this data expected to grow?

Some applications remain fairly constant in this aspect; however, most will grow. New data may get added on a regular basis, and this will impact the physical devices needed to store this data, as well as the algorithms for accessing it. This growth may also warrant special procedures for regularly deleting or archiving the data to keep the active data manageable.

Therefore, gathering information about the growth of data is another essential part of requirements analysis. In particular, three types of information should be gathered regarding the growth of data: what data will grow, how often will it grow, and how much will it grow?

Growth In Cycle Of Use

In addition to knowing the number of users and the amount of data, the *cycle of use* is another important factor in specifying scalability. An application that runs once a month as a background task might make very little impact on the use of system resources. However, these requirements may change significantly when a number of concurrent users attempt to run this application online to produce and print these same reports on a daily basis.

Practice Questions

Question 1

> Which of the following statements best describes the current business problem at Action Aerospace?
>
> ○ a. The IT staff has little experience developing client/server applications.
>
> ○ b. The company cannot accurately track and account for time spent on various contracted projects in a timely fashion.
>
> ○ c. Many employees have difficulty submitting time card data using terminal emulation software.
>
> ○ d. The time card system is currently centralized on a mainframe system, and employees have desktop computers.

Answer b is correct. Answers a, c, and d are all correct statements; however, they are not necessarily business problems.

Question 2

> The following types of factors must be analyzed to determine the requirements for a business information system:
>
>
>
> Scalability
>
> Availability
>
> Security
>
> Maintainability
>
> Identify the appropriate category for each of the following requirements:
>
> Only the employee who owns the time card can enter hours for time worked.
>
> The system will be deployed across the company as soon as three departments complete beta testing.
>
> Employees will enter data into the system during their normal work shift.
>
> The system must be able to handle four transactions per second.

The correct answer is

Scalability

> The system will be deployed across the company as soon as three departments complete beta testing.

Availability

> Employees will enter data into the system during their normal work shift.

Security

> Only the employee who owns the time card can enter hours for time worked.

Maintainability

The fact that the system must be capable of handling four transactions per second is a *performance* requirement. None of the requirements listed are a maintainability requirement.

Question 3

> Which of the following requirements are maintainability requirements? [Check all correct answers]
>
> ❑ a. The IT staff will maintain and enhance the system after it has been deployed.
>
> ❑ b. System maintenance can be done between midnight and 6 A.M., because no one will have access to the system at that time.
>
> ❑ c. Each department will maintain a separate department database on its own server.
>
> ❑ d. Each employee will maintain his own time card, and will not have access to the time card of any other employee.

Answers a and c are correct. Answers a and c are maintainability issues, because they relate to the knowledge of the staff as well as to the breadth of application distribution, which are both key considerations when determining the maintainability requirements. Answer b is actually related to system availability. Answer d is a security requirement.

Question 4

When gathering performance requirements, you discover that the system will process no more than 10,000 transactions in any given 24-hour period, which averages out to less than one transaction per second. You, therefore, specify a performance requirement for five transactions per second. Which of the following statements is the best description of this requirement?

○ a. The requirement of 5 TPS is sufficient, because you have more than doubled the anticipated transaction rate.

○ b. Bandwidth would provide a more meaningful measure and requirement for this type of application.

○ c. Regardless of the number of transactions processed in any 24-hour period, 5 TPS is a good ballpark number, because it satisfies the requirements for 80 percent of the online systems that are implemented.

○ d. The analysis that this requirement is based on is incomplete, because it assumes a uniform distribution of transactions across the 24-hour period that may not be the case.

Answer d is correct. The anticipated peak transaction rate should also be incorporated into the requirements. Answer c is interesting but not the best choice. It's true that many online systems actually average five or fewer TPS. In fact, if all 10,000 transactions for the proposed system occurred in a one-hour period, the average transaction rate would still be less than three TPS. If the 10,000 transactions occurred within a 30-minute period, then the average transaction rate is 5.5 TPS. TPS is an appropriate metric for this type of application. Bandwidth is not.

Question 5

Which of the following statements best describes the relationship between legacy applications and new applications?

○ a. If at all possible, legacy applications should be rewritten and incorporated into the new application to take advantage of properties, methods, and events.

○ b. Encapsulating a legacy application requires less software development than using a terminal emulator to access the application.

○ c. Terminal emulation is a poor alternative for accessing legacy applications, because it does not provide a graphical interface to the legacy system.

○ d. Terminal emulation often offers a cost-effective method for accessing a legacy application from the desktop.

Answer d is correct. Answer a could involve a substantial amount of development work. Although encapsulating a legacy application does require less development than a total rewrite, using a terminal emulator usually requires no development effort.

Question 6

Based on the situation at Action Aerospace, which of the following seems like a viable approach to the problem?

○ a. Rewrite the reporting applications using a tool like Microsoft Access that can access the data in the DB2 database directly from the desktop.

○ b. Migrate the mainframe applications to the NT Server platform.

○ c. Develop a front-end application that can interface the users to the legacy system.

○ d. Enhance the mainframe applications and acquire additional mainframe hardware.

Answer c is correct. An integrated solution consisting of new applications that smoothly interface with the legacy applications is a viable approach. Although Microsoft Access might be used for prototyping or even play a part of the solution, answer a is not a good choice. Answer a deals with the reporting applications, and rewriting the reporting applications will have no effect on the current business problem. Answer b is not a good choice because of the complexity and expense of rewriting the applications. And answer d does not support the overall Action Aerospace business strategy, which is to slowly migrate off the mainframe system.

Question 7

Which of the following statements best describes a true fault-tolerant system?

○ a. A system that provides greater than 95 percent availability.

○ b. A system that provides greater than 99 percent availability.

○ c. A configuration using multiple clustered systems.

○ d. A configuration having redundant hardware, software, and data, and no single point of failure.

Answer d is correct.

Need To Know More?

Kano, Nadine. *Developing International Software for Windows 95 and Windows NT.* Redmond, WA: Microsoft Press, 1996. ISBN 1-57231-311-0. This book presents a very thorough description

of the issues related to developing and distributing software applications for international use. Chapter 1 covers the topic "Localization," and Chapter 2 covers the topic "Identifying Localization Requirements in Specs." Both of these provide useful information for helping define the business requirements for an international solution. This documentation is also available on the Microsoft Developer Network Library.

The Enterprise Edition of Visual Studio V6 contains an online book entitled *Developing for the Enterprise.* This online documentation is also available on the Microsoft Developer Network Library. "Part 1: Enterprise Design and Architecture" discusses application requirements and design methodologies. In Chapter 1, "What is an Enterprise Application," the section "Business Model" describes the business model and identifies some of the questions to be addressed by the business requirements. "Part 1: Enterprise Design and Architecture" discusses application requirements and design methodologies. In Chapter 3, "Tools for Enterprise Application Design," the section "Identifying Business Requirements" explores business model tasks and how they relate to the business requirements. "Part 2: Data Access and Security Strategies" discusses application performance. In Chapter 9, "Data Access Performance Tuning," the section "What is Application Performance" describes real and perceived performance, as well as some of the design trade-offs to consider regarding performance.

http://search.microsoft.com/dev/

Dedo, Doug and Greg Nelson. "Integrate the Enterprise." Redmond, WA: Microsoft Corporation, 1997. This background paper covers the topic of integrating legacy systems with new applications.

http://search.microsoft.com/dev/

Lowney, Greg. "The Microsoft Windows Guidelines for Accessible Software Design." Redmond, WA: Microsoft Corporation, 1995. This is a thorough specification on designing and building applications that are usable by people with disabilities. It describes what accessibility is, how it's incorporated into software, and why it's important to do so.

 http://search.microsoft.com/dev/

Microsoft Corporation. "Database Replication with the Microsoft Jet Database Engine: A Technical Overview." Redmond, WA: Microsoft Corporation, 1997. This background paper on database replication provides a good description of the replication facilities provided by the Jet database engine.

 http://search.microsoft.com/dev/

————. Microsoft Corporation. "Securing Microsoft Windows NT Installation." Redmond, WA: Microsoft Corporation, 1997. This background paper identifies a number of security considerations for the Windows NT environment and presents good overviews of security roles, security levels, and auditing.

 http://search.microsoft.com/dev/

Smith, Will. "Managing Infrastructure Deployment Projects". Paper presented at TechEd 97. This paper describes the different project documents, including those for business requirements. Many of the factors addressed during a requirements analysis are also discussed in the paper.

 www.microsoft.com/enable

This is Microsoft's Web site for providing news and information on accessibility. The site features a section for designers and developers, as well as a download capability for accessibility tools.

Defining
Solution
Architectures

5

Terms you'll need to understand:

√ Presentation services
√ Business services
√ Data services
√ Logical three-tier model
√ Single-tier application
√ Two-tier application
√ Three-tier application
√ *n*-tier application
√ Component Object Model (COM)

√ Distributed Component Object Model (DCOM)
√ Internet Information Server (IIS)
√ Microsoft Transaction Server (MTS)
√ COM Transaction Integrator (COMTI)
√ Active Server Pages (ASP)
√ Deployment topology
√ Message Queue Server (MSMQ)

Techniques you'll need to master:

√ Differentiating between single-tier, two-tier, and three-tier applications
√ Describing the Windows Distributed interNet Applications model (DNA)
√ Describing the logical three-tier model
√ Describing the characteristics of the Component Object Model
√ Describing how to modularize an application based on the logical three-tier model

√ Describing the differences between server-side scripting and client-side scripting in a Web-based application
√ Identifying the factors to consider when choosing a solution technology
√ Identifying the factors to consider when choosing a data storage architecture
√ Identifying the strengths and weaknesses of a given deployment topology

The solution architecture provides the overall design of how the business problem will be solved. Design is a compromise between business requirements and technological capabilities. This means design decisions are management decisions and designers need to be aware of business requirements.

Chapter 4 introduced some of the problems at the fictitious company, Action Aerospace. The CIO at Action Aerospace asked you to help them design a solution. After gathering the business requirements, you engaged the support of Dave, a fellow consultant and Microsoft Certified Solution Developer. Dave reviewed the business requirements with you and helped you propose a solution architecture.

CASE STUDY: **Action Aerospace**

Business Requirements

After reviewing the results of the business requirements analysis at Action Aerospace, you and Dave produce a list of some of the key factors that will influence your solution. The list includes the following:

➤ The company is growing, so the solution must be scalable to handle the growth.

➤ The budget is limited, so new development effort can't be extensive.

➤ The existing legacy system plays a key role in the business, so the solution must include interoperability with the IBM environment.

➤ The current staff has little or no experience in building desktop/server types of applications.

➤ The intended audience will require a familiar graphical user interface similar to the other applications on their workstations.

➤ The system will experience periods of peak loading when everyone tries to submit time card data just before the deadline.

Solution Architecture

Dave proposes to design the Employee Time Card System based on the three-tier logical model. To do this, you'll partition the solution into three logical pieces. Each piece will provide a particular type of service. In your design, these will be presentation services, business services, and data services.

As the code is developed, it will be modularized following the same structure of the logical model. To do this, code modules will only contain the code necessary for supplying the intended service of the module. In particular, different types of services won't be included in the same module. For example, the presentation services will be responsible for filling a form with data, but the presentation services module won't directly access the database to retrieve the data. The data services module will handle all access to the database, and the presentation services module will request data from the data services model when data is required.

You've built several client/server applications in the past using a Visual Basic application on the client and a SQL Server database on the back end. You ask Dave why this classic two-tier architecture wouldn't work.

Dave explains that although the two-tier architecture works on a small scale, he's run into problems with it as more users are added to the system. He's actually built applications using the logical three-tier model and explains more about it.

"By isolating the different service, we will have a great deal of flexibility for implementation. For example, we might want to consider using a Web browser as a key component of the presentation services. Or we might want to use a traditional Win32 application written in Visual Basic. By using a modular design, we can use either and not worry about having to make changes in other parts of the application.

"We also have a great deal of flexibility when it comes to actually deploying the application. We can start out using a single system and later distribute the application across different systems as the need arises. From a development perspective, small development teams can work independently on the different modules. You and I can function as mentors to the current staff. With this approach, the learning curve is not nearly as steep, because each team focuses on only one part of the problem. We will have to help them build the application, but once implemented, the current staff should be able to support it."

Dave continues to describe the solution. "Several different technologies exist for building this type of solution; however, I would use the Component Object Model (COM) as the fundamental piece. We would also use Microsoft Transaction Server (MTS). Together, these two technologies will provide a scalable infrastructure and facilities for supporting concurrent users. MTS will provide many facilities that we would otherwise have to implement ourselves."

"Data services will provide two different types of data. We will use a relational database, but we also need to access the mainframe environment. When information is needed from the mainframe, the COM Transaction Integrator (COMTI) feature in SNA Server can be used to communicate with the host. No changes will be required to the mainframe applications, because COMTI

will enable us to execute Customer Information Control System (CICS) transactions on the mainframe and obtain the results. All of these details can be
embedded in the data services layer."

Dave sketches out a design, which is shown in Figure 5.1.

You like Dave's proposal and schedule a meeting with the CIO at Action Aerospace to discuss your ideas.

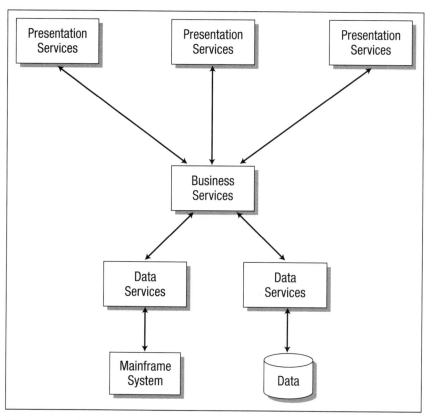

Figure 5.1 Action Aerospace's proposed solution.

Solution Architecture Options

As you start planning the solution architecture, you'll have many configuration options and deployment options. Your final design will be a balance between the business requirements and technology. Cost, schedule, and development resources will drive business requirements. Performance, scalability, and development tools will drive technology requirements.

One of the first considerations you'll need to determine is where the processing is going to be done. You have many options from which to choose. For example, will the processing be:

➤ On a single system?

➤ Distributed across multiple systems?

➤ Mostly in a client application?

➤ Mostly in a server application?

➤ As stored procedures in a database?

To understand the advantages and disadvantages of all these options, you must first understand some of the basic guidelines for structuring an application. This is best described using an application logical model.

Logical Three-Tier Model

Applications perform many different types of tasks and processing. However, a general model that's true for most business applications groups the application functions into three general categories: *presentation services*, *business services*, and *data services*. This is referred to as the *logical three-tier model*.

Presentation services, sometimes referred to as *user services*, establish the user interface and provide the facility for interacting with users. For example, in the Employee Time Card System at Action Aerospace, displaying a form for an employee to enter, view, and modify time card data would be classified as one of the presentation services.

Business services apply business rules and perform the logic behind the business task. Sometimes the business services provided by the application are also referred to as application services. For example, in the Employee Time Card System, processing an employee time card entry for hours worked on a specific project constitutes a business service. It involves getting data, which the user has entered, and adding it to the database. Before the entry can be added to the database, it must also be verified. The project code must be valid, and it must be a project code that the employee is authorized to use. These types of validation checks are also part of the business services.

Data services manage the storage of persistent data. Persistent data is data that is permanently stored even though the application is not in use. For example, the database used to track employee time card data must store the data each employee enters. Later, the employee or supervisor will want to look at that data. The data must be available, and it must be the same data originally entered.

Figure 5.2 depicts these three services.

The earliest business applications performed these functions. However, finding where these functions were performed was not always easy. Early applications were usually written as a single piece of monolithic code, and this code was very difficult to manage and maintain. The concept of building an application out of multiple modules, rather than a single module, reduced some of the management and maintenance problems.

Although applications became modularized, presentation, business, and data services weren't necessarily used as the basis for modularization. In other words, a single module might present the user with a form for entering data, validate the data once it was entered, and store the data after it was validated. As a result, it's often difficult to maintain these applications even though they've been broken into separate modules.

Imagine what's required to change the application because the database storing the data has changed. It's necessary to change the code in all places where the data is accessed. This might be spread across many modules, and without a good understanding of what each module does, it's difficult to find all the places where the code accesses the database.

Restructuring the application so it's modularized according to the three functional services makes the application more maintainable, and it also makes the application more scalable and extensible.

The rule is not to produce a single source module for each service but to *isolate the three fundamental services into separate groups of modules*. Each group of

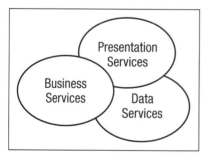

Figure 5.2 The logical functions performed by a business application.

modules providing a specific service can be thought of as a *logical tier*. Modules in one tier communicate with modules in another tier. Thus, any module displaying data in a form wouldn't directly access the data store to get that data. Instead, the module providing the presentation services would access a data services module that would retrieve the data. Specific details on how to access the data from the data store would be found only in the data services module.

This is precisely the solution that's been proposed for Action Aerospace. Figure 5.3 shows the services grouped into separate tiers.

The real power and flexibility of using this logical model is that there are a number of *different physical models you can use to implement an application based on the logical three-tier model*. You might implement the three logical tiers in:

➤ A single physical tier

➤ Two physical tiers

➤ Three physical tiers

➤ *n* physical tiers

The business requirements will help you determine which physical model is appropriate for your solution architecture.

When services are separated into physical tiers a boundary exists between the tiers. Some type of communication mechanism is required to exchange data and messages between the tiers. The communication mechanism used depends on the type of boundary.

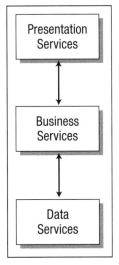

Figure 5.3   The logical services of an application grouped into tiers.

It's possible that the separate tiers can be implemented as *separate processes running on the same machine*. In this case, an interprocess communication facility can provide the communication mechanism. However, it's also possible that the separate tiers can be implemented as *separate processes running on different machines*. In this case, a network connection is required to provide the communications.

Single-Tier Implementation

One implementation option is to group all three services into the same physical tier. This is referred to as a *single-tier physical implementation*. In a single-tier physical implementation no special communication mechanisms are required to cross the boundaries between the services. Standard procedure calls are used to provide communication between the various modules in the application. This implementation is depicted in Figure 5.4.

One advantage of this model is that it's the simplest model to implement. For some applications, such as a single user system, it's a good solution.

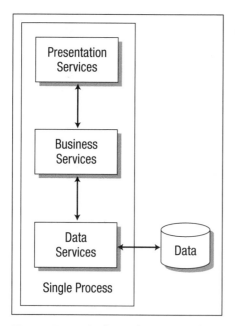

Figure 5.4 The logical services of an application implemented in a single tier.

Although single-tier implementation resembles the monolithic applications created in the past, it's different. If you've actually partitioned the source code and structured the application around three logical tiers, with very little effort, you can migrate these logical tiers to another physical model.

Two-Tier Implementation

One of the most common implementations is to separate the services into two physical tiers: a client and a server. This is referred to as a *two-tier physical implementation,* and it represents the classic client/server architecture.

Typically the communication mechanism between the client and the server is a database connection. When the client and server are deployed on separate systems, a network provides the database connection between the tiers.

 A two-tier client/server application typically uses a database connection as the communication mechanism between the client and the server.

Often the presentation and business services are grouped together in the client, and the data services are deployed in the server. This implementation, which is referred to as a *fat client*, is depicted in Figure 5.5.

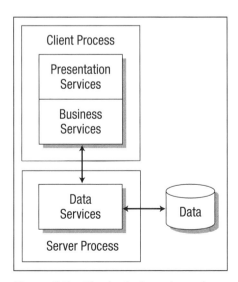

Figure 5.5   The logical services of an application implemented in two tiers as a fat client.

This solution is popular for several reasons:

➤ Many development tools support the implementation of this model.

➤ Relational database management systems function well as the server.

➤ For a modest number of users, the model performs well.

Not surprising, it also has some limitations:

➤ The server determines application performance and scalability.

➤ Each client requires at least one connection to the database; therefore, growth is limited to the number of connections the database can support.

➤ Each client usually holds its database connection, which requires database resources, even though the database isn't being accessed.

➤ When the client and server are on separate machines, network traffic is usually heavy because all data must be transferred over the network to the client for processing.

➤ Adequate processing resources, such as memory and central processing unit (CPU) power, are required for each client.

 In a fat client, most of the processing occurs on the client system, because this is where the bulk of the application code resides. This often leads to added expense, because each client requires sufficient memory and CPU power to run the application.

An alternate two-tier physical implementation groups the business services with the data services on the server. This implementation, which is referred to as a *fat server*, is depicted in Figure 5.6.

Fat servers are usually implemented using the stored procedure capabilities of a relational database management system. Business logic is written as a stored database procedure.

This model has advantages over the fat client:

➤ Network traffic is reduced, because some computing is performed on the server.

➤ Resource requirements for the client may not be as demanding, because less processing is done on the client.

Likewise, there are also limitations:

➤ The language used for stored database procedures and the facilities provided by stored database procedures are determined by the relational

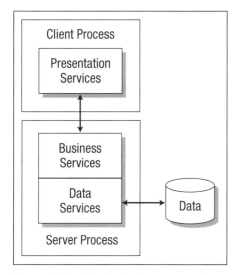

Figure 5.6   The logical services of an application implemented in two tiers as a fat server.

database management system (RDBMS). Therefore, once implemented, it may be difficult, or even impossible, to migrate the stored procedures to a different database system.

➤ The programming language used for implementing stored procedures is usually limited and not as powerful as other development languages.

 Two-tier applications have two major limitations: they don't scale well and they often require excessive resources on the client workstation.

Three-Tier Implementation

By implementing the three logical services in three tiers, some of the limitations of the two-tier physical model can be addressed. This is referred to as a *three-tier physical implementation*. Sometimes this physical model is assumed to be the only implementation possible for the three-tier logical model. However, this assumption is incorrect, given the examples above. Figure 5.7 depicts a three-tier implementation.

The key characteristic that distinguishes the three-tier physical implementation from other implementations is a boundary between the presentation services and business services as well as a boundary between the business services and the data services.

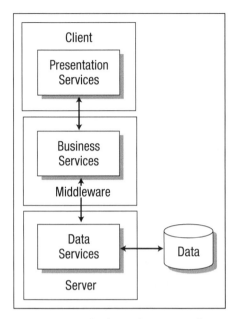

Figure 5.7   The logical services of an application implemented in three tiers.

As shown in Figure 5.7, a new tier exists between the client and server. This tier is referred to as *middleware*. In addition to hosting business services, the middleware tier also provides an infrastructure for tying the application together.

Some of the advantages of the three-tier implementation include:

➤ Greater scalability and improved performance

➤ Flexibility to partition and distribute the application

On the downside:

➤ Management of the application is more difficult because of the distributed pieces.

➤ Developing the infrastructure can be complex and a major part of the development effort.

n-Tier Implementation

The *n*-tier application is a logical extension of the three-tier application. It's a distributed application in which one or more of the three original tiers have been separated into additional tiers. This provides another level of abstraction for describing the model.

Implementing A Multitiered Application

Developing the solution architecture is part of the design process; however, there must be a way to actually implement the architecture if your solution is to be viable. Therefore, to design the architecture, you'll need to conceptually understand the technologies that can be used to implement it.

Implementing n-tier physical models can be time consuming and complex to manage. These constraints are typically inconsistent with the business requirements.

However, over the last few years, several enabling technologies are being used successfully to facilitate the implementation. Two examples are the Component Object Model (COM) and application services that support the middle tier.

Component Object Model (COM)

The fundamental concept of the Component Object Model (COM) is the ability to create reusable parts or components. These binary components are the building blocks used to develop applications. Using the COM model, a component encapsulates a specific piece of application functionality and exposes a set of methods and properties that can be used by other applications and components.

COM enables software developers to build three-tier distributed applications from components that can be deployed in any tier. In the presentation tier, components manage user interaction and make requests for other services by calling components in the middle tier. In the middle tier, business service components perform business logic and call components in the data services tier. Components in the data services tier interact with the particular data store to access data and return it to the calling component.

The COM Specification defines how to call COM objects in a language-independent and location-independent manner. The platform supporting COM provides the services of locating, identifying, and creating objects from the components. The platform also provides facilities for supporting communications between components.

In summary, COM provides a standard model for:

➤ Building reusable binary components and creating objects from those components

➤ Building components independent of source language

➤ Enabling components that interact with one another independent of location

➤ Creating new versions of components

In particular, COM addresses many of the issues that application developers must solve, allowing the developer to focus more attention on the actual business problem.

When you use Visual Basic to create a COM component, you have several options for enhancing your components over time. When you update a component, you can specify whether the component interfaces are *version identical*, *version compatible*, or *version incompatible*. This will determine whether or not existing applications can use the new version of the component.

 Compiling the component with No Compatibility ensures that the new executable won't contain any global universal identifications (GUIDs) that reference the previous version.

Distributed COM (DCOM)

A key part of COM is defining and providing the facilities that support component interaction. This interaction is defined such that a client and the component can connect without the need of any intermediary system component. The client simply calls methods in the component.

However, components may run:

➤ On the same thread within the same process

➤ On different threads within the same process

➤ In different processes on the same computer

➤ On different computers

For true location independence, all of these options must be supported.

A client needing to access a component in the same process has no problems. The client can directly access the properties and methods of the component.

However, when the client and component are in different processes, special steps must be taken. A client that needs to communicate with a component in another process can't call the component directly but has to use some form of interprocess communication provided by the operating system. COM provides this communication in a completely transparent fashion: it intercepts calls from the client and forwards them to the component in another process.

The Distributed Component Object Model (DCOM) extends the Component Object Model to support communication between a client and component on different computers. When client and component reside on different machines, DCOM simply replaces the local interprocess communication with a network protocol. Neither the client nor the component is aware that the communication link spans multiple computers.

DCOM allows you to access remote components in exactly the same way you access local components. Thus, components can seamlessly interact across a local area network (LAN), a wide area network (WAN), or even the Internet.

 Windows NT 4.0 supports DCOM, which provides an efficient, transparent mechanism for interprocess communication between two components located on different computers.

Presentation Services

The primary purpose of the presentation services tier is to provide the graphical user interface and logic so the user can interact with the application. You'll need to evaluate several considerations when you design presentation services. These include:

➤ Target audience

➤ Capabilities and facilities of the user interface

➤ Development effort

➤ Deployment and maintenance concerns

Until recently, most presentation tiers were implemented using a *native user interface* that relies on user interface services provided by the underlying operating system. On Windows, native user interfaces employ the Microsoft Win32 application programming interface (API). A Win32-based user interface is usually deployed as an application (EXE file) that runs on the client platform. Using native user interface, you can provide a robust interface with rich functionality.

The growth of the Internet has not only created new demands for access to information, it's also opened up new possibilities for implementing presentation services. A *Web-based user interface* employs an Internet browser to deliver the presentation services for an application. They're typically based on HTML and deployed as a Web page, which can be rendered on any operating system by a Web browser.

There are, of course, multiple options for implementing presentation services. Four options, which also provide an Internet or intranet interface, are shown in Figure 5.8.

Browser Neutral

Browser-neutral client applications are page-based applications that use standard HTML for presentation services. The services run in the context of the browser. To achieve the greatest compatibility with all browsers, browser-neutral applications rely on standard HTML, not on the browser supporting a particular technology. The downside of a browser neutral application is that the interface will be limited in the functionality and features it can provide.

Browser Enhanced

Browser-enhanced client applications are page-based applications that take advantage of specific features found in a particular browser. The services run in the context of the browser, but they exploit browser capabilities to provide maximum functionality. Sometimes these applications will determine the browser type dynamically, so they can identify what features are available.

A browser enhanced application might use dynamic HTML (DHTML), Java applets, ActiveX controls, or *client-side scripting*, depending on what the browser

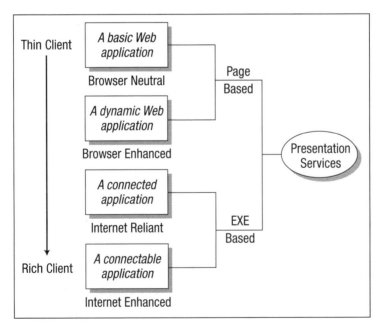

Figure 5.8   Implementation options for presentation services.

supports. Although browser enhanced applications are limited to a specific set of browsers, they can provide a robust user interface.

Internet Reliant

Internet-reliant applications are application based rather than page based. They're built using the services provided by the operating system (such as the Win32 API), but they also *rely* on data and services provided via the Internet. Presentation services can be implemented as an Internet-reliant application on the client.

Internet Enhanced

Internet-enhanced applications are also application based and built using the services provided by the operating system. These applications leverage Internet connectivity to provide robustness, but they don't depend on it. For example, an application that provides the capability to seamlessly download a file from the Internet is usually an Internet-enhanced application.

Application Services Supporting The Middleware

The middle tier of the three-tier model hosts business services. This tier also hosts a large part of another important piece, the *middleware*. Middleware provides the infrastructure that ties the application together.

Unfortunately, part of the complexity of developing multi-tier applications stems from development of the middleware. Middleware handles connectivity, security, and directory issues, as well as process and thread management and database connection management. When developed from scratch, middleware can account for 30 to 40 percent of the total development effort.

Furthermore, middleware code is complex, requiring highly skilled developers and thorough testing. Often middleware must be customized for the specific application and can't easily be reused elsewhere.

You can reduce the development effort of middleware facilities by utilizing the capabilities provided by several enabling technologies. The facilities described here provide Web services, messaging services, and transaction and resource management services.

Internet Information Server (IIS)

The Internet Information Server (IIS) provides facilities for Web publishing and file transfer and enables intranet and Internet-based applications.

In addition to standard HTML pages, IIS supports Active Server Pages (ASP), a language-neutral server-side scripting environment that's used to create and run Web server applications. An ASP is a mix of script and HTML. ASP makes it possible to generate dynamic Web pages.

 ASP uses server-side scripting. Because script processing occurs on the server, the client receives only standard HTML. Thus, ASP-based applications typically have few browser dependencies and can work with a wide variety of browser software.

Microsoft Transaction Server (MTS)

Microsoft Transaction Server, an extension of the COM programming model, simplifies the development, deployment, and management of distributed applications.

From the programming perspective, developers can prepare components that contain the business logic. These components can be written as if they'll be used serially by a single user. Developers can focus on the business problem rather than the application infrastructure details needed to support scaling and access by concurrent users.

MTS provides a run-time environment for these server-side components. MTS services include thread pooling, multiuser synchronization, instance management, scaling, and database connection management. When the components are run within the MTS run-time environment, MTS handles the instance management and automatically scales to support large numbers of concurrent users.

MTS also provides automatic transaction services. A settable attribute of the component indicates the level of transaction support required. MTS will automatically create and manage the required transactions. Once a component completes its work, it then makes a function call to MTS specifying whether or not the operation completed successfully. MTS can then commit or roll back the transaction.

Microsoft Message Queue Server (MSMQ)

Microsoft Message Queue Server provides services that allow you to manage queues of messages and route messages between queues. It provides a technology for interoperability between two different applications.

One application creates a message and sends it to a queue. Another application, or another part of the same application, retrieves the message from the queue and processes it. An application can write to data queues without waiting for a response.

MSMQ provides reliable transport services between physical servers that may be disconnected at times. This enables application support for occasionally connected clients. With third-party middleware, MSMQ can communicate with IBM's MQ Series.

MSMQ facilitates robust architecture solutions such as allowing you to take your legacy databases down for backup, while still continuing to take orders.

Data Services

The primary purpose of the data services tier is to provide access to the persistent data that the application will use. If you've worked with client/server applications, the application data is often stored in a relational database. In addition to an RDBMS data might be stored in a traditional file system or even be managed by another computer system.

In the three-tier model, the actual details of where and how the data is stored is isolated from the other tiers. Only the data services tier has this information. The other tiers make all data requests through the data services tier, which knows how to access the data. Figure 5.9 shows several options for storing persistent data.

For the Action Aerospace solution, data service components will be used to access a relational database as well as the CICS environment on the mainframe.

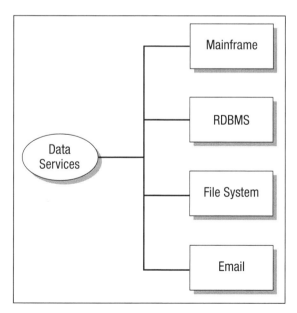

Figure 5.9   Data services are more than simply accessing a database.

Microsoft Windows DNA

Microsoft Windows Distributed interNet Applications (DNA) is a multi-tiered distributed application model based on the concept of *cooperating components*. These components are built using COM.

The technologies and architectural concepts described in this chapter are exactly what Windows DNA is all about.

Windows DNA:

➤ Provides a model for producing scalable, manageable, and maintainable multiuser applications.

➤ Provides a comprehensive and integrated platform for distributed applications.

➤ Provides interoperability with existing applications and legacy systems.

➤ Facilitates the development of distributed applications.

Distributed applications require an underlying infrastructure that provides communication. In the past, the creation of this infrastructure was usually rolled into the solution development. It was common for the development of the infrastructure alone to account for 40 percent of the total development effort. Thus, a significant part of development wasn't developing software to solve the business problem but, instead, developing the software that would support the solution.

Distributed applications built using the Windows DNA model rely on a common set of infrastructure and networking services provided by the Windows application platform. Internet Information Server, Transaction Server, and Message Queuing supplement the Windows NT operating system services, which include security, systems management, directory services, networking, and hardware support. Together, these facilities provide a powerful infrastructure, allowing developers to focus on how to solve business problems.

Solution Technologies

To determine the final solution technology, you'll need to consider the following:

➤ **Standards**   Many businesses will require that the solution support certain standards. This may be due to technology requirements, or it may simply be a matter of company policy. In any case, the support of a specific standard (or lack thereof) may be the determining factor for selecting a particular technology.

➤ **Proprietary Technologies**   Because most solutions are prepared for an existing environment, proprietary technologies may also exist that your solution will need to support. This, too, can be a determining factor for choosing a particular technology.

➤ **Technology Environment**   In addition to proprietary technologies, existing technologies will influence your technology options. For example, at Action Aerospace, interoperability with the mainframe environment was a critical requirement. This was addressed by selecting a technology that provided a smooth interface into the CICS application.

➤ **Development Tools**   The particular development tools you choose will strongly influence the technology supported by the solution. Often, development tools are chosen because of availability or developer familiarity. As a result, existing or familiar development tools are often used to create code that doesn't support the solution architecture. Therefore, the development tools must support the facilities and technologies required by the solution architecture.

➤ **Solution Type**   As described earlier, you can use a number of different physical models to implement a logical model based on presentation, business, and data service tiers. Your final solution type may be distributed, centralized, desktop, or enterprise. Some of the key factors that will help you determine the solution type include:

➤ Number of users

➤ Number of databases

➤ Concurrent access to shared data

➤ Security

➤ Availability

➤ Scalability

Data Storage Architecture

The data storage architecture is a key part of most business solution architectures because the data storage contains the persistent data that reflects the state of the business. Rarely will access to this data be limited to only one user at a time. In most cases, this data will be a shared resource that must be capable of concurrent access by many users. The design of the data storage architecture will determine if this is possible.

You'll want to consider a number of factors to determine the right data storage architecture. These include:

➤ Volume

➤ Transactions

➤ Connections

➤ Business requirements

➤ Extensibility

➤ Reporting

➤ Users

➤ Databases

Volume

Volume refers to the amount of data. You'll not only want to consider the current amount of data but how the data will grow and what the growth rate will be. Volume will strongly influence how you physically store the data. For example, you might be able to store it on a single disk, or you may decide to distribute the data across multiple disks.

In general, it's usually better to spread the data over multiple disk drives rather than storing it all on one large disk. This enables concurrent access to different parts of the database, and when properly designed, can increase database performance. It's common to find high performing database servers with the data spread over sixty or more disk drives.

Transactions

A *transaction* is the fundamental unit of work performed by the database system. Any time you access a database you'll perform a transaction. The application design will determine what operations, and how many, are actually performed in the context of a single transaction. Transactions, by definition, have atomicity. All the database operations performed in the context of a transaction either succeed or fail as a group.

Two important aspects of transactions will affect your solution design: the transaction rate (the number of transactions per unit of time) and the transaction length (how long the transaction takes to complete). High transaction rates will require computing resources capable of handling the load.

Ideally, transaction lengths should be as short as possible, because during the transaction, database resources are allocated to the transaction. These resources aren't available to other users who may end up waiting for them. Furthermore, depending on the specific operations, the data itself may be locked during the transaction and, therefore, inaccessible to other users.

In the real world, not all transactions will be short, and you'll probably discover that the transactions in the application vary in length. Your storage architecture must allow for this. If at all possible, you'll want to prevent a lengthy transaction from blocking a number of short transactions. Sometimes this can be accomplished by providing different environments for the different transactions. For example, one server might be dedicated to long transactions, and another server could be dedicated to shorter transactions. That way, a long transaction would not prevent a shorter transaction from running.

When a business maintains multiple databases, which it usually does, it's often necessary to access and, perhaps, to modify data in one or more databases as part of the same transaction. This is accomplished using a *two-phase commit*. The distributed transaction coordinator (DTC) coordinates all the resources involved and handles all the details of the commit and abort processes.

 A two-phase commit allows the scope of a single transaction to span multiple databases. To accomplish this, each database system first confirms that it's prepared to commit the transaction. If any of the participants fails to do this, the transaction can't be completed. However, if all database systems are prepared to commit, the operation proceeds to its second phase. At this point, each database commits the changes that have been made during the transaction.

Connections

A *database connection* is the path between the user of the database services and the database management system. For an application to access a database and retrieve or update data, the application must first establish a connection to the database management system. An application will often establish more than one connection.

Several aspects of database connections are significant, because they can play a key role in total system performance. They are as follows:

➤ Each connection requires dedicated computer resources

➤ Establishing a connection to a database requires processing time for the allocation of the needed resources

➤ A database system can support only a finite number of connections

➤ The number of connections a database can support is often controlled by the database license. More connections cost more money.

 In a two-tier application, database connections usually constitute the performance bottleneck and limit the scalability.

One of the popular implementation techniques for database applications is to establish a connection to the database as part of the application initialization process. The connection remains open until the application ends. This minimizes the overhead in connection creation because the connection is created only once, and it also ensures that a connection is ready when the application needs to access data.

However, a hefty penalty is incurred with this model because of the inefficient use of database resources. Most of the time the connection will be idle. However, the database resources allocated for the connection are dedicated to a single user and aren't available to any other users.

The consequences of using a separate dedicated connection for each user are:

➤ The total number of users is limited to the total connections the database will support.

➤ The database could be idle, yet no more users can log on, because the connections are exhausted.

➤ As the number of connections increases, performance decreases because computer resources are dedicated to the connections.

➤ To support more connections, additional processing power and memory must be added to the database server.

Figure 5.10 shows a database that's accessed by a number of users, with each user maintaining a separate connection to the database.

For a limited number of users, this model works well, and it's one of the easiest to implement. Many existing applications are based on this model; however, these applications have poor scalability.

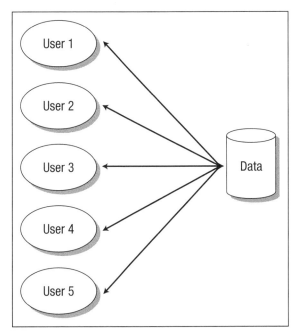

Figure 5.10 Multiple users accessing a database using separate connections.

Scalability usually ranks high on the requirement list. This is especially true of Internet-based applications where thousands of users might be online at the same time. Therefore, an alternative to the dedicated connection model is needed.

One approach is to limit the number of database connections to a number that the database management system can efficiently handle given the specific hardware environment. These connections are, then, shared by a number of users. *Connection pooling* is based on this concept. Figure 5.11 depicts a situation in which five users can access the same database using only two connections.

For this concept to work, a connection manager functions as the gatekeeper to the database. Furthermore, all application requests for a database connection don't go directly to the database but, instead, are routed through the connection manager.

Applications must cooperate with the connection manager by requesting a connection only when it's needed. The application then releases the connection as soon as the database access completes. It has always been possible to write applications that do this, but it was rarely done because of the performance overhead in establishing a database connection. Finally, the application should try to minimize the length of time it holds a connection. Limiting the processing activities to those actually required for accessing the data does this.

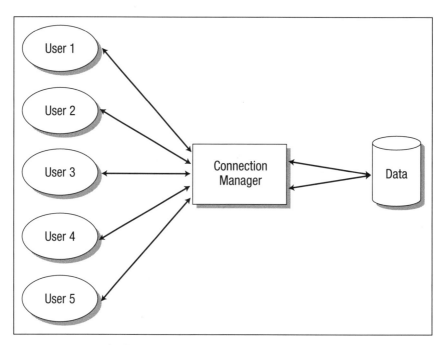

Figure 5.11   Multiple users accessing a database using shared connections.

For its part, the connection manager maintains a set of open connections to the database. When an application requests a connection, the connection manager assigns it one of the open connections that's not in use. Because the connection is already connected to the database, no initialization overhead is incurred. When the application releases the connection, the connection manager can reassign the same connection to another user.

 One of the biggest advantages of the shared connection concept is that you can configure a database server to handle a specific number of connections. Once the server has been tuned, the performance will be consistent and predictable.

Business Requirements

Remember, there may be specific business requirements that require a specific characteristic in the data storage architecture. For example, availability, maintainability, security, or geographic distribution could all influence the data storage architecture.

Extensibility

You'll also want to make sure that the data storage architecture you choose supports the enhancements that are envisioned for the future.

Reporting

Most business information systems will produce reports. In fact, reporting requirements often represent a significant portion of the overall business requirements.

Ironically, there's usually a conflict between the *informational* (reporting) requirements and the *operational* (production) requirements.

The operational requirements are the basis for an online system with many concurrent users. This system always reflects the current state of the business and usually has a high level of availability. System response time is very important, and the transactions being processed are often very short in duration.

On the other hand, the reporting requirements are the basis for a batch-oriented system. Reports can usually be generated in the background and may require significant amounts of processing time to read and summarize data. A data snapshot as of yesterday's close of business is often more desirable than the current state of the business, which changes from minute to minute. The transactions that produce the reports are usually very lengthy and access large amounts of data.

In recent years, many businesses have started supporting both an operational environment and an informational environment. Data from the operational environment is used to create the informational environment that can be used for reporting and data analysis. A *data warehouse*, the database used to store the informational data, is usually a key component of the informational environment.

 Having two separate environments, one for production and one for reporting, often represents a viable solution. The data warehouse can be optimized for reporting, while the production database can be optimized for online transaction processing.

Users

Although the number of users indirectly affects the load on the database, as previously mentioned, the number of connections really represents the key factor for determining how many users can concurrently be supported.

Databases

Most businesses will have data stored in multiple databases. Sometimes this is done because a single database is *partitioned* into multiple databases. For example, the Western Region database and the Eastern Region database might logically represent the same data, but for performance reasons, the data has been split into two separate databases. These databases could even be geographically distributed.

Businesses also have multiple databases, because they deal in many different types of data. The human resources database would most likely be separate from the order entry database.

Replication is often used to maintain multiple copies of the same database. As changes occur in one database, they're automatically replicated to the duplicate databases. Replication is used to maintain a backup copy in case of failure, as well as to provide a higher level of availability.

Sometimes replication is used to move just part of a database to another geographic location to provide faster access to the data. For example, replication could be used to create the Western Region and Eastern Region databases described previously. Replication can also be used to roll up the changes in the regional databases into a single corporate sales database.

Solution Feasibility

Once you've determined a solution architecture, you'll need to demonstrate that it's, indeed, a feasible solution to the business problem. To do this, you'll need to:

➤ Demonstrate that business requirements are met

➤ Demonstrate that usage scenarios are met

➤ Demonstrate that existing technology constraints are met

In addition to demonstrating the hows and whys of feasibility, you can't overlook the fact that the solution will also have deficiencies. Solution feasibility also requires that you're able to *assess the impact of shortfalls in meeting requirements*.

Deployment

Once your application has been designed, implemented, and tested it's ready to be deployed. That is, the necessary pieces will be delivered to the destination system, and the software will be installed. Usually, a system manager handles this job.

Application deployment consists of two important parts:

➤ *Deployment topology* that defines what systems will host what application components

➤ *Deployment process* that describes the steps for actually distributing the pieces to the target systems

 When you incorporate an application into MTS, application components are assembled into location-transparent modules known as packages. MTS packages provide the system manager with a great deal of flexibility for deploying application modules across multiple systems.

The Deployment Topology

Several important factors will help you determine the topology:

➤ Existing systems and infrastructure

➤ Performance needs

➤ Availability needs

➤ Scalability needs

The deployment topology identifies the systems that will host the database and other application components. If additional application support services are needed, such as IIS, SNA Server, or MSMQ, the deployment topology will also identify the systems that will host these services.

To gain performance, you may consider distributing the load across multiple machines. Scalability is often achieved by choosing a topology that can easily be expanded by adding additional systems as the need arises. High reliability and high availability are often achieved by using *clusters* of systems.

Several sample deployments are described next. However, these are only a few of the possible options.

Figure 5.12 shows an application that's been deployed to a single-server system. Both the business and data services components are on the same server system, while the presentation services are located on each client.

Figure 5.13 shows an application that's been deployed to two server systems. One of the server systems hosts the business services, and the other server system hosts the data services components. Presentation services are located

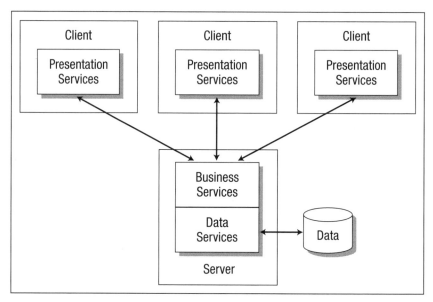

Figure 5.12 The business and data services deployed on a single-server system.

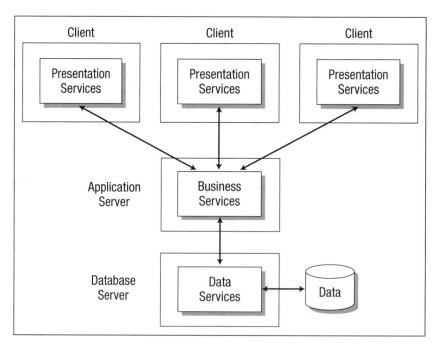

Figure 5.13 The business and data services each deployed on a separate server system.

on each client. This configuration provides improved performance by distributing the processing load across two server systems.

Figure 5.14 shows another deployment topology using two server systems. The server systems are identical, with business services and data services components on each one. Presentation services are located on each client.

This configuration provides high availability. If one of the server systems experiences a failure, the entire load can be diverted to the other server. MTS and clustering facilities provided by Microsoft Cluster Services facilitate deploying this type of configuration.

It's also possible to achieve improved performance with this configuration by balancing the client load between the two servers. However, trying to share a single database between two different servers presents another problem. Additional software, such as a distributed lock manager, must be used to coordinate database activity between the two server systems.

Figure 5.15 shows another deployment topology using multiple server systems. The business services are located on one server, and data services components are deployed on two different servers. Each data services server accesses its own database. This model allows you to partition a large, single database into multiple smaller databases. It is even possible to deploy the databases using different RDBMSs. This configuration has an advantage over the

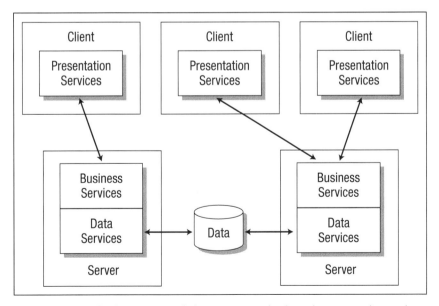

Figure 5.14   The business and data services deployed on two identical servers for high availability and load balancing.

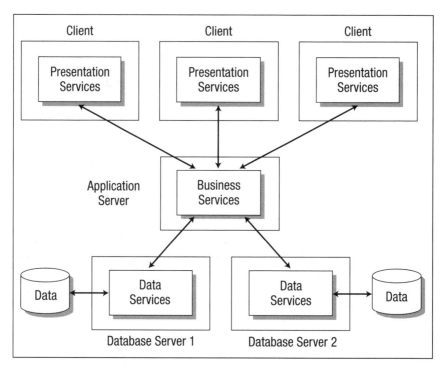

Figure 5.15   The business and data services deployed using a partitioned database.

configuration shown in Figure 5.14 in that the partitioned database model won't require a distributed lock manager.

You'll need to evaluate numerous trade-offs before deciding on a final distributed deployment topology. As you distribute the application across more machines, scalability and availability might increase. However, system management and security might become more complex, and network traffic will likely increase. Distributing an application is also likely to introduce more processing overhead causing degradation in overall performance. Your solution architecture will need to balance all of these factors.

The Deployment Process

Deploying the application to its destination involves two types of deployment:

➤ Deploying the files to the server systems

➤ Deploying the files to the client systems

Deploying the files to the server systems involves transferring the files to the target machine, then installing the software. A semiautomated procedure is usually used to perform the installation. When more server systems are involved, this process becomes more complicated, because files must be deployed to multiple machines, and multiple installation operations must be performed.

Deploying the files to the client systems is very similar to the process of deploying the files to the server systems. Namely, the files are transferred to the target machine and installed using an install program. When multiple clients are involved, the software must be installed on each client machine.

However, some architectures, such as those utilizing a Web browser in the client, may not initially require any additional software to be loaded and installed on the client. When the application is run and client components are needed, they'll automatically be downloaded from the server by the browser. For this to work, the components will have to be installed on the server, so they can be downloaded on demand.

For example, a Web page may require a particular ActiveX control on the client system. When the browser downloads the page from the server, it can determine if the control is already installed on the client. If it is, then the page is ready to be rendered. However, if the browser finds that the control is not available on the client, or an outdated version is installed, it will automatically download the control from the server and install it on the client system. This all happens without any special intervention from the user.

Usually applications are distributed as .cab files. Depending on how you plan to distribute the application, this can be a single .cab file or a series of .cab files.

Practice Questions

Question 1

> Which of the following characteristics describes the two-tier application model?
> [Check all correct answers]
>
> ❑ a. Scalability and performance are primarily determined by the database.
>
> ❑ b. Scalability and performance are primarily determined by the client application.
>
> ❑ c. Program-to-program communications are used between the tiers.
>
> ❑ d. Program-to-database communications are used between the tiers.

Answers a and d are correct. The database and the server limit performance and scalability. In the two-tier application model, program-to-database communications (for example, open database connectivity [ODBC]) are used between the tiers.

Question 2

> In the three-tier physical model, which of the following provides the infrastructure that ties the pieces together?
>
> ○ a. Presentation services
>
> ○ b. Middleware
>
> ○ c. Business services
>
> ○ d. Data services

Answer b is correct. Middleware provides the infrastructure that ties the application pieces together. The presentation services provide a user interface. The business services provide the business logic, and the data services manage the storage of persistent data.

Question 3

> Which of the following terms best describes the Microsoft Office 97 products?
>
> ○ a. Internet enhanced
>
> ○ b. Internet reliant
>
> ○ c. Browser enhanced
>
> ○ d. Browser neutral

Answer a is correct. The Office 97 products do not rely on the Internet but are enhanced to utilize Internet facilities.

Question 4

> Which of the following characteristics apply to the Component Object Model (COM)? [Check all correct answers]
>
> ❑ a. Location transparency
>
> ❑ b. Source language independent
>
> ❑ c. Binary building blocks for developing applications
>
> ❑ d. Allows encapsulation of application functions

Answers a, b, c, and d are all correct.

Question 5

> Which of the following would you most likely use to provide reliable asynchronous communications between two applications?
>
> ○ a. Electronic mail
>
> ○ b. MSMQ
>
> ○ c. IIS
>
> ○ d. MTS

Answer b is correct. Message Queuing allows an application to prepare a message and place it on a queue where it can later be retrieved by another part of the same application or a different application.

Question 6

One of the advantages of modular components is that they can be easily deployed across multiple computer systems. What technology makes this location transparency possible?

○ a. TCP/IP

○ b. NetBUI

○ c. DTC

○ d. DCOM

Answer d is correct. Distributed COM is the technology. DCOM can use either TCP/IP or NetBUI network protocols.

Question 7

It is often necessary to include more than one database in a transaction. What technology makes a two-phase commit possible?

○ a. TCP/IP

○ b. NetBUI

○ c. DTC

○ d. DCOM

Answer c is correct. The Distributed Transaction Coordinator makes two-phase commit possible.

Need To Know More?

 Kirtland, Mary. *Designing Component Based Applications*. Redmond, WA: Microsoft Press, 1999. ISBN 0-73560-523-8. This book presents a thorough discussion of building-distributed applications based on COM. Chapter 2 provides detailed information about the technology, and Chapter 14 discusses several different topologies.

 http://msdn.microsoft.com/library/backgrnd/html/ msdn_bldcli~1.htm

 Vaughn, Bill. "Building Successful Client/Server Applications". Redmond, WA: Microsoft Press, 1997. This paper describes the characteristics of client/server architectures, the factors determining the design, and the "Top Ten Design Mistakes". The paper is available on the Microsoft Developer Network Library.

 http://msdn.microsoft.com/library/backgrnd/html/ msdn_dcomtec.htm

 Microsoft Corporation. "DCOM Technical Overview". Redmond, WA: Microsoft Corporation, 1996. This technical paper provides a good description of the COM architecture and describes the communication facilities that support the architecture, and it also describes many of the design issues such as performance, security, and scalability that DCOM addresses. The article is available on the Microsoft Developer Network Library.

 http://msdn.microsoft.com/library/backgrnd/html/ msdn_windnapps.htm

 Rauch, Stephen. *Windows DNA: Building Windows Applications for the Internet Age*. Redmond, WA: Microsoft Corporation, 1998. This background paper provides an excellent high-level description of Windows DNA and the underlying technologies. The paper is available on the Microsoft Developer Network Library.

 http://msdn.microsoft.com/library/conf/pdc97/ dcom_solutions.htm

 Microsoft Corporation. "DCOM Solutions in Action". Redmond, WA: Microsoft Corporation, 1996. This is a technical paper available on the Microsoft Developer Network Library. This paper describes several business scenarios and the technical architectures that were chosen to provide solutions. These case studies all involve distributed applications and the use of DCOM technology.

http://msdn.microsoft.com/library/conf/tech97htm/
off501ef.htm

 ———. "Database Replication with the Microsoft Jet Database Engine: A Technical Overview". Redmond, WA: Microsoft Corporation, 1997. This technical paper provides a good description of the concepts of database replication, and it also describes how replication is implemented for the Jet database engine. The paper is available on the Microsoft Developer Network Library.

 http://msdn.microsoft.com/library/sdkdoc/dasdk/
desi4jzm.htm

 Hussey, Peter. "Designing Efficient Applications for Microsoft SQL Server". Microsoft SQL Server Developer's Resource Kit. Redmond, WA: Microsoft Corporation, 1997. This paper provides complete descriptions of multitier architectures and database access techniques.

 http://msdn.microsoft.com/library/techart/
msdn_bldvbcom.htm

 Salmre, Ivo. "Building, Versioning, and Maintaining Visual Basic Components". Redmond, WA: Microsoft Corporation, 1998. This article provides the philosophy and the guidelines for building COM objects with Visual Basic, and it also identifies advantages and disadvantages of many design alternatives. The paper is available on the Microsoft Developer Network Library.

Developing
Data Models

. . . .

Terms you'll need to understand:

- √ Relational database
- √ Entities
- √ Attributes
- √ Tables
- √ Columns
- √ Primary key
- √ Foreign key
- √ Normalization
- √ First normal form

- √ Second normal form
- √ Third normal form
- √ Denormalization
- √ Referential integrity
- √ Constraints
- √ One-to-one relationships
- √ One-to many relationships
- √ Many-to-many relationships

Techniques you'll need to master:

- √ Designing a database
- √ Organizing data into entities
- √ Identifying attributes for each entity
- √ Identifying a primary key for an entity
- √ Normalizing data

- √ Identifying relationships between entities
- √ Enforcing referential integrity
- √ Denormalizing data
- √ Developing an entity-relationship diagram

Almost all information systems perform some type of operation on stored data. In the business environment, this is especially true, because the main function of business information systems is to model and track some aspect of business activities. Based on the business climate, the state of the business is always changing. As a result, the data about the business is also continually changing, so it must be easy to enter, update, and delete this data. Just as important as entering the data is being able to retrieve the data. A business typically makes critical decisions based on its data, so it must be possible to quickly retrieve, summarize, and report on the business data.

Often, changes in the business practices will require changes in the underlying data model. The ability to adapt the data model in a timely fashion, so that it accurately reflects the current business environment, is crucial to the operation of the business.

Most legacy information systems use data files to store the data. Some of these files simply store the data as a set of sequential records while other file storage schemes are more sophisticated and use indexes to speed up the search for particular data records. Although the use of file systems is widespread, they tend to be inflexible. When the business model changes, it's often difficult to implement all of the corresponding changes to the software in a timely manner.

Most new applications utilize relational database management systems (RDBMSs) to store and manage the data. These systems are based on the relational data model. Microsoft SQL Server is an example of a RDBMS.

This chapter describes the relational data model and identifies the considerations you use to design a relational database. It also identifies some of the advantages the relational model has over conventional file systems. To better understand the relational model, you'll examine the Southwestern Specialties database.

CASE STUDY: Southwestern Specialties

Southwestern Specialties is a fictitious company that imports and exports specialty foods from around the world. It handles a large number of products in different categories, and it does business with multiple suppliers. To track and manage the business, Southwestern Specialties designed and built a database based on the relational data model, and several applications have also been developed that utilize this database.

The Southwestern Specialties database contains all the sales and order data for the company. Before the database was designed, management identified some of the tasks they wanted to be able to do once the database and supporting applications were in place. These included:

➤ Add and edit complete product information

➤ Add and edit product supplier information

➤ Add and edit customer information

➤ Add and edit employee information

➤ Enter, view, and edit an order to Southwestern Specialties

➤ View product information about items in an order

➤ Produce an invoice for a Southwestern Specialties order

➤ Produce an alphabetical list of products

➤ Print a catalog of products using photos for each product category

➤ Print customer names and addresses on mailing labels

➤ Print a monthly report showing the top 50 customers based on total order value

➤ Print sales grouped by country and employee

➤ Print annual sales by product category

➤ Print quarterly sales

➤ Print summary reports showing sales from multiple years for each quarter

➤ Print sales in descending order by amount

In this chapter, you'll look at the design of the database that was devised for Southwestern Specialties.

NWIND.MDB

To get some hands-on experience with a sample relational database, open the file NWIND.MDB using Microsoft Access. This file is distributed with Microsoft Access and several other products. The file contains a database for the Northwind Traders, another fictitious company. The Northwind Traders database is very similar to the database in the case study.

NWIND includes a Help facility called Show Me that displays the main features in the Northwind application. You can access this facility using the Show Me item on the menu bar.

Another file distributed with Microsoft Access, ORDERS.MDB, uses the same database and provides additional facilities for Northwind Traders.

What Is A Relational Database?

Edgar F. Codd developed the relational database model in the late sixties. It's actually based on set theory and predicate logic, which are branches of theoretical mathematics. The basic concept behind the relational model is that data is organized into a series of tables, and mathematical operations can be performed on these tables to produce new tables. Codd referred to these tables as *relations*, meaning a related set of information. As a result, the term *relational database* was used to describe this data model.

Originally, Codd identified 12 rules to which a database system must adhere in order to support the relational model. Since then, other theorists have expanded on Codd's work, and now there are hundreds of rules. This book won't go in to any of these rules, because many books are available on database design theory that discuss these topics in detail.

As a means for storing and manipulating data, the relational model provides many advantages over the file systems that have been used in the past.

 Structured Query Language (SQL) is a relational database query and programming language originally developed by IBM. It's used for accessing and updating data in relational database systems and for querying, updating, and managing relational database systems.

The popularity of relational databases and the relational model is mainly attributed to a number of advantages a relational database has over file systems for storing data. These advantages include:

➤ Separation of application and data

➤ Support for the client/server model

➤ Stored procedures in the database

➤ Data integrity

➤ Transaction support

Separation Of Application And Data

In a relational database, the data about the data, the *metadata*, is stored in the database rather than in the application. A clear separation exists between application and data, and as a result, applications can obtain data about the tables and columns that make up the database. To retrieve a data item, the application still needs to provide the name of the data item; however, detailed format information isn't required. Because the metadata is stored in the database, it's easy to make changes to the database.

When using the relational model, the application requires less detailed information about the data storage. However, when using data files for data storage, even though the data files are also separate from the applications that process them, the application must have detailed information about the physical organization of the files. For example, the application must know the record structure of the file and the format details of each field. Changing either of these in the data file almost always requires a change to the application (or applications). Because each change may require numerous other changes, the process can be error prone and time consuming.

Support For The Client/Server Model

Most relational database systems provide an interface that supports the client/server model, therefore, it's fairly straightforward to implement a desktop application that accesses data stored in a relational database on a server. Many desktop tools are also available that make it easy to query the data in a relational database.

Stored Procedures In The Database

Most relational database systems provide a facility for *stored procedures*, which are coded procedures stored within the RDBMS. The first advantage to stored procedures is that the procedure executes on the system with the database, therefore, processing that formerly was done by the application is now off-loaded to the database server. By performing the data manipulation operations on the server, it's often possible to significantly reduce the network traffic between a client application and the database server. Data that would otherwise have to be delivered over the network for processing by the application is now processed directly on the server. Only the results are transmitted over the network. A second big advantage to stored procedures is that the data and calculations used by a particular procedure can be completely isolated from the application.

Data Integrity

Relational database systems also provide facilities to help maintain the validity of the database. RDBMSs provide mechanisms so you can define rules that the data must adhere to before it's accepted and entered into the database.

Transaction Support

Relational database systems support the concept of *transactions*. In a transaction, a series of operations either succeeds or fails as a unit of work. This is particularly useful in business scenarios where multiple tasks correspond to a single business transaction. If any single task fails, then the entire transaction should fail. When using file systems, any transaction support is typically provided by the application. Without transaction support, the data can easily become inconsistent. That is, some of the data looks as if a particular transaction occurs, and some of it doesn't. Chapter 4 provides additional information on transactions.

MDB files, which are processed by Microsoft Access, are often referred to as databases. Don't confuse the objects found in an MDB file with the relational database model described here. MDB files do contain database objects—tables, for example—which correspond to the tables found in the relational model. However, MDB files also contain other *application* objects, such as forms and reports, that are unique to Access and have no counterpart in the relational data model.

Designing A Relational Database

Relational databases model something in the real world. In particular, they store facts about different things. The key to designing a relational database is determining what the things are, determining what facts are needed for each thing, and, finally, ensuring that these facts can be used to provide the information that's desired.

For example, you know that Southwestern Specialties has a base of customers. So, it makes sense to think of customers as one of the things to be represented in the database. The next question to deal with is: what facts do you need to have about the customers? Two obvious choices here might be a name and address for each customer. Finally, you want to ensure that you have all the facts needed to provide the information expected from the database.

The management at Southwestern Specialties has asked for a monthly report showing the 50 customers placing the largest orders during the last month. Somehow, you need to get this data from the database. One possibility would be to keep an additional fact about each customer, namely the amount of all orders placed during the last month. But what if you need to get information about other orders the customer has placed, and not just those placed in the last month? Although these facts are about the customer, they're also facts about another thing: orders. Suddenly, organizing all these facts becomes a little more complicated.

Fortunately, a systematic process can be used for designing relational databases. Although you still need to make a number of decisions and trade-offs, using the following methodology will help minimize the problems you'll encounter:

1. Determine the purpose of the database.

2. Organize the data into entities.

3. Identify attributes for each entity.

4. Define relationships between entities.

5. Refine the design.

Determine The Purpose Of The Database

When you determine the purpose of the database, you'll find out what kind of information is expected from it. This is essential to the overall success of the database. During this step you'll want to identify the reports that are anticipated. You'll also want to understand the interactive forms and the data items that need to be entered.

Another important piece of information is determining the volume of data that the database will store. Will all the data be loaded initially, or will the database grow over time?

Finally, it's important to find out how the database will be used. Will access be limited to a small number of applications generating reports, or will the database be supporting hundreds of online users doing data entry? This type of information is critical to creating a design with optimal database performance.

Organize The Data Into Entities

Once you understand the purpose of the database, it's time to start determining how the data will be organized. Identifying the subjects or categories of information that will be stored in the database accomplishes this. This is discussed in more detail in the section "Tables and Columns," later in this chapter.

Identify Attributes For Each Entity

After you've identified the categories of information, you can start defining the facts that go with each category. The details for doing this are discussed in more detail in the section "Tables and Columns," later in this chapter.

Define Relationships Between Entities

As you go through the process of determining the categories of information for the database, you'll find that many categories seem to overlap. In the Southwestern Specialties example, information about orders is related to information about customers. Establishing relationships between the different categories of information is one of the key concepts behind the relational data model. The section later in this chapter "Relationships Between Tables" provides details on how to do this.

Refine The Design

Database design is an iterative process. Once you've come up with an initial design, try it out with some sample data, then plan on reviewing and revising the design a few more times. After completing the revision process, you'll be mapping the *logical design* into a *physical design*. The section "Refining The Database Design" provides more details on this topic.

The database design process is often broken into two distinct parts: the logical design and the physical design. Logical design refers to planning and designing. The result of this process is a logical view of the data entities and associated relationships between them. Logical database design includes determining the purpose of the database, organizing the data into entities, identifying attributes, and defining relationships between entities. The physical database design is based on this logical design. The physical database design determines how the database will be physically mapped to the data storage devices so that optimal performance is achieved. During the physical design process, indexes are defined that will improve the performance for the various transactions that the database will execute.

Tables And Columns (Entities And Attributes)

After you have a good understanding of what the database is to provide, you can start organizing the data. As mentioned earlier, a database simply models things in the real world. Therefore, it seems logical to start out by identifying what these things are.

Real-world things are more formally referred to as *entities* or *tables* in the database. Tables are made up of *rows* and *columns*. Columns are used to store the different *attributes* about the table. Rows are used to store all the attributes for each entry in the table.

Many terms are used to describe the relational model, and this often leads to confusion. Most mathematicians and database theorists use the terms *relations*, *attributes*, and *tuples*. Rather than using these formal terms, this book will use the more common terms *tables*, *columns*, and *rows* to describe the same relational concepts. The term *entity* is another term that's often used and refers to a database table.

Sometimes the terms *files*, *fields*, and *records* are used. Although these terms do correspond to the physical implementation of the relational model, they more accurately describe the file systems that preceded relational technology. Thus, they're less preferable for describing a relational database.

Tables

Determining the tables for the database can be the most difficult part, because you usually start out with many different alternatives. Systematically, you'll need to evaluate these alternatives, determine the trade-offs, and make some preliminary decisions. Later, you'll probably revisit some of these decisions to refine the database design.

In general, all tables have the following characteristics:

➤ They describe one entity.

➤ They have no duplicate rows.

➤ There is a primary key.

➤ The columns are unordered.

➤ The rows are unordered.

After studying the requirements for the Southwestern Specialties, three categories seem like good candidates for tables. These are:

➤ Customers

➤ Employees

➤ Orders

These tables are depicted in Figure 6.1.

Once a table has been identified, the next step is defining the columns for the table.

Columns

Columns store the characteristics or attributes about the table. That is, they store the facts about the items. Each table will have a fixed number of columns.

To determine the columns for a table, you'll need to identify all the facts you need to track for it. The Customers table in the Southwestern Specialties database keeps track of all the companies that are Southwestern Specialties' customers. In the Customers table, it seems likely that you'll need information on the company name, contact name, address, city, and phone number.

In general, table columns have the following characteristics:

➤ They describe the subject of the table.

➤ They don't contain derived or calculated data.

➤ They contain data broken into the smallest logical parts.

Rows

Three different tables have been initially identified for the Southwestern Specialties database. The Customers table will contain the data for all Southwestern Specialties' customers. Each customer is a separate entry in the table or a row

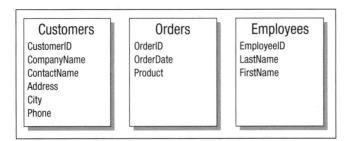

Figure 6.1   A preliminary design for tables in the Southwestern Specialties database.

in the table. The number of rows a table contains varies and is determined by the number of data items for the particular table.

Figure 6.2 shows a sample Customers table for the Southwestern Specialties database. The table contains four rows and five columns. Each row represents a single customer of Southwestern Specialties. The five columns contain the attributes for each customer.

Primary Key

The relational model requires that each row in a table be unique. If you allow duplicate rows in a database table, there's no way to identify one from the other. This creates a number of problems when trying to access the data in the table. To avoid the problem of having duplicate rows, you identify a value that will be unique for each row. Many times, a single column will contain this value. However, there will be situations when this isn't the case. When this happens, you can use a combination of columns to provide the unique value. This unique value is the *primary key*.

The rules for the primary key are quite simple: each table can have only one primary key, and the value of the primary key must be unique for each row in the table. When selecting a primary key, you often have several choices. These are referred to as candidate keys. Only one of these will become the primary key.

Let's examine the Customers table in the Southwestern Specialties database for a suitable primary key. One choice might be the Company Name. However, this would introduce a limitation of doing business with two different companies, each having the same name. Although this situation is unlikely, it's probably a restriction that you want to avoid. By combining the Company Name column with the Contact Name column to form a primary key, you reduce the chances of encountering duplicates, but it's still not guaranteed. The phone number for each customer is a unique value, so it's definitely a candidate key. A final possibility is to create a new column solely for the purpose of being a primary key. Many times, when this is done, a unique sequential number is used for each row.

Company Name	Contact	Address	City	Phone
Southwest Distributors	Charles Snyder	11228 W. Central	Phoenix	(602) 555-0751
The Big Tortilla	Richard Sanchez	1716 N. Speedway	Tucson	(502) 555-6683
International Specialties	Wendy Hardy	143 S. Main	Nogales	(502) 555-9963
Molina Foods	Edward Molina	45 Market St.	San Francisco	(415) 555-3872

Figure 6.2   An initial version of the Customers table for the Southwestern Specialties database.

When using a numeric value for a primary key, use a whole number rather than a real (floating-point) number. Real numbers tend to be inexact.

As a database designer, you'll examine all these possibilities, evaluate the trade-offs, and choose a primary key. Several guidelines to follow for choosing a key are:

➤ Use the minimal number of columns possible

➤ Use a value that's unlikely to change

➤ Use a numeric or short text value

The relational model requires that each row in a table be unique. To determine this uniqueness, you identify a column or group of columns where the unique value is found. This unique value is the *primary key*.

The primary key chosen for the Customers table is the field CustomerID. This is a five-character text field derived from the Company Name. This column was created specifically for the purpose of being a primary key. Figure 6.3 shows the Customers table with the primary key field.

Data Normalization

One of the design goals for a relational database is to eliminate redundant data in the database. Obviously, redundant data will increase the size of the database, because additional storage is required to store the duplicate data items. But more importantly, redundant data makes the management and maintenance of the database more difficult, and it can lead to inconsistencies in the database.

Suppose, for example, customer data was not tracked in the Customers table but was tracked with each order in the Orders table. If this were the case, the

CustomerID	Company Name	Contact	Address	City	Phone
SWDIS	Southwest Distributors	Charles Snyder	11228 W. Central	Phoenix	(602) 555-0751
BGTOR	The Big Tortilla	Richard Sanchez	1716 N. Speedway	Tucson	(502) 555-6683
INTSP	International Specialties	Wendy Hardy	143 S. Main	Nogales	(502) 555-9963
MOLFD	Molina Foods	Edward Molina	45 Market St.	San Francisco	(415) 555-3872

Figure 6.3 A version of the Customers table with a primary key field.

database could contain duplicate data. For example, when a customer placed multiple orders, a lot of duplicate data would be stored for the same customer. If the customer should move or change phone numbers, all the order entries would need to be updated. Furthermore, if a customer had only placed a single order, it would be very undesirable to delete the customer data just because the order was cancelled and deleted.

Normalization is the process of eliminating data duplication within the database. Five different levels of normalization, or *normal forms*, are defined. Each level presents an increasingly restrictive set of rules or constraints on the design of the database tables.

If the first set of rules is satisfied, the database is said to be in *first normal form*. Likewise, if the second set of rules is satisfied, the database is said to be in *second normal form*. As with most formal rules, real-world requirements won't always allow full compliance. However, as a general rule, most database designers try to achieve a *third normal form* for the database design. In third normal form, all redundant data will be eliminated from the design.

If you have normalized your database into third normal form, by definition, it is also in first normal form and second normal form.

First Normal Form (No Repeating Groups)

First normal form requires that an individual table will have no repeating groups. Furthermore, each column can contain only a single value; lists of values aren't allowed for a column value.

For example, in the Southwestern Specialties database, you've defined an Orders table to track customer orders, and you've included a Product column to identify the product in the order. However, an individual order can contain requests for several different products. The single field you've provided won't work for multiple product orders.

The first approach might be to incorporate additional product columns into the Orders table. These columns could be used for additional products in the order. For example, the table could contain the following fields: OrderID, Product1, Product2, and Product3. This is shown in Figure 6.4.

The first drawback to this design is that an order is limited to a maximum of three products. Even though you can certainly add additional product fields to the design, there will always be a maximum number of order items allowed.

OrderID	Product1	Product2	Product3
1	Sonoran Hot Sauce	14" Flour Tortillas	Southwest Salsa
2	14" Flour Tortillas		
3	Spicy Refried Beans	Southwest Salsa	

Figure 6.4   A first attempt at creating the Orders table.

However, the situation becomes more complicated very quickly. In addition to tracking the products in the order, you'll need to track the quantity of each product ordered, and you'll also need to track the unit price of each product. Figure 6.5 shows this.

This example contains *repeating groups,* and, as such, it violates the rule for first normal form. The use of repeating groups is popular in some application models and record structures, but it causes many problems in the relational model.

To eliminate repeating groups, the information in the initial Orders table is broken into two tables: an Orders table and an Order Details table. The Order Details table is used to keep track of each item in the order. An order for one item will have only one entry in the Order Details table. An order for three items will have three entries in the Order Details table. The use of an additional table not only solves the problem of having repeating groups, it also eliminates the restriction of limiting an order to a specific number of items.

Each entry in the Order Details table has a column called OrderID. This column refers to a specific order entry in the Orders table. This is shown Figure 6.6.

For a table to be in first normal form, the table can contain no repeating groups.

Second Normal Form (No Partial Dependencies)

Second normal form requires that tables contain data only related to the table. Nonkey columns depend on the primary key for their value. Specifically, columns depend on the primary key, the whole primary key, and nothing but the primary key.

Order ID	Product1	Unit Price1	Quantity1	Product2	Unit Price2	Quantity2	Product3	Unit Price3	Quantity3
1	Sonoran Hot Sauce	$18.20	5	14" Flour Tortillas	$ 9.60	6	Southwest Salsa	$12.00	0
2	14" Flour Tortillas	$ 9.60	10		$ 0.00	0		$ 0.00	0
3	Spicy Refried Beans	$15.30	5	Southwest Salsa	$12.00	10		$ 0.00	0

Figure 6.5   The Orders table with repeating groups.

Figure 6.6   Two tables, the Orders table and the Order Details table, eliminate the use of repeating groups.

For example, in the Southwestern Specialties database, you've created a table called Order Items to track the individual items for each order. The first question you want to address is what is the primary key for the Order Details table. Using the OrderID field alone isn't enough. There can be multiple order detail entries with the same OrderID. However, the values from both the OrderID and the Product columns together do result in a unique value for each Order Detail entry. Therefore, these two columns are used as the primary key for the table. This is a *composite* or *compound* primary key, because it's based on two columns.

After creating the Order Details table, you find that you need to determine the customer for each entry in the table. To do this, you add another field, the Customer ID, to the Order Details table. You've done this because you want to be able to determine the customer for each entry in the table. The CustomerID field allows you to find the customer in the Customers table. The resulting table is shown in Figure 6.7.

The new Order Details table contains no repeating groups, therefore, it's in first normal form. For the table to be in second normal form, every nonkey field must be completely dependent on the full primary key. This is, indeed, true for the two columns, UnitPrice and Quantity. That is, given both an OrderID and a Product, you'll know the UnitPrice and Quantity values.

Figure 6.7   The Order Details table with a new field, CustomerID.

However, it's not true for the CustomerID field that you just added. The CustomerID field is dependent only on the OrderID. This is referred to as a *partial dependency*. That is, all order details belonging to the same order are for the same customer.

Because the CustomerID field is dependent on only part of the primary key, and not the entire primary key, the proposed Order Details table is not in second normal form.

 For a table to be in second normal form, it must be in first normal form and each nonkey column in the table must be fully dependent on the entire primary key.

The solution to this situation is to move the CustomerID field from the Order Details table to the Orders table. Doing this results in both tables being in second normal form. No information has been lost, because it's still possible to determine the customer for each order detail entry. However, to get this data, you'll also need to access the Orders table. The resulting tables are shown in Figure 6.8.

If the primary key of a table contains only one column and if the table is in first normal form, then the table is automatically in second normal form as well. Only when the primary key consists of more than one column is it possible to have partial dependencies in the table. When this is the case, a table in first normal form is not necessarily in second normal form as well. Sometimes, as shown in Figure 6.8, additional steps are required to achieve a second normal form.

Third Normal Form (No Transitive Dependencies)

Third normal form requires that all nonkey columns are mutually independent.

The Order Details table you've created contains information about each line item in the order. The columns include a unit price and a quantity. As stated

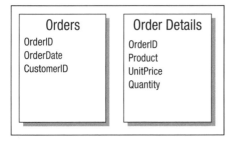

Figure 6.8 Two tables, the Orders table and the Order Details table, in second normal form.

previously, these columns are completely dependent on the full primary key, therefore, the table is in second normal form.

A number of reports will also require knowing the total cost of each line item in the order. Let's consider the ramifications of including another column, TotalCost, in the Order Details table. The value for the TotalCost column is calculated by multiplying the UnitPrice by the Quantity. With the new column, the table is still in first normal form, and it's also in second normal form. However, the new column violates the rules for third normal form.

The new column, TotalCost, is dependent on two other nonkey columns in the table. Therefore, all nonkey columns are not mutually independent, and the table is not in third normal form. The column TotalCost is a calculated column, and including a calculated column in a table always introduces some undesirable consequences. For example, every time the Quantity or UnitPrice values change, the TotalCost column must also be updated. In general, it's better to avoid putting calculated values directly in the table. An alternative is to perform the calculation as part of the query statement when the data is retrieved, and return the computed value as part of the result set.

 For a table to be in third normal form, it must be in second normal form and all nonkey columns in the table must be mutually independent.

Calculated columns are not the only way to introduce columns that aren't mutually independent. Looking again at the Order Details table, you've used the column Product to identify the particular product being ordered; this column contains the product name. However, you now find that most reports also require a short product description. Including another field, ProductDescription, in the Order Details table will introduce a nonkey column that isn't mutually independent. This option is depicted in the Figure 6.9.

In addition to violating third normal form, this choice has other disadvantages. For example, if the product description should change, this change

Figure 6.9   The Order Details table with a dependent nonkey field.

would have to be propagated to all the OrderDetail entries where that product was ordered.

A better option seems to be creating a new table, Products, with one entry for every product that is handled by Southwestern Specialties. Then if the product description changes, only one entry needs to be updated. All references to that particular product will then use the new ProductDescription value. This table is shown in Figure 6.10.

Denormalization

Now that you've gone to great lengths to normalize the database, its time to consider *denormalization,* that is, intentionally modifying the design and violating the normalization rules. The motivation for doing this is to *improve database performance.*

In theory, a fully normalized database represents the ultimate database design. However, in practice, fully normalizing the database almost always introduces performance degradation. Consider, for example, an order entry database that has two tables: Orders and Customers. In its normalized form, all customer data is found in the Customers table and all order data is found in the Orders table. A CustomerID field in the Orders table will identify the customer associated with a particular order. So it's possible to get the customer name by finding the row in the Customers table with the matching CustomerID from the Orders table.

This operation represents a database *join,* which is discussed in more detail in the next section. However, most of the time when you reference an order, you'll also want the customer name. In a fully normalized database, this will require accessing data from two different tables. Simply joining two different tables to get the desired information may not make a significant impact on performance. However, as data requests become more complex and as you need to join four or more tables together, performance is likely to suffer.

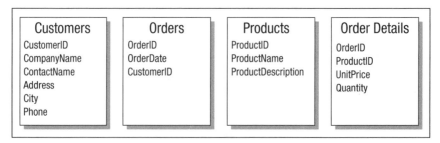

Figure 6.10   Using a Products table with the Order Details table maintains third normal form.

When this starts to happen, look for ways to eliminate some of the tables from the join. If you find that tables are providing a single column of data, you may want to consider duplicating this information in one of the other tables. However, if you do this, remember to document what was done and why it was done. Also remember that this could impact application code, because the same data will be stored in two different places.

Relationships Between Tables

When you initially examined the requirements for the Southwestern Specialties database, you identified three categories that seemed like good candidates for the database tables. These were Customers, Employees, and Orders. You also started defining columns for each table.

However, as you reviewed the requirements further and began applying rules for normalization, you began modifying the original design. As a result, you now have five tables:

➤ Customers

➤ Employees

➤ Orders

➤ Order Details

➤ Products

This new design was achieved by creating new tables and moving columns from tables in the earlier design into these new tables. New columns were also introduced so that values in one table could be linked to values in another table. In other words, you defined a series of *relationships* between the tables. The database design is depicted in Figure 6.11. Lines have been added between the columns that form the relationships between the tables.

From the figure, you see that all tables are related except for Employees. It's possible, in a relational design, to have tables that aren't related to other tables. However, in our design, this situation has occurred because the design is still incomplete.

Examining the requirements further, you find that you also need to know the employee that processed a specific order. To add this capability to our database, you add another column to the Orders table. This column identifies the EmployeeID for the employee associated with the order. Figure 6.12 shows the new design.

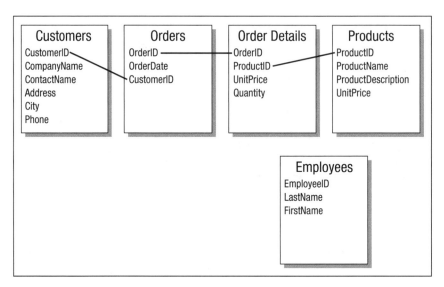

Figure 6.11 The current design of the Southwestern Specialties database.

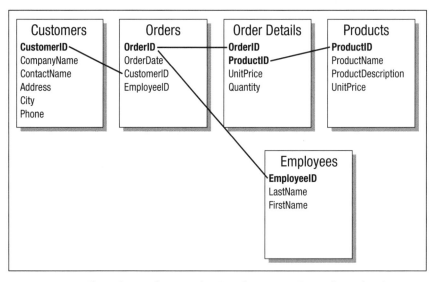

Figure 6.12 The relationships in the Southwestern Specialties database.

One of the key concepts of the relational model is this ability to define relationships between the tables. This enables the RDBMS to retrieve rows of data from one table and *join* them with the related data from another table.

For example, it you wanted to see a complete order, you would instruct the database system to obtain data from both the Orders table and the Order Details table. By supplying the database system with the OrderID for the desired order, the appropriate rows could be obtained from each table. Figure 6.13 shows the results obtained by joining the Order and Order Details tables. The OrderDate value comes from the Order table and the ProductName comes from the Order Details table.

For the database management system to join two tables together, you must define the columns that are used to relate the tables. One way of accomplishing this is by using a *primary key* and a *foreign key*.

The primary key has already been discussed; it identifies a unique row in a table. To relate data from another table to this unique row of data, the other table must also contain a key that matches this primary key. This matching key is called the foreign key.

 A foreign key is a column (or group of columns) in one table that references the primary key in another table.

Foreign Keys

A *foreign key* is a column, or group of columns, in one table that references the primary key in another table. For the primary key–foreign key relationship to be valid, both keys must contain the same number of columns, and the corresponding columns must be the same data type. Although the table with the primary key will always have only one row of data for any primary key value, the table with the foreign key can, and usually does, have multiple rows with the same foreign key value.

All the relationships developed during the data normalization processes described in the last section were based on the use of a foreign key. Look again at Figure 6.12. The Orders table actually contains two foreign keys. The CustomerID column is a foreign key that establishes a relationship with the Customers table. The CustomerID column in the Orders table is linked to the CustomerID column in the Customers table. CustomerID is also the primary

Order	Order	ProductName
10250	3/22/1999	Extra Crispy Taco Shells
10250	3/22/1999	14" Flour Tortillas
10250	3/22/1999	Spicy Refried Beans

Figure 6.13 The Orders table joined with the Order Details table to show related data from both tables.

key in the Customers table. In a similar fashion, the EmployeeID column is a foreign key that's used to link the Orders table to the Employees table.

Another variation on the use of foreign keys is found in the Order Details table. Here the OrderID is used as a foreign key to the Orders tables, and the ProductID is used as a foreign key to the Products table. In this example, the columns OrderID and ProductID make up a compound primary key for the Order Details table.

The concept of using primary and foreign keys is the most common technique for establishing relationships between two tables. In general, you can define three types of relationships between two tables:

➤ One-to-many relationships

➤ One-to-one relationships

➤ Many-to-many relationships

These different types of relationships are described in the section.

One-To-Many Relationships

Two tables have a one-to-many relationship if for every row in the first table, there can be zero, one, or many rows in the second table. However, for every row in the second table, there's only one row in the first table. One-to-many relationships are the most common type of relationship found in the relational data model. Sometimes the tables in a one-to-many relationship are referred to as a parent-child or master-detail relationship.

 A "one-to-zero or one-to-many" relationship is the same thing as a one-to-many relationship, except that there may be cases where the parent table has no corresponding rows in the child table.

In the Southwestern Specialties database, the following tables have one-to-many relationships:

➤ Orders-to-Orders Details

➤ Customers-to-Orders Details

➤ Products-to-Orders Details

➤ Employees-to-Orders Details

One-To-One Relationships

Two tables have a one-to-one relationship if, for every row in the first table, there is at most one row in the second table. And, for every row in the second table, there is at most one row in the first table. The two tables in a one-to-one relationship will most likely have the same primary key, which is used to define the relationship. This particular relationship isn't very common, because, in most cases, the data from the second table can simply be included in the first table.

From the perspective of a theoretical relational model, you would never have a one-to-one relationship. However, occasionally, there will be times when you can justify maintaining two separate tables. Perhaps this is done for security reasons to isolate some sensitive data, or it might be done to track some temporary data that you don't want to add to the main table. In these situations, the one-to-one relationship is used.

Many-To-Many Relationships

Two tables have a many-to-many relationship when, for every row in the first table, there can be many corresponding rows in the second table, and for every row in the second table, there can be many corresponding rows in the first table. A many-to-many relationship is modeled by breaking it into multiple one-to-many relationships.

In the Southwestern Specialties database, the relationship between the Employees table and the Customers table is a many-to-many relationship. Each time a customer places an order, any employee can take the order, so it's possible for a single customer to work with many employees. Likewise, any employee can process orders for many different customers. Therefore, the relationship between these two tables is many-to-many.

To relate two tables in a many-to-many relationship, you must have an intermediate table for linking the two tables together. Many times, you can use existing tables in the database to serve as linking tables. However, if none exists, you must then create a linking table explicitly for the purpose of supporting the many-to-many relationship.

In the Southwestern Specialties database, the Orders table links the Customers table and the Employees table in a many-to-many relationship. This is shown in Figure 6.14.

There is a one-to-many relationship between the Employees table and the Orders table. That is, each employee can be associated with many orders, but each order is processed by a single employee. There is also a one-to-many

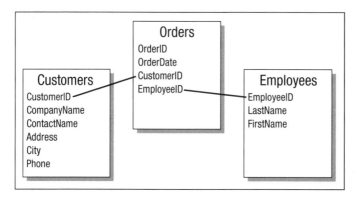

Figure 6.14 A many-to-many relationship between the Customers table and the Employees table. The Orders table serves as a linking table between the two.

relationship between the Customers table and the Orders table. That is, each customer can be associated with many orders, but each order is for a single customer.

Final Database Design

The final database for Southwestern Specialties consists of seven different tables:

➤ Customers

➤ Orders

➤ Order Details

➤ Shippers

➤ Employees

➤ Products

➤ Suppliers

In this chapter, you haven't gone through the process of developing all the tables and columns. However, you can see that the final database design is based on the five tables developed in this chapter.

It's often useful to graphically represent the tables and the relationships between the tables that you've designed for your relational model. This provides a good form of documenting the design. *Entity-Relationship diagrams* (E-R diagrams) are used to graphically depict the tables in a database and the relationships between them.

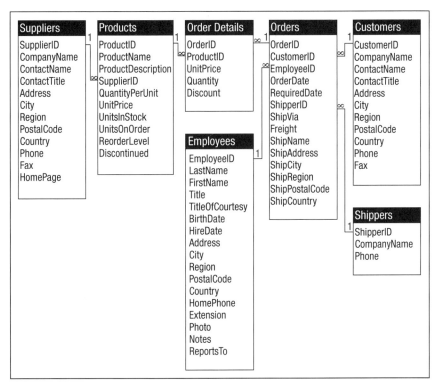

Figure 6.15   An Entity-Relationship diagram for Southwestern Specialties database.

An E-R diagram for the Southwestern Specialties database is shown in Figure 6.15. All the *one-to-many relationships* between tables in the database are shown.

Data Integrity And Constraints

After organizing the data into tables and defining relationships between the tables, you've created a database that accurately models your business environment. However, you must now ensure that the data which gets entered into the database also provides an accurate representation of the state of the business. In other words, you need to ensure that the *business rules* are enforced and that the *integrity* of the database is maintained.

For example, the Southwestern Specialties database tracks orders in the Orders table and customers in the Customers table. It's unlikely that the business will take orders without knowing what customer is placing the order. The business rule, "Orders will only be accepted for current Southwestern Specialties customers," must also be followed when orders are entered into the database.

A stack of paper orders having invalid or incomplete customer information will certainly impede the order fulfillment process. Similarly, having orders in the Orders table with no matching customer in the Customers table will create the same kinds of problems.

Although each order can be manually verified by looking the customer up in the database before the order is entered, relational database management systems provide a number of facilities to help automate this process.

Business Rules

Information systems usually implement a set of business rules that define how the business operates. Business rules might be a set of steps needed to execute a specific business task, or they could simply be validity checks used to ensure that only valid data gets entered into the system.

Business rules can be implemented as part of the application, or they might be implemented directly in the database. Putting the rules in the database means that the rules are enforced for all database users, not just those users accessing the database using a particular application that has the rules coded into it.

Most RDBMSs provide facilities for:

➤ Supplying default values

➤ Validating data before writing it to the database

➤ Enforcing the relationships between tables

➤ Ensuring unique values

➤ Storing procedures directly in the database

These facilities can all be used to implement business rules directly in the database.

 Business rules can be implemented as part of the application, or they might be implemented directly in the database.

Referential Integrity

Referential integrity is a set of rules to ensure that the relationships between two related tables are valid. In particular, referential integrity ensures that the relationship between the tables is preserved when you enter new rows or delete existing rows from the tables. Referential integrity is usually used to enforce the primary-foreign key relationships discussed earlier.

In the Southwestern Specialties database, you could use referential integrity to ensure that an order detail entry doesn't refer to an order that doesn't exist. Perhaps more importantly, you can use referential integrity to prevent deleting an order from the Orders table while leaving the associated details in the Order Details table. When such situations do occur, the remaining records are referred to as orphan records. Orphan records indicate that the integrity of the database is no longer valid.

Referential integrity is a type of *constraint* that can be defined for your database. Other types of constraints are discussed in the next section.

Constraints

Constraints are rules that the relational database management system automatically enforces for you. Constraints limit the possible values that you can enter into a column or columns. Constraints can be used to:

➤ Supply default values

➤ Validate data values

➤ Enforce the relationships between tables

➤ Ensure unique values

Stored Procedures

Stored procedures are a precompiled collection of SQL statements and optional flow control statements stored within a database. Stored procedures can be used to define business rules, and they allow you to specify more complex processing than can usually be accomplished by just using constraints.

Stored procedures can contain program flow logic as well as queries against the database. They can accept parameters and return result sets as well as return a value.

When stored procedures are compiled, the data access plan is saved. This gives stored procedures a performance advantage over regular database queries because the database system does not need to determine the data access strategy every time the query is executed.

Stored procedures are stored in the database and execute on the database server. They're usually faster than SQL statements because they're already compiled.

Refining The Database Design

The first version of your database design is really a "rough draft" of what will become the final design. The database design process is iterative in nature. Once you've established your initial design, you can test the database with some sample data, then change the design as needed. See if you can create the necessary reports from your database.

This is the time when you might consider denormalizing the database. Denormalization, the process of deliberately violating the normalization rules in order to improve performance, was discussed earlier in this chapter.

One advantage of the relational model is the flexibility it provides. Changing the table structures, adding new fields, and modifying relationships is fairly straightforward. This is the point in time when you can try different alternatives and easily evaluate the design. However, once all the tables are loaded with data, the forms and reports are designed, and the application is created, changing the database can have an impact on other system components that can make the process more difficult.

If you're designing a database that will be used concurrently by a large number of users, you'll want to spend time ensuring that your database design will provide a level of performance that's acceptable.

Although the logical design will impact the overall database performance, the physical design of the database provides the most influence on database performance. Two critical factors make up the physical design:

➤ The physical organization of the data on the storage devices

➤ The use of indexes to expedite accessing the data

 Relational database management systems are complex pieces of software. In addition to the design factors listed here, the database system itself usually provides a number of configuration options that can be used to help tune the database performance. However, configuration tuning alone usually can't compensate for the deficiencies introduced by a poor database design.

This book doesn't go into the details of physical database design; however, the general rule of thumb is to minimize the number of read/write operations that the database management system must perform as well as to distribute the processing of those operations as much as possible.

By using an appropriate index, the database system may be able to locate a record after performing only several read operations on the index to a table. In order to find a record without the use of an index, the database system must sequentially read every record in the table in order to find desired records.

Although indexes can greatly reduce the processing and amount of time required to locate and read a record, they also carry a performance penalty for updating and adding new records. These operations require additional processing for managing the indexes. As a database designer, you will have to determine if the benefits of having a particular index outweigh the overhead required to maintain it. A general guideline is to create an index for fields when the index will improve the performance of frequently used queries.

Using multiple physical devices to store the data can also result in improved performance by allowing some read/write operations to overlap and execute simultaneously. To accomplish this, data from different tables is distributed over different physical drives. Sometimes it's also possible to split data from a single table onto separate drives. A large production database used for transaction processing might use over one hundred separate physical drives for data storage.

Transaction analysis is often used to optimize the physical database design. When using this technique, every transaction that the database will perform is identified and analyzed. In particular, the tables and fields affected by each transaction are identified, and the path to that data is determined. Minimizing the operations required to retrieve the data will most likely improve database performance.

Detailed transaction analysis is possible for online transaction processing (OLTP) systems where all possible transactions are known in advance. However, transaction analysis isn't possible for systems that support ad hoc queries.

Practice Questions

Question 1

In a relational database, each row has a column or group of columns that makes the row unique. What is this called?

- ○ a. Index key
- ○ b. Foreign key
- ○ c. Primary key
- ○ d. Secondary key

Answer c is correct. The value of the primary key is unique for each row.

Question 2

The following two design processes are used for developing a relational database:

Logical

Physical

Identify the appropriate design process in which each of the following steps would be done:

A primary key is identified.

An index based on multiple columns is defined.

The data is grouped into tables.

Storage space on drive F is allocated for customers with last names starting with A through M.

A relationship using a foreign key is established.

The correct answer is

Logical

A primary key is identified.

The data is grouped into tables.

A relationship using a foreign key is established.

Physical

An index based on multiple columns is defined.

Storage space on drive F is allocated for customers with last names starting with A through M.

Question 3

> After evaluating your initial database design, you discover that by adding an additional column to one of your tables you can reduce the number of joins required to produce many of the reports. However, the new design creates duplicate data in the database. If you make this modification, which of the following statements is true?
>
>
>
> ○ a. You have normalized the data.
>
> ○ b. You have denormalized the data.
>
> ○ c. You have added a foreign key to the table.
>
> ○ d. You have violated relational rules, so the database results are no longer predictable.

Answer b is correct. You have deliberately violated some of the normalization in the database to improve operational performance. Changes like this need to be carefully evaluated and documented so others are aware of them, but this is a practice that is often done to improve database performance. Answer d is not correct. Even though relational rules have been violated, the relational model will still work; however, applications will need to be aware of this violation so it can be accommodated. Some relational rules can't be broken. For example, having duplicate rows in a table can cause unpredictable results.

Question 4

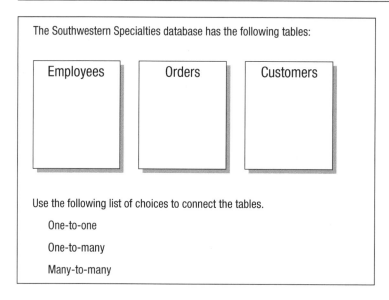

The Southwestern Specialties database has the following tables:

| Employees | Orders | Customers |

Use the following list of choices to connect the tables.

One-to-one

One-to-many

Many-to-many

The correct answer is:

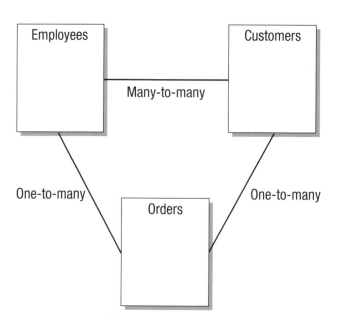

| Employees | | Customers |

Many-to-many

One-to-many   One-to-many

Orders

Question 5

You have created a database with two tables: Orders and Customers. In your model, customers can place multiple orders, which are tracked in the database. The CustomerID column in the Orders table references the CustomerID column in the Customers table. Which of the following statements is correct?

- ○ a. CustomerID in the Customers table is a primary key and CustomerID in the Orders table is a foreign key.

- ○ b. CustomerID in the Customers table is a foreign key and CustomerID in the Orders table is a primary key.

- ○ c. CustomerID in the Customers table is a primary key and CustomerID in the Orders table is a primary key.

- ○ d. CustomerID in the Customers table is a foreign key and CustomerID in the Orders table is a foreign key.

Answer a is correct.

Question 6

Which of the following methods can be used to enforce business rules? [Check all correct answers]

- ❑ a. Stored procedures in the database
- ❑ b. A primary key
- ❑ c. A foreign key
- ❑ d. An index

Answers a, b, c, and d are all correct. Stored procedures can be used to validate specific data. A primary key can be used to ensure unique entries. Although an index is typically used for performance, a unique index is another mechanism for ensuring unique values. A foreign key can be used to prevent the creation of orphan rows in the child table of a parent-child relationship.

Question 7

> Reorder the following steps into the sequence recommended for designing a relational database.
>
>   Defining the indexes
>
>   Defining the tables
>
>   Mapping the data tables to physical data storage
>
>   Defining the columns
>
>   Defining the primary keys
>
>   Defining the foreign keys
>
>   Defining the purpose of the database

The correct order is

>   Defining the purpose of the database
>
>   Defining the tables
>
>   Defining the columns
>
>   Defining the primary keys
>
>   Defining the foreign keys
>
>   Defining the indexes
>
>   Mapping the data tables to physical data storage

The order of the last two steps could be interchanged; however, you will usually define the indexes first. That way, you know if additional physical data storage is needed for the indexes.

Need To Know More?

 Date, Chris J. *An Introduction to Database Systems.* Sixth Edition. Addison-Wesley Publishing Company, 1994. ISBN 0-2015-4329-X. This classic textbook, written by one of the original researchers of the relational model, provides a comprehensive description of database concepts and technology.

 Getz, Ken, Paul Litwin, and Mike Gilbert. *Access 97 Developer's Handbook.* Third Edition. Alameda, CA: Sybex, 1997. ISBN 0-7821-1941-7. Chapter 4, "Database Design," provides a practical description of the database design process.

 Microsoft Access provides several sample databases. These can be installed when you install the Microsoft Access software. In addition, you can use the Database Wizard to create many types of databases, such as a Contact Management database. By studying the design of these databases, you can gain some practical knowledge about organizing data into tables and creating relationships.

 http://support.microsoft.com/support/kb/articles/q100/1/39.asp

This paper, "Database Normalization Basics", found in the Microsoft Knowledge Base, provides a description of database normalization, as well as several examples.

 http://support.microsoft.com/support/kb/articles/q110/3/52.asp

This paper, "Optimizing Microsoft SQL Server Performance", found in the Microsoft Knowledge Base, provides useful information on factors that affect database performance. This paper discusses normalization and index design as well as several other key areas that affect performance.

Developing The Conceptual And Logical Design For An Application

7

Terms you'll need to understand:

- √ Application architecture
- √ Conceptual design
- √ Usage scenarios
- √ Context model
- √ Workflow process model
- √ Task sequence model
- √ Physical environment model
- √ Logical design
- √ Single document interface

- √ Multiple document interface
- √ Console application
- √ Dialog application
- √ Web application
- √ Presentation objects
- √ Business objects
- √ Data objects
- √ Model
- √ Components

Techniques you'll need to master:

- √ Developing a conceptual design for an application
- √ Augmenting the conceptual design with diagrams that depict the workflow or task sequence of an application
- √ Developing a logical design for an application

- √ Describing the object types of the logical design
- √ Describing the guidelines for designing the application objects
- √ Evaluating the impact of the logical design on performance, maintainability, extensibility, scalability, availability, and security

Developing a business application that truly satisfies business requirements and can evolve as the business grows involves much more than simply writing a computer program. To develop a solution to a business problem, several steps are required.

You must first determine the business requirements, which was discussed in Chapter 4. After determining the requirements, you can evaluate what types of solution architecture might be appropriate for the solution. Chapter 5 presented many of the solution architecture options, along with their strengths and weaknesses.

You'll also need to know how the persistent data is going to be organized and stored. Chapter 6 discussed the topic of data modeling.

Armed with all this information, you can now begin to focus on the application or applications that will need to be developed to implement the solution.

CASE STUDY: Power Patterns

Company Background

Power Patterns is a startup company that's trying to make a business by helping other businesses analyze their energy usage. The CEO at Power Patterns states, "When a business can see where the energy dollars are going, they are able to take steps toward energy conservation. As a result, they not only use less energy, but they also save money. It's a win-win for everybody."

By showing its customers how to better manage their energy usage, Power Patterns hopes to divert some of the savings dollars into its own revenue stream.

Business Model

Power Patterns has developed a software application that generates reports of energy usage. These reports graphically display energy-related statistics, such as kilowatts and kilowatt hours, as well as computed statistics, such as kilowatts used per square foot and cost per day. Each month, Power Patterns prepares a printed report for each customer, which is then mailed to the customer.

To create these reports, Power Patterns also developed a database for storing customer data as well as energy usage data for each customer. Power Patterns isn't an energy provider; therefore, to get the data needed for the reports, Power Patterns must obtain it from the energy providers that actually deliver the energy to the customers.

Six major energy providers serve the area that Power Patterns has identified as its customer base. Power Patterns has special arrangements with all of them for obtaining energy usage data.

Once Power Patterns enrolls a new customer for their service, several steps must be followed:

1. Power Patterns must obtain the energy usage data for that customer from the utility company that provides energy services to the customer.

2. The energy usage data for this customer must be added to the database that Power Patterns maintains for generating the energy usage reports.

3. Energy usage reports must be created for the customer.

The process is depicted in Figure 7.1.

The EnergyReporter Application

A key component of the business operations at Power Patterns is the EnergyReporter application. This application produces all the energy usage reports that get printed and mailed to customers. This application does the following:

➤ Allows users to pick a customer

➤ Allows users to identify the reports to be created for that customer

➤ Allows users to specify parameters specific to each report, such as reporting period

➤ Creates and prints the customer reports

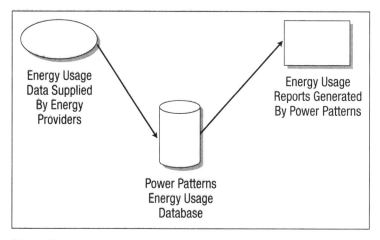

Figure 7.1   Power Patterns' flow of data.

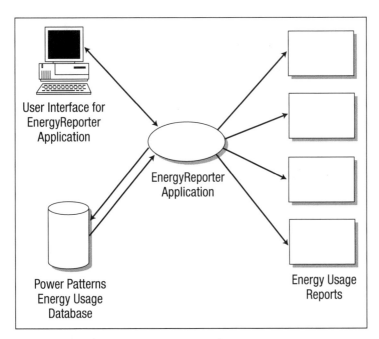

Figure 7.2 The EnergyReporter application.

This application is depicted in Figure 7.2.

Power Patterns engaged the services of an outside consulting firm to help them write the EnergyReporter application. The consultants suggested that the application be written using the logical three-tier model, which is what Power Patterns did. This technique modularized many of the functions and allows them to be reused in other applications as the business grows.

The Energy Usage Database

The Energy Usage database presented several problems for Power Patterns. Defining the table structure was fairly straightforward, and creating the database from the logical design presented no problems. Defining the data objects for the EnergyReporter application also went smoothly. To load the database, procedures were developed to import the data supplied by the energy providers directly into the database.

However, difficulties occurred in loading data into the database for several reasons:

➤ Data was obtained from six different energy providers.

➤ Although Power Patterns specified a format for the input data, some of the providers would only deliver it in their own unique format.

➤ The data often contained errors or omissions that caused the EnergyReporter application to produce errors.

Power Patterns asked the consultants to help them address these problems.

The DataLoader Application

The consultants proposed developing another application, the DataLoader application. The main purpose of this application would be to take input data from the energy providers and load it into the Energy Usage database. In particular, this application:

➤ Reads input data supplied by energy providers in a number of supported formats.

➤ Loads the input data into a Staging database.

➤ Validates the input data and produces an error log showing the data items that are invalid.

➤ Allows users to examine and edit data in the Staging database.

➤ Uploads valid data from the Staging database to the Energy Usage database.

Two main objectives of the DataLoader application are to allow different energy providers to supply data in different formats and to prevent erroneous data from being loaded into the Energy Usage database. To accomplish its tasks, the DataLoader application temporarily stores the input data in a Staging database. This allows the data to be examined and edited before it's loaded to the Energy Usage database.

The steps performed by the DataLoader application are depicted in Figure 7.3.

The DataLoader application solved many of the problems that Power Patterns had been trying to address.

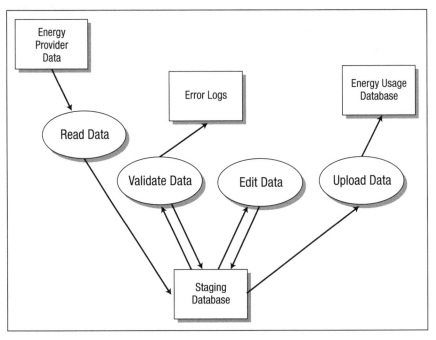

Figure 7.3 The DataLoader application workflow.

Application Types

Application development consists of designing, modeling, prototyping, and, finally, implementing and testing. During the designing and modeling phases, you'll develop an *application architecture*. Almost all applications contain presentation code, data processing code, and data storage code. The application architecture defines how this code will eventually be organized and packaged.

Analysis and design are essential activities of application development. As you develop the application architecture, you must carefully consider the impact of your design decisions. Don't skimp on the time allotted for design; it's an iterative process. You'll need to plan for multiple iterations of analysis and design to refine your architecture. Remember that an application based on a poor design will be a bad application.

Before designing your application, you'll want to determine the *type* of application you're going to build. A broad range of terms is used to describe the application characteristics or the type of application. These include:

➤ SDI

➤ MDI

➤ Console

➤ Dialog

➤ Desktop

➤ Distributed

➤ Single-Tier

➤ Two-Tier

➤ n-Tier

➤ Client/Server

➤ Web

➤ Collaborative

It's not surprising that there's an overlap in the definition of these application types. In fact, your application will probably be some combination of the various types. To help you understand these various application types, each is characterized in the following sections.

Desktop And Distributed

Desktop applications are applications run by a single user on a single computer. These applications reside on the hard drive of the user's computer and use local resources. A desktop application might utilize a two-tier architecture that accesses data from a server.

Distributed applications are multiple applications running separately and working together. They utilize multiple computer systems to solve a problem or accomplish a task.

Client/Server

Client/server applications are distributed applications based on a model of computing whereby a client requests services from another entity, the server. The server responds to the client. This model is popular for creating client/server applications in which a client running on a desktop or personal computer accesses information on remote servers or host computers. The client portion of the application is typically optimized for user interaction, whereas the server portion provides the centralized functionality shared by multiple users.

In a client/server environment, application processing is performed by components on both the client and the server. This can be differentiated from a file server environment where no application components run on the file server.

 Many distributed applications are implemented as client/server applications. In this model, a requestor (the client) requests services from a provider (the server). Client/Server applications are usually implemented as separate applications running on separate systems; however, this isn't a requirement. The different applications can also run on the same computer system. The interaction between the two applications, in which one requests services that the other provides, determines the nature of a client/server application.

Single Document Interface (SDI)

Two basic user interface styles are used by Windows applications. Some applications, such as Notepad, allow you to work with only one document at a time. If you want to open another document, you must first close the document with which you are working.

An application, such as Notepad, that uses a single, primary window with a set of supplemental secondary windows is referred to as a *single document interface (SDI)* application. SDI is a single-instance model. It's always possible to bring up multiple instances of an SDI application when you need to display different objects at the same time. In an SDI application, you can display one or more windows on the desktop, each of which can be minimized or maximized independently of each other. If a user reopens an object, you activate the existing window.

SDI applications are the most common style found under Windows 95, because the operating system has adopted a "document-centered" view.

Multiple Document Interface (MDI)

Other applications, such as Microsoft Word, allow you to work with multiple documents at a time. Each document is displayed in a separate window, and the *Window menu* on the menu bar allows you to easily switch between windows.

The *multiple document interface (MDI)* presents a standard way of writing applications for Windows in which a single, primary window, called a parent window, is used to visually contain a set of related child windows. An MDI application allows the user to display multiple documents at the same time, with each document displayed in its own window.

Each child window is essentially a primary window but is constrained to appear within the parent window. In MDI applications, child windows minimize within the bounds of the parent's window and show an icon when minimized.

Microsoft Access and Microsoft Excel are examples of MDI applications. For example, Microsoft Excel allows you to create and display multiple-document windows of different types. When the child windows are of different types, such as chart windows and spreadsheet windows, the menu bar changes as MDI child windows of different types are activated. Each individual window is confined to the area of the Excel parent window. When you minimize Excel, all of the document windows are minimized as well; only the parent window's icon appears in the task bar.

Although SDI and MDI are the most common styles of user interface, there are certainly other possibilities. The *explorer-style* interface is a single window containing two panes or regions. The left pane usually consists of a tree or hierarchical view and the right pane consists of a display area. This in the interface style utilized by Microsoft Windows Explorer. This type of interface lends itself to navigating or browsing large numbers of documents, pictures, or files.

Console

Console applications have no graphical user interface but have a *command interface* that allows users to interact with the application. Each console application usually has a set of commands that can be used to invoke the application procedures. However, users sometimes find it difficult to remember the exact commands and their syntax.

Most mainframe and legacy applications fall into the category of console applications. These applications were designed and built for use with character cell terminals. Console applications are often run from the Windows environment using terminal emulation programs.

 Console applications are appropriate when the user interface is command-line oriented rather than graphically oriented.

Dialog

A *dialog application* guides a user through a sequence of steps to accomplish a task. Dialog applications usually interact heavily with the user, presenting a series of screens (or dialog boxes) for which the user supplies a response. The *wizards* utilized by many of the Windows tools are good examples of dialog applications.

Single-Tier

A *single-tier application* refers to an application that's been implemented in a single physical tier. That means its running as a single process on one machine. A single-tier application might be based on a multiple-tier, logical model in which the different types of services are all separate. Or, a single-tier application might also be based on the monolithic model in which there's no clear distinction between the types of services.

In a single-tier application, standard procedure calls are used to provide communication between the various modules in the application. Therefore, it's not subject to the overhead processing associated with distributed applications. However, performance is limited by the hardware used to run the application.

One advantage of a single-tier application is that it's one of the simplest models to implement. For this reason, single-tier applications are very popular.

Two-Tier

A *two-tier application* is a good example of a distributed application using the client/server model. In a two-tier application, the application is implemented using two separate physical tiers. This model became very popular for implementing applications that required access to a database.

In this model, an application running on a desktop (the client) accesses the data in a centralized database on a back-end system (the server). The server supports numerous distributed clients. Although this model enables the sharing of computer resources and also provides a centralized database, management of the client applications is still more complex than the centralized systems of the past.

Two-tier applications are limited in scalability, which is usually caused by the performance limitations of the database on the server. A typical implementation strategy for two-tier applications is to have the client connect directly to the database server. This requires one or more database connections, which the client then holds for the lifetime of the application. Although easy to implement, this strategy has serious performance ramifications.

n-Tier

A *multi-tier application architecture* is a software design based on splitting the application into separate functional components. Generally, the application is designed around three tiers of service—user, business, and data services—referred to as a three-tier application.

A logical extension of the three-tier application is the n-tier application. An n-tier application is a distributed application in which one or more of the three original tiers have been separated into additional tiers. This provides another level of abstraction for describing the application model.

Web

Web applications usually consist of a series of Web pages that are displayed in a Web browser. Although Web browsers were initially used for downloading and displaying static Web pages, Web applications utilize technologies that support *dynamic Web pages*. Web applications integrate Internet technologies with traditional programmed applications. Web pages provide the presentation content of the application. A Web application might be deployed locally over a corporate intranet or globally on the Internet.

Most Web applications are a hybrid of Hypertext Markup Language (HTML) pages and executable code. The executable code might be part of a script on the Web page, or it could be included in programs or components that are invoked from the Web page.

A number of different models exist for combining HTML and program logic. Some models support code that runs entirely on the server, which allows a wide variety of browsers to work with the application. Other models support code that runs on the client, allowing the client to share in the processing, reducing network traffic and providing a more responsive user interface. However, not all browsers support all the different implementation models.

 Active Server Pages (ASP), Internet Server API (ISAPI), and Common Gateway Interface (CGI) scripts are all different technologies for creating Web applications that perform processing on the server.

Collaborative Applications

Collaborative applications are distributed applications that work together. An application that's used as part of a collaborative application is usually a full functioning application that can also be used independently.

For example, a collaborative application might consist of an application written in Visual Basic, Microsoft Word, and Microsoft Excel. The Visual Basic application could use automation to invoke the services of Word and Excel. Lotus Notes and Microsoft Exchange are two other examples of collaborative applications.

Conceptual Design

Conceptual design is the process of acquiring, documenting, and validating user and business perspectives of a problem and its solution. The goal of conceptual design is to understand what users do and to identify business needs. The output of conceptual design is *scenarios*. A scenario documents a sequence of steps necessary to complete a user-assigned task.

When you create a conceptual design for an application, you'll describe what a user will be able to do with the application. You'll also be describing the tasks the application performs in response to user actions. The conceptual design is documented in the various project documents using scenarios.

Usage Scenarios

One common scenario is the *usage scenario*. It's particularly useful if an existing application is to be enhanced or if an existing process or manual procedure is to be automated.

Usage scenarios help validate and complete user profile information as well as offer a better understanding of how users will interact with an application. Usage scenarios can be used to:

➤ Understand how the target audience works with the current applications, which will also help identify training requirements.

➤ Identify new user functionality needs—what do users want to do that they can't do now?

Several different techniques are used for gathering the data needed for usage scenarios:

➤ Observation (shadowing users on the job)

➤ Interviewing users

➤ Consulting with the help desk

➤ Referring to documentation

Documenting Scenarios

Several different methods are used to describe and document a scenario. To document the conceptual design of your application, you'll construct scenarios consisting of narrative documents, context diagrams, physical environment diagrams, workflow/process models, and task/sequence models.

A *narrative document* describes the scenario in text. Diagrams and figures might be included, but the primary description comes from the narrative text. A *functional specification* is a document that describes what an application is expected to do from a user's perspective. Therefore, the functional specification documents the tasks the application is required to perform.

 The functional specification is a narrative document describing what an application is expected to do from a user's perspective. Like the requirements document, it's a key document for every software development project.

Often, it's difficult to convey exactly what is going on using only narrative text. Therefore, *diagrams* are frequently used to convey what is happening during a scenario.

For example, in the case study for Power Patterns, a narrative description provides information about the company and its applications. However, to augment the narrative text, diagrams are also included. No formal methodology has been used for the case study. But the narrative text and diagrams convey the types of information that are fundamental to the conceptual design.

Scenario Diagrams

A number of different diagrams and models are utilized for conceptual design. In addition, many tools are also available to support the methodologies of the various design models. These include:

➤ Data flow diagrams

➤ Physical environment diagrams

➤ Context diagrams

➤ Workflow/process diagrams

➤ Task/sequence diagrams

Data Flow diagrams are used to represent the flow of information throughout the system.

Physical Environment diagrams depict a physical representation of the system. Usually physical environment diagrams consist of two parts—current and proposed diagrams. A *current* diagram shows the system as it currently exists. A *proposed* diagram shows the system that is anticipated.

A *context diagram* is another representation of an application. It represents the highest level of the view of the application, depicting the application as a single process. The context diagram also shows the external components that interact with the application. The external components may provide information to the application as well as receive information from the application.

For example, Figure 7.2 is a type of context diagram for the EnergyReporter application. It depicts the various external components that interact with the application.

Workflow/Process diagrams show the various processes used to accomplish a task. Typically, multiple steps are required, and often, different people or processes perform these steps. The workflow/process diagram depicts these different steps.

For example, Figure 7.3 is a type of workflow/process diagram. It shows the various processing steps of the DataLoader application and also shows the flow of data through the steps.

Task/Sequence diagrams are another type of diagram used for conceptual design that display interactions between objects from a temporal standpoint. The representation focuses on expressing object interactions.

Conceptual design is best described by using scenarios. A scenario defines a sequence of steps necessary to complete a user task. Narrative documents, context diagrams, physical environment diagrams, workflow/process diagrams, and task/sequence diagrams are all different methods used to describe a scenario

Logical Design

From the conceptual design, you'll have a high-level abstraction of what the application is supposed to do. You'll be able to describe the different interactions the user will have with the application. Furthermore, you'll be able to describe the different tasks the application is expected to perform for each of those interactions. With the conceptual design in place, you'll now want to move forward and define the next level of abstraction: the *logical design*.

Logical design is a view of the solution from the project team's perspective. It defines the solution as a set of cooperating objects and their services. Based on the MSF Application Model, these services are grouped into the categories of user (or presentation), business, and data services.

The goal of logical design is to describe the structure of the solution and the communication among its elements.

Logical design is best described by using *models*. Using the most basic definition, a model is a simplification and representation of a real-world entity. By using a model, you'll be able to better understand the application you're designing. A model will help you accomplish four things:

➤ To visualize the application, as it is or as you want it to be

➤ To specify the structure or behavior of the application

➤ To provide a template that guides you in building the application

➤ To document the decisions you've made

In particular, the logical design produces four important models:

➤ Database logical design

➤ Data services logical design

➤ Business services logical design

➤ Presentation services logical design

The database logical design has already been described in Chapter 6. Here you'll focus on the logical design of the application: namely, the presentation, business, and data services.

Modeling The Logical Design

A number of software development tools are available to help you prepare the logical design of your application. These *modeling tools* allow you to interactively develop the database and application designs. Usually, these tools provide a graphical interface that allows you to define and modify the different elements that will comprise the design.

Microsoft Visual Studio includes a design tool called Visual Modeler, a modeling tool based on the Unified Modeling Language (UML). Visual Modeler is useful for designing three-tier distributed applications using class and component diagrams. With Visual Modeler, you can visually design models of the classes and components your application needs, and then convert these models to Visual Basic or Visual C++ code.

Grady Booch, one of the UML architects, describes UML as "a graphical language for visualizing, specifying, constructing, and documenting the artifacts of a software-intensive system. UML gives you a standard way to write a system's blueprints, covering conceptual things, such as business processes and system functions, as well as concrete things, such as classes written in a specific programming language, data base schemas, and reusable software components. UML is a widely adopted standard that represents best practices and lessons learned from well over a decade of experience of modeling complex software-intensive systems."

Principles Of Modular Design

In Chapter 5, the logical three-tier model was introduced and described. As you may recall, the fundamental design principle of the logical three-tier model is *modularization*.

The logical design will define the modularization for the logical three-tier model. From the functional specification, you'll know the various tasks the application must handle. The logical design will identify the *presentation objects*, *business objects*, and *data objects* that will perform these tasks. Each object will have properties, the characteristics of the object; and methods, the tasks the object performs.

In general, the logical design is totally independent of how the application will eventually be deployed. In fact, you should try to design the application so it has a high level of flexibility and supports a number of different deployment options. Modularity will make this possible.

Keep in mind that design is an *iterative process*. You'll initially define a set of objects, and start evaluating how well they satisfy the requirements and interact with other objects. As you find flaws, you'll *refine* your design, defining new objects and modifying existing ones. And then you'll reevaluate the new design. Although you'll probably make numerous changes to your design, making these changes is much easier during the application design rather than after the implementation has begun.

You'll be designing four basic kinds of objects:

➤ *Interaction objects* are used in the presentation tier and allow the user to interact with the application, view data, and update data. Because these objects are in the presentation tier, they're *presentation objects*.

➤ *Query objects* are used in the business tier and retrieve data according to the business rules. Because these objects are in the business tier, they're *business objects*.

➤ *Update objects* are also used in the business tier and update data according to the business rules. Often an update object will compute the updated data. Because these objects are in the business tier, they're *business objects*.

➤ *Data objects* are used in the data tier and encapsulate the access to persistent data. Because these objects are in the data tier, they're *data objects*.

Figure 7.4 depicts the logical three-tier model and the objects found in each tier.

Figure 7.4 also shows the fundamental interactions between the layers and the logical flow of data in the logical three-tier model.

The user views the data through the presentation services tier. Using forms and controls or interactive Web pages, the user interacts with the presentation services of the application.

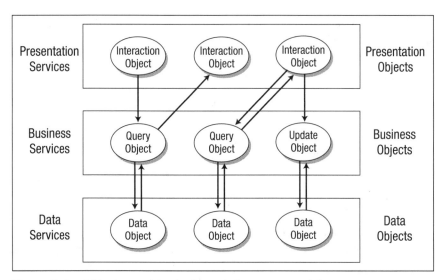

Figure 7.4 Objects used in the logical three-tier model.

Presentation services use presentation objects to obtain data from the business services tier and present it to the user. The presentation objects display the data obtained from the business services.

Business services use business objects to obtain data from the data services tier and present it to the presentation tier. The business objects also allow data provided by the user via the presentation tier to be passed to the data services tier.

The data services tier uses data objects to access the data in the physical data store. Only the objects in the data services tier know where and how the data is stored. By *isolating the three fundamental services (presentation, business, and data) into separate groups of objects*, you can achieve a modular design.

The primary applications developed by Power Patterns are based on a modular design and the logical three-tier model.

 Logical design defines the modularization for the logical three-tier model. By isolating the three fundamental services (presentation, business, and data) into separate groups of objects, you can achieve a modular design.

Deriving Objects And Services Of The Logical Design

Now that you know the purpose of the logical design is to identify a set of objects for each of the three service tiers, the next question is obvious. How do you decide what these objects are?

There is no simple answer and no single answer for all situations. However, you can follow some guidelines that work in many situations. Data objects and business objects are discussed here. Chapter 8 discusses presentation services.

When you've identified the objects and the properties and methods that each object requires, you can begin creating the *components* that implement the object *classes*. The actual objects get created at runtime as instantiations of an object class.

Data Objects

Data objects are responsible for pieces of data. Therefore, one approach for defining data objects is to have each data object manage a logical unit of data in the data store. In a relational database, this corresponds to *defining a separate data object for each table in the database.*

A data object of this type is going to perform four basic operations:

➤ Add a new record

➤ Delete an existing record

➤ Read an existing record

➤ Update an existing record

Therefore, it makes sense to provide methods for the data object to perform these operations. Depending on the requirements, data objects may need to support additional methods.

This is exactly the way Power Patterns defined the data objects for their EnergyReporter application. They created one data object for each table in the Energy Usage database. For example, one of the tables defined in the Power Patterns Energy Usage database is the Customers table. This table keeps track of customers who are utilizing the services provided by Power Patterns. The EnergyReporter application, which is based on the logical three-tier model, utilizes a data object called **db_Customers**. This data object manages the data in the Customers table of the database.

The **db_Customer** object supports several methods:

➤ **Add** Adds a new customer record.

➤ **Delete** Deletes an existing customer record identified by the CustomerID.

➤ **Update** Updates an existing customer record identified by the CustomerID.

➤ **Read** Reads and returns an existing customer record identified by the CustomerID.

➤ **GetCustomerList** Returns a list of customer names. Parameters to the method allow the client to request a list of only those customers within a particular zip code.

Remember, the general rule is to have each data object manage a logical unit of data. Usually, this will correspond to a specific database table, but this isn't always the case. Sometimes a logical unit of data may correspond to columns from several different tables. Many relational database systems support this by allowing you to define a *view*, which is a "logical table," derived from items in other tables. A view doesn't require any additional storage for the data items. Therefore, it may be appropriate to have data objects corresponding to views as well as tables.

As you determine the data objects, keep the following guidelines in mind:

➤ Data objects are responsible for the accuracy, completeness, and consistency of the data they own.

➤ Data objects should work within the context of a transaction as well as outside a transactional context.

➤ Data objects can't retain their state across transaction boundaries.

➤ Data objects should minimize network traffic. Carefully consider the amount of data your objects will send across the network, as well as the overhead processing involved in accessing object properties and methods.

One approach for defining data objects is to have each data object manage a logical unit of data in the data store. In a relational database, this corresponds to defining a separate data object for each table or view in the database.

Business Objects

Business objects encapsulate the tasks of business operations. The business objects are the brains of the application, controlling the sequencing of tasks, enforcing business rules, and ensuring transactional integrity for the operations they perform. Business objects will usually perform multistep operations and access multiple data objects.

One way to define business objects is to relate business entities to business objects. In general, each business object should encapsulate functionality for one business entity. The functional specification will identify the business tasks the business object must perform. Business object methods should do exactly one unit of work, and each unit of work should be implemented in exactly one method. By calling methods on other business objects and data objects, you can define higher-level operations.

Granularity is a term used to describe a component's capacity to handle activities. A component's granularity can range from coarse to fine; the more functionality contained in the component, the more coarse the granularity.

Power Patterns defined a set of business objects for their EnergyReporter application, and they created one business object for each real world object. For example, two of the business objects created were the **bus_Report** object and the **bus_Customer** object.

The **bus_Report** object processes all the customer reports. A key method of the **bus_Report** object is **CreatePrintedReport,** which is used to create all the printed Energy Usage reports produced by the application.

As you determine the business objects, keep the following guidelines in mind:

➤ Business objects encapsulate real-world business operations, independent of how the data they use is actually stored.

➤ Business objects control sequencing and enforcement of business rules, as well as the transactional integrity of the operations they perform.

➤ Business object methods should do exactly one unit of work, and each unit of work should be implemented in exactly one method. Higher-level operations are composed by calling methods on other business objects and data objects.

➤ Business objects should minimize network traffic. Carefully consider the amount of data your objects will send across the network to remote presentation layers, as well as the overhead processing involved in accessing object properties and methods.

➤ Business objects are the gatekeepers that control access to your data.

One approach for defining business objects is to have each business object encapsulate a real-world business operation. Business object methods should do exactly one unit of work, and each unit of work should be implemented in exactly one method.

Evaluating The Logical Design

As you create your logical design, you'll want to continually evaluate it to ensure that it meets the stated business requirements. In particular, you'll want to consider how your design affects the key application factors including:

➤ Performance

➤ Development

➤ Maintainability

➤ Extensibility

➤ Availability

➤ Scalability

➤ Security

There are a number of major advantages to the logical three-tier model. From a *performance* perspective, the modularity allows distributing applications across multiple systems. Although this does include additional overhead processing, it also allows multiple computer systems to process the application.

One of the biggest performance gains comes in the area of database access. Rather than having each user maintain a *connection* to the database, only the data objects will require database connections. When carefully designed, all the business objects can share the data objects, so the number of connections the database is required to support is minimized.

From a *development* and *maintenance* perspective, application functionality is isolated, so a broad range of skill sets isn't necessary for working on a particular module. For example, the developer working on presentation objects doesn't need to know anything about SQL. Modularity also means that different developers can work on different parts of the application at the same time without interfering with one another.

The functional isolation provided by modularity also makes it easier to enhance the application. This enables better application *extensibility*.

Application *availability* and *scalability* are also made easier by the logical three-tier design. By supporting many different physical deployment options, the physical configuration can be adjusted and tuned to the desired level.

Finally, the modular approach also makes it easier to incorporate *security*. Using facilities of the Windows NT operating system, the system administrator can establish users and groups. Developers can define permissions for application components based on these same users and groups. In addition, an executing application can contain the logic code that allows it to determine the permissions of the current user and grant or deny access to a facility based on this information.

Practice Questions

Question 1

> Which of the following statements best describes conceptual design?
>
> ○ a. A view of the solution from the developer's perspective
>
> ○ b. A view of the solution from the project team's perspective
>
> ○ c. The process of acquiring, documenting, and validating user and business perspectives of a problem and its solution
>
> ○ d. Definition of the solution as a set of cooperating objects and their services

Answer c is correct. Answer a describes physical design and answers b and d describe logical design.

Question 2

> Which of the following statements best describes logical design?
>
> ○ a. A view of the solution from the developer's perspective
>
> ○ b. A view of the solution from the project team's perspective
>
> ○ c. The process of acquiring, documenting, and validating user and business perspectives of a problem and its solution
>
> ○ d. Output is scenarios

Answer b is correct. Answer a describes physical design and answers c and d describe conceptual design.

Question 3

> Which of the following statements best describes physical design?
>
> ○ a. A view of the solution from the developer's perspective
>
> ○ b. A view of the solution from the project team's perspective
>
> ○ c. The process of acquiring, documenting, and validating user and business perspectives of a problem and its solution
>
> ○ d. Output is scenarios

Answer a is correct. Answer b describes logical design. Answers c and d describe conceptual design.

Question 4

In which of the following applications would you most likely find a Window menu?

○ a. Client/Server

○ b. SDI

○ c. MDI

○ d. n-tier

Answer c is correct. A multiple document interface application will almost always have a Window menu because it supports multiple windows for displaying different documents. A single document interface will not need a Window menu, because it supports only one window for displaying one document at a time. Client/Server and n-tier applications could be either SDI or MDI applications.

Question 5

Based on the four types of objects used in the logical design of a three-tier application, what are the query and update objects?

○ a. Presentation objects

○ b. Business objects

○ c. Data objects

○ d. Stored procedures

Answer b is correct. Query objects and update objects are types of business service objects. Therefore, they are business objects. From their name, you might assume they are data objects, but this is not the case. As business objects, these objects retrieve and update data in accordance with business rules. They communicate with the data objects that actually access the data. Business objects have no knowledge of how the data is physically stored.

Question 6

Which of the following terms describe a Web application? [Check all correct answers]

❑ a. Desktop

❑ b. Distributed

❑ c. Client/Server

❑ d. Single-Tier

Answers b and c are correct. A Web application is a distributed application and also a client/server application. It is neither a desktop nor a single-tier application, because it uses the processing capabilities of multiple computer systems.

Need To Know More?

 Egremont, Carlton. *Mr. Bunny's Guide to ActiveX*. Reading, MA: Addison-Wesley, 1998. ISBN 0-20148-536-2. When you have finally reached the point where you can no longer study the exam preparation material, you'll want to start reading this book. You can gauge your understanding of the technologies by your amount of laughter.

 Booch, Grady. "The Visual Modeling of Software Architecture for the Enterprise." Microsoft Corporation: Redmond, WA, 1998. This background paper describes software architectures, modeling, and the Unified Modeling Language (UML). It also includes a case study that models a three-tier architecture. This paper is available on the Microsoft Developer Network Library.

 The Enterprise Edition of Visual Studio V6 contains an online book entitled *Developing for the Enterprise*. This online documentation is also available on the Microsoft Developer Network Library. "Part 1: Enterprise Design and Architecture" discusses application requirements and design methodologies. In Chapter 3, "Tools for Enterprise Application Design," the section "Meeting User Needs" describes tasks and tools for the conceptual modeling phase of application design. The section "Defining Application Logic" describes tasks and tools for the logical modeling phase of application design.

 msdn.microsoft.com/vstudio/downloads/solutions.asp

This is Microsoft's Web site for the Visual Studio Solutions Center. Here you can find case studies and samples for building end-to-end solutions based on architectures that utilize the latest Microsoft technologies. Microsoft describes the functions of the Web site as a source for learning how to properly architect complex applications, how to approach application development with documented design decisions and tradeoffs that were made, and how to use the integrated tools in Visual Studio.

www.fmcorp.com

This is the Web site for the fictional company Fitch and Mather. From here you can access sample applications that were developed to support the Fitch and Mather business. Visual InterDev and other Visual Studio tools were used to develop the sample applications. A set of design documents is also available, as well as sample code. This is a good reference site for studying how to design and build a Web application.

Designing A User Interface And User Services

Terms you'll need to understand:

√ User interface

√ User services

√ Primary window

√ Secondary window

√ Prototype

√ Shortcut key

√ ToolTips

√ Status bar

√ Contextual help

√ Task help

√ Wizard

√ Dialog box

√ Help menu

√ Menu bar

√ Drop-down menu

√ Pop-up menu

Techniques you'll need to master:

√ Differentiating between a native user interface and a Web-based interface

√ Differentiating among the various mechanisms available for providing user assistance

√ Describing the guidelines for designing a user interface

√ Describing the steps for prototyping and evaluating a user interface design

√ Describing the major facilities for navigating the user interface

√ Describing how input validation could be integrated into the user interface

√ Describing the difference between modal and modeless windows

√ Designing a dialog box and laying out the controls

√ Designing a wizard

√ Describing the different types of menus

√ Describing how to localize your application

In addition to preparing a logical design for your application and modeling the data, you'll also need to address how the end user is going to interact with the application. This is handled by the presentation services. The user interface, a key part of the presentation services, dictates how the end user will see the application. The user interface can mean the difference between acceptance and rejection of the entire application. Therefore, a well-designed interface is imperative to the ultimate success of your application.

CASE STUDY: **Power Patterns Wants More**

Additional Requirements

The CIO at Power Patterns really liked the modularity in the solution that was developed. It provided a great deal of flexibility for internally managing and deploying the application. In the current version of the application, printed reports are generated on a monthly basis and mailed to the customers. This has been working well.

However, as the business has started to grow, some of the customers are asking for better access to the data. Customers are now asking for more frequent reports. In particular, many of the customer sites utilize meters that record energy usage on an hourly basis. Power Patterns' customers would really like to see this data every day so that they can perform a more timely analysis of energy consumption.

In fact, Power Patterns receives this data on a daily basis from the energy providers. The CIO explains, "Based on the data-loading procedures we have implemented, we have no problem getting the data and updating our database on a daily basis. However, it's impractical to create a set of new reports and mail them every day."

The CIO has scheduled a meeting and asked you to attend to help them determine how to address this new requirement.

Solution Options

Two different approaches have been proposed to address this problem. Bob, a senior developer, suggested developing another user interface that could be distributed to each customer. "We could write it in Visual Basic and it would have no problem working with the rest of our application because of our modular design. We would distribute this to all our customers. Our customers would need to install only this component on their systems. They could use a dial-up connection to get on our network and generate the data reports right on their own system."

Betty, another senior developer has another idea: "All our customers have access to the Internet. Why don't we consider creating the reports here and publishing them on our Web site? That way, the users can access them directly. We could generate the HTML pages each day after we loaded the latest set of data. Bob has a good idea, but this way we don't really need to develop any new software, and we don't have to worry about any of the deployment issues associated with distributing an application front end."

After listening to this discussion, the CIO asks you to provide some input.

Your Solution

Your suggestion is to build on the idea of using the Internet: "Although the application modularity certainly supports creating another user interface in Visual Basic, you may not want to do this. With this type of user interface—a *native* interface—you're going to have to deal with the installation and maintenance issues, and your business is not really set up for that.

"Of course, the Web pages approach also has its own set of drawbacks. Someone is going to have to create and publish all the HTML pages every day. Although this can be automated, it will involve work and require managing the areas for storing each customer's reports.

"There is, however, another alternative worth exploring. That is, rather than generating a number of *static* Web pages, you could consider generating *dynamic* Web pages. This approach would not require creating all possible reports in advance, because the Web pages would be generated dynamically only when a customer requests a report.

"Active Server Pages technology makes this possible. An Active Server Page is a Web page written in HTML and a scripting language. You could use Visual Basic as the scripting language. Because the development team already knows Visual Basic, they can easily develop the VB scripts. You would actually be able to access the business services of your application directly from the ASP script and insert data into the HTML that gets sent to the customer's browser. New code will be required, but this will all be deployed in the server environment as part of the script in the Active Server Pages. Having all the code located here is important for maintenance concerns. Active Server Pages is also attractive because it supports a wide variety of browsers."

Your solution is depicted in Figure 8.1.

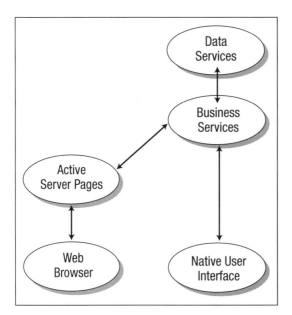

Figure 8.1 Two implementations of presentation services.

The CIO and the rest of the group like this idea. They ask you to help them produce a prototype Web page for evaluation.

Presentation Services

The primary function of the presentation services tier is to provide the graphical user interface (GUI) and logic so that the user can interact with the application. The GUI facility is referred to as simply the *user interface*. The logic supporting the GUI is referred to as the user services. Another important function of the presentation services tier is to link the *user services* logic to the business services. The presentation services tier is depicted in Figure 8.2.

Functions Of The Presentation Services Tier

Although the primary function of the presentation services tier is to manage the user and business services, this tier also performs several other important functions. These include controlling task flow, facilitating the propagation of events, providing user assistance, and managing state.

➤ **Managing User And Business Services** The presentation services tier links the different user services with the appropriate business services. User services direct the flow of data and information between the business services and the user interface.

➤ **Controlling Task Flow** An important function of the presentation services is to ensure that tasks do not occur out of context and that a specific sequence of operations will not violate the business rules. You

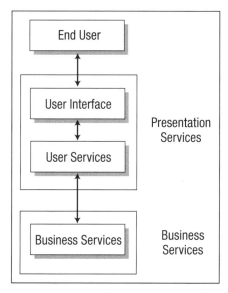

Figure 8.2 The logical structure of presentation services.

can accomplish this by designing the user interface so that the user is only allowed to perform tasks that are appropriate for the given situation or context. For example, hiding or disabling controls constrains the user from inadvertently performing inappropriate actions.

➤ **Facilitating Event Propagation** As the user interacts with the application, events will be triggered. This is usually the result of a specific user interaction with the user interface. However, events can also be triggered as a result of a requested business service operation. Depending on the current state of the application and the context of the user action, the presentation services tier may respond to events differently. User services facilities determine the meaning of the event and initiate the appropriate course of action.

➤ **Providing User Assistance** A key aspect of user interface design is to ensure that the user can get help when he or she encounters difficulty. Two mechanisms are usually used to provide these facilities: online help and intelligent assistants. In addition, tooltips and the status bar can provide valuable user feedback that guides the user along. These facilities are described in more detail later in this chapter.

➤ **Managing State** The presentation services tier may need to maintain the state of the different activities being performed by the user as well as the state of the operations performed by the different business services. Furthermore, this state information may need to persist from one invocation of the application to the next. By doing this, you can restore the application to the state it was in when last used. Therefore, the application is able to finish any pending asynchronous request processing for business services that may not have completed the last time the application was run. Maintaining state information also makes it possible to restore a user's personal preferences.

Presentation Services Tier Implementation Considerations

As described in Chapter 5, where the presentation services tier was introduced, there are two primary ways of implementing and, hence, distributing this tier:

➤ **A Native User Interface** This method relies on user interface services provided by the underlying operating system. In Windows, native user interfaces use the Microsoft Win32 API. A Win32-based user interface is usually deployed as an application (EXE file) that runs on the client platform. Using a native user interface, you can provide a robust interface with rich functionality.

➤ **A Web-Based User Interface**   This method uses an Internet browser to deliver the presentation services for an application. Web-based user interfaces are typically based on HTML and deployed as a Web page, which can be rendered on any operating system by a Web browser.

Of course, it's also possible to develop presentation services based on a combination of both technologies.

You have several considerations to evaluate when you start to determine how to implement the presentation services. These include the following:

➤ **Target Audience And Environment**   The target audience and the capabilities of the client systems that the target audience will use are critical factors for determining the presentation technology. For example, if the only users for the application will be company employees accessing the application via the corporate network, you can make a number of assumptions, and the number of unknowns is fairly limited. You'll know the operating systems involved and whether the company has standardized on a particular Web browser. On the other hand, it's very difficult to limit the unknowns with Web-based applications. This type of application can be used by thousands of users who might access it using a number of different browsers.

➤ **Application Model**   The application model will help determine the implementation strategy for the presentation services tier. For example, will the application use a single document interface (SDI) window or does it require multiple-document interface (MDI) windows because it supports multiple documents?

➤ **Desired Richness**   If your target audience demands the richness of the native user interface, such as menu bars, toolbars, and direct manipulation, your only option might be to implement the presentation services tier with a native user interface such as Win32. Web-based applications provide a different user interface experience from the classical desktop application. Although a number of familiar desktop user interface controls and behaviors can be emulated in Web-based applications, sometimes this is not easily accomplished.

➤ **User Interface Objects**   In addition to the desired richness, you need to determine what views are required to present the user interface objects. For example, will there be outlines, text, folders, tables, pictures, graphs, or even animations? The level of support required will influence what presentation services tier technology is used.

➤ **Control Facilities**   Command buttons, menus, and direct manipulation of objects are all different types of control facilities that the user might use. If the user must supply input, how will it be entered and validated? If message and dialog sequences are needed, how will they be done? All these aspects of the interface will also influence what presentation services tier technology is used.

➤ **Development Effort**   You'll also want to consider what development tools and technologies are available to build the user interface. A number of tools are available, and the list is continually growing. However, familiarity with the tool and its ease of use are just as important as having the tool. If the team must learn a new tool, this must be factored into the development schedule.

➤ **Deployment And Maintenance**   Deployment and maintenance also enter into the decision. If you plan on frequently updating the presentation services tier, minimizing the number of pieces that must be installed on the client seems desirable. Likewise, technologies that support the automatic downloading of updated components eliminates the need for explicitly installing software updates. However, if most clients access the application using a slow link, requiring frequent downloads of application components will be unacceptable. You'll need to balance all these factors when choosing your design.

Presentation Services Tier Technologies

A number of different technologies exist for creating the presentation services tier. They are summarized here:

➤ **Native**   Native presentation services tiers can be written in any language that supports COM. Client systems of the target audience must be running an operating system that supports COM. Win32 is such an environment, and development languages such as Visual Basic and Visual C++ can be used to produce native user interfaces.

The major advantage of native user interfaces is that they support a rich set of features, and powerful development tools are usually available to create the software. However, deployment is usually an issue. Native interface components must be manually downloaded and installed on the target system. Installation can be simplified by using an automated procedure.

➤ **Static HTML**   Static HTML is a Web-based technology, and it supports the largest target audience of Web users, because virtually all Web browsers support at least the basic features of HTML. Deployment issues for static HTML are minimal because the browser on the client downloads the HTML objects and renders them on the client. However, static HTML is limited to static content, which restricts the capabilities of the application.

➤ **Active Server Pages**   Active Server Pages (ASP) is a Web-based technology that supports a large target audience of Web users. ASP enables dynamic content of Web pages by combining HTML with a scripting language. Because script processing occurs on the server, the client sees no difference between a static HTML page and an ASP page.

The Active Server object model exposes an object model that allows you to gather data that a user entered into a form, output an HTML response to a browser's request, and maintain session and application-level state.

Another feature of ASP is that the server script can determine the capabilities of the target browser. Therefore, if certain features are available in the browser, the server is able to exploit them. Deployment issues are minimal with ASP because all the important activity takes place on the server.

➤ **Client-Side Scripting**   Client-side scripting is a Web-based technology that supports most Web users. Like ASP, client-side scripting enables dynamic content of Web pages by combining HTML with a scripting language. However, because the script is processed on the client, the client must have a scripting engine that can process the script lines in the Web page.

➤ **Java Applets**   Another Web-based technology that supports most Web users is Java applets. However, in order to run a Java applet, the Java Virtual Machine must be installed on the client. Furthermore, the version of the Java Virtual Machine must support the features you've used in the Java applet. The Java language is used to develop a Java applet.

➤ **ActiveX Controls**   ActiveX is another Web-based technology, but it only supports some Web users. In order to use an ActiveX control, the browser must support ActiveX functionality. Some browsers provide native support for this; other browsers achieve it by using a plug-in. Deployment is not an issue, because the browser automatically downloads controls as they are needed. However, the operating environment for ActiveX is restricted to the Win32 platform.

User Interface Design Guidelines

A well-designed user interface is a user-centric interface that's built around the users and the tasks they will perform. In general, a well-designed interface has the following features:

➤ Supports user initiation of actions

➤ Supports user customization of the interface

➤ Supports an interactive and modeless environment

➤ Supports direct manipulation

➤ Uses familiar, appropriate metaphors

➤ Is internally consistent

When you design the user interface, you'll want to consider the following areas:

➤ Business requirements

➤ Standards

➤ Navigation and control

➤ User assistance

➤ Directness

➤ Consistency

➤ Forgiveness

➤ Feedback

➤ Aesthetics

➤ Simplicity

 An overall design goal of the user interface is to create an interface that's both useful and elegant. The user interface should empower the user to exploit the capabilities of the application.

Business Requirements

When designing a user interface, start by checking the business requirements for any special requirements that will impact the user interface. This could include but is certainly not limited to the following items:

➤ Target audience

➤ Technology requirements

➤ Accessibility requirements

➤ Internationalization requirements

Standards

You'll also want to incorporate any standards into your user interface design. This will include existing standards and practices of the business as well as standards of the operating system environment.

For example, the company may have standards for the screen layout and use of function keys. Similarly, if you're developing a Windows 95 application, it should look like a Windows 95 application. Remember the case study involving Action Aerospace in Chapter 4? Users who were familiar with the Windows 95 environment had a difficult time using the mainframe-oriented user interface in the pilot version of the Timecard application.

Navigation And Control

The graphical user interface introduced a new paradigm for how a user interacts with an application. In particular, the control of the application shifted from the program itself to the user. Rather than always assuming a *reactive* role to the program operations, the user now plays an *active* role and controls the application. Therefore, when you design your user interface, remember that the user must feel in control of the application.

Part of feeling in control means that the user is able to "personalize" the user interface. Your software should allow the user to specify colors, fonts, and other preferences. For initial colors, follow the standard Windows guidelines and make special considerations for color blindness. Another aspect of putting the user in control means that the software is highly interactive and as responsive as possible.

Finally, the concept of control requires you to provide the user with multiple ways to accomplish the same task. This allows the user to choose the method with which he or she is most comfortable.

Different users think and work in different ways. Some prefer menus; others prefer buttons and toolbars. Your application needs to accommodate all users by supporting all the standard ways of doing things.

Shortcut keys, also known as *accelerator* keys, provide a convenient way to invoke a task with a single keystroke. Shortcut keys are usually a combination of the Ctrl key and a letter or one of the function keys (F1 through F12).

By definition, shortcut keys provide an alternate way of accessing application functionality. Therefore, don't use a shortcut key as the only way to perform a specific operation.

 If you have a command button for a task, you should also have a shortcut key for that command button. You should also have a menu item for the same task and, if appropriate, a toolbar button. You should also have a status bar that indicates which task will be performed in response to any of these actions as well as a Help file topic that provides further information.

User Assistance

Online user assistance is an important part of the user interface, so you'll want to incorporate it into your design. A variety of mechanisms are available, ranging from the automatic displaying of information based on the current context to the explicit requesting of assistance initiated by user action.

Online Help

The two types of online help are contextual help and task help. *Contextual help*, also referred to as *context-sensitive help*, provides information about the object with which the user is interacting. Contextual help takes into consideration the context of the activity the user is currently performing. Contextual help tries to answer questions such as "What is this?" and "Why should I use this?".

The What's This? command provides contextual help. This command can be accessed from the following areas of a program:

➤ The Help drop-down menu of a primary window

➤ A button on a toolbar

➤ A button on a title bar of a secondary window

➤ A pop-up menu for an object

Task help, on the other hand, provides an explanation to the user on how to accomplish specific tasks or activities. It can involve a number of procedures. Task help is presented in task Help topic windows.

 When you provide a Help menu in the menu bar, make the Help menu the last item in the list.

ToolTips

ToolTips are small pop-up windows that display the name of a control when the control has no text label. ToolTips are often used for toolbar buttons that have no graphic labels, but they can be used for any control. ToolTips provide a form of contextual user assistance.

A ToolTip should display after the pointing device remains over the control for a short period of time. The ToolTip should continue to display until the user clicks on the control or moves off it. If the user moves to another control, the short timeout period should be ignored and the new ToolTip displayed immediately.

Status Bars

The *status bar*, located on the bottom edge of the window, can be used for displaying messages, progress indicators, and state information. Because the status bar might not be near the area of user activity, messages displayed in the status bar may sometimes go unnoticed. For this reason, use the status bar as a supplemental means of providing user assistance. The status bar provides another form of contextual user assistance.

Wizards

A *wizard* is a series of pages displayed in a secondary window that helps a user complete a task. The pages may request the user to supply data that's then used to complete the task.

Wizards usually have four command buttons that allow you to navigate through the wizard:

➤ **Back**   Returns to the previous page

➤ **Next**   Moves to the next page

➤ **Finish**   Applies all the setting from all the pages and completes the task

➤ **Cancel**   Discards any user-supplied settings, terminates the process, and closes the wizard window

Directness

Your design should allow users to directly manipulate software representations of information. Furthermore, you'll want to provide feedback so users can see how their actions affect objects on the screen.

A primary mechanism for providing directness is using familiar metaphors to direct the users with their tasks. Metaphors give the user a cognitive bridge by allowing them to recognize an object with which they are already familiar. Examples of metaphors include the Windows folders, the Recycle Bin, and the Windows desktop itself.

Consistency

Consistency provides a sense of stability and makes the user interface familiar and predictable. It allows users to focus on the task at hand rather than learning new interactions. Consistency allows the user to take their current knowledge and apply it to your application.

Consistency in the user interface applies to the naming of commands, the visual presentation of information, and the operational behavior. To incorporate consistency fully into your design, you'll need to account for it at three different levels:

➤ Consistency within the product

➤ Consistency within the operating environment

➤ Consistency with metaphors

Forgiveness

Even with a well-designed interface, users can make mistakes. Some of these may be accidental, such as hitting the wrong key. Others may be the result of a bad decision. In either case, an effective interface design will allow for such errors and make it easy for the user to recover.

Another important aspect of the interface design is to avoid giving the user the option of making a potentially dangerous mistake. If a particular task should not be performed in the current context, the user should not have access to a button that invokes the task.

Remember, users like to explore and will often experiment with the interface, learning by trial and error. A well-designed interface will support this.

Feedback

Nothing is more frustrating to a user than a dead screen. Therefore, you'll want to supply ample feedback so that the user has a sense of what the application is doing. Providing detailed feedback reinforces the feeling that the application is responding the way the user intended. Feedback might be provided by a pointer change or status bar message, or it may require displaying a message in another window. The "flying pages" display for the Copy command is an example of effective user feedback.

Aesthetics

The visual design is also an important aspect of the user interface. Visual attributes of objects provide important cues to the object's behavior. In addition, the visual design creates an impression of the entire application. You might want to consult with a graphics designer to help with this part of the design.

Simplicity

Although the interface must provide access to all the application functionality, it must also be simple, easy to learn, and easy to use. One way of achieving simplicity is to keep the presentation of information to a minimum. Consider using *progressive disclosure* by hiding information and not displaying it until it's appropriate. This reduces the amount of information the user is required to process.

Common Mistakes

In the September 1995 issue of *Microsoft Developer Network News,* Tandy Trower describes the "Top 10 List" of major mistakes developers make when designing user interfaces:

10. **Using an ellipsis for every menu command that results in a window**
    If the command requires the user to specify or confirm any parameters in order to complete a task, you should use an ellipsis. However, if no parameters are required to complete the command—because the command has no parameters or they were already specified before selecting the command—you should not use an ellipsis.

9. **Secondary windows appearing in the taskbar**   Taskbar entries are only for primary windows. Titles for dialog boxes, message boxes, and property sheets should never have entries in the taskbar.

8. **Using Ok instead of OK**   Both letters should be capitalized.

7. **Including icons in title bars of secondary windows**   Icons should appear only in the title bars of primary windows.

6. **Displaying read-only information as static text or disabled text**
    Read-only information should be displayed in a normal text box with the background matching the background of the secondary window.

5. **Using Exit instead of Close**   Exit implies quitting a process. Close means removing a window.

4. **Using incorrect title bar icon and text**   In the title bar, you have to define what its window represents. If it's a data object, use the icon defined for the data file type. If it's an application that has no data files,

use the icon for the application. In multiple-document interface (MDI) applications, the application's icon typically appears in the title bar of the parent window, whereas the data file's icon appears in the title bar of the child's window. When you've determined the title bar icon, you can then determine the title text. The first name in the title bar corresponds to the icon you used. If it's a data file icon, the name of the data file should be the first name in the title text, optionally followed by the application's name.

3. **Supporting multiple instances**   Sometimes, rather than always creating another instance of a window, it's better to first check whether an instance of the window is already open, and if it is, activate that window. This is often less confusing to users.

2. **Failing to include pop-up menus for title bar icons**   The icon in the title bar is an access point to the commands of that icon. Your application should support right-clicking the icon to bring up a pop-up menu that contains commands for the object represented by that icon. Right-clicking anywhere else in the title bar should bring up the pop-up menu for the window.

1. **Failing to register**   Failing to register your file types, primary verbs, OLE information, and icons will certainly make your application's user interface seem poorly integrated with Windows.

Design, Prototype, Test, Repeat

Designing an effective user interface involves four important steps:

➤ Design

➤ Prototype

➤ Test

➤ Repeat

This process is depicted in Figure 8.3.

The first step in designing a user interface is to prepare a *design*. To do this, you'll want to factor in the requirements and develop a design that's suitable for the target audience. Base your design on the conceptual model of the tasks to be performed. Use metaphors that will enable the user to carry out those tasks.

After the design is complete, you'll want to build a *prototype* of your design. By doing this, you create an effective means of communicating your design to others. Prototyping also helps you to better understand your design, and it

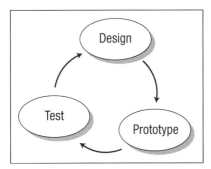

Figure 8.3   The user interface design process.

provides a good mechanism for others to effectively provide feedback to you. At this point, keep the prototype independent of the application so you're not waiting for any application code to test your prototype.

Testing the design allows the user to get involved with the design process. At this point, the testing focus is on the *usability* of the design. In other words, you want to determine how well the design fits user needs and expectations.

Once you've completed testing, you can begin the refinement process. In other words, *repeat* the process, incorporating user feedback into the design. As the prototype evolves, you may want to start introducing actual application components into your prototype.

Windows, Menus, And Controls

Users will view data and interact with the application through windows. Windows provide the fundamental framework of the user interface. By incorporating Windows conventions and guidelines into your design, you'll allow users to focus on the tasks rather than learning the nuances of a new user interface. Some of these conventions are described in the following sections.

Primary Windows

The *primary window* is the main window in which most viewing and editing activity takes place. A primary window consists of the following components:

➤ A frame or border that surrounds the window

➤ A title bar that identifies what's being viewed in the window

➤ Scrollbars (if the viewable content exceeds the current size of the window)

➤ A menu bar

➤ Toolbars

➤ A status bar

Secondary Windows

In addition to the primary window, you can also use multiple *secondary windows*. These windows supplement the primary window, allowing users to specify parameters or options or providing more specific details about the objects in the primary window.

Secondary windows are often used for the following tasks:

➤ Validating input

➤ Displaying property sheets

➤ Displaying dialog boxes

➤ Displaying message boxes

➤ Displaying wizards

Modeless And Modal Windows

A secondary window can be either modal or modeless. A *modeless* secondary window allows the user to switch between it and other windows, including other secondary windows or primary windows.

A *modal* secondary window requires the user to complete all activity within the window and close it before switching to another window. A secondary window can be modal with respect to the application, or it can be modal with respect to the system.

Remember that an important aspect of the user interface is that the user should feel in control of the application. Modal secondary windows restrict the user, so you'll want to carefully consider when you should use them.

Validation Of Input

Secondary windows can be used to validate user input. In general, it's best to validate data as soon as it's entered so the user can correct any errors. A number of techniques can be used to enforce entering only valid data. For example, you might use field masks or controls that limit the input to only valid choices.

A message box displayed in a secondary window can guide the user if he or she encounters difficulty supplying a valid data item.

Property Sheets

A *property sheet* is a modeless secondary window that displays the user-accessible properties of an object. It's displayed when the user chooses the Properties command for the object. The property sheet allows the user to view and edit the object properties. Some of the properties displayed in the property sheet may be read-only. Although they can be viewed, the user will not be able to edit read-only properties.

 Property sheets usually have three command buttons:

➤ **OK**   This button applies all pending changes and closes the property sheet window.

➤ **Apply**   This button applies all pending changes but leaves the property sheet window open.

➤ **Cancel**   This button discards any pending changes and closes the property sheet window.

Dialog Boxes

A *dialog box* provides a mechanism for the exchange of information between the user and the application. Dialog boxes are often used to obtain additional information from the user in order to complete an operation. A dialog box usually contains an OK button as well as a Cancel button. The OK button applies the values and closes the window. The Cancel button ignores any changes made, closes the window, and cancels the operation that invoked the dialog box.

 When you create a dialog box, orient the controls in the way people read information. This may vary from country to country.

Common Dialog Boxes

In addition to creating your own customized dialog boxes, you may want to utilize some of the common dialog boxes used by most Windows applications. Doing so will maintain a level of consistency between your application and the Windows environment. This also allows you to easily provide robustness to your user interface.

Common dialog boxes include the following:

➤ Open dialog box

➤ Save As dialog box

➤ Find And Replace dialog box

➤ Print dialog box

➤ Print Setup dialog box

➤ Page Setup dialog box

➤ Font dialog box

➤ Color dialog box

Menus

A *menu* provides a list of commands available to the user. By supplying a list of visible commands from which to choose, you assist the user by not forcing him or her to remember command names and syntax.

The *menu bar* is the most common type of menu. It's displayed across the top of a window, beneath the title bar, and provides a set of menu titles, each of which produces a drop-down menu of items or choices.

Pop-up menus provide an effective way to access the commands for a particular object. Pop-up menus are displayed on demand at the location of the mouse pointer, and because they refer to a specific object in its immediate context, the number of commands displayed for the user is limited to only relevant items.

Controls

Controls are graphic objects that represent the properties or operations of other objects. Some controls are used to initiate an operation. Other controls are used to enter, view, and edit data values. Some of the standard controls include the following:

➤ Command buttons

➤ Menu buttons

➤ Option buttons

➤ Checkboxes

➤ List boxes

➤ Text fields

Windows Common Controls

In addition to the standard types of controls, Windows also provides a set of more advanced controls. These controls are used throughout Windows, and they're packaged so you can easily incorporate them into your user interface. These controls are referred to as the *Windows Common Controls* and include the following:

➤ Animation control

➤ Image list control

➤ List view control

➤ Progress bar control

➤ Rich text box control

➤ Slider control

➤ Status bar control

➤ Tabstrip control

➤ Toolbar control

➤ Tree view control

➤ Updown control

Internationalization

Although all applications are not going to be globally deployed, there are a number of conventions that, if followed, facilitate the task of adapting your application to another language. This will require localizing the user interface to the target environment.

In her book *Developing International Software for Windows 95 and Windows NT*, Nadine Kano identifies several important steps for developing a user interface that can be easily localized:

➤ Put all native language localizable elements in one or more resource files.

➤ Link the resources to the program executable or put them in a DLL.

➤ Translate text elements and resize dialog boxes using localization tools.

➤ Test the localized program and change the localized files if necessary.

➤ Add, delete, or change all localizable elements in the native language resources.

➤ Merge the changes into localized resources.

Practice Questions

Question 1

> Which of the following are functions of the presentation services tier? [Check all correct answers]
>
> ❑ a. Providing user assistance
>
> ❑ b. Linking the graphical user interface to the business logic
>
> ❑ c. Validating input data
>
> ❑ d. Binding controls on a form to elements in a database

Answers a, b, and c are correct. In a three-tier model, the presentation services tier is isolated from the physical structure of the data store. Therefore, controls on a form would not be bound to elements in a database. The presentation services tier obtains data for controls by requesting it from the business services or the data services tiers.

Question 2

> What's the recommended order for laying out the controls for a dialog box?
>
> ⭕ a. Left to right
>
> ⭕ b. Top to bottom
>
> ⭕ c. Across the top first, then continue down the right edge
>
> ⭕ d. In the way people read information

Answer d is correct. The controls should be oriented in the same way people read information. This may vary from country to country. This question is tricky because the correct answer might not even be considered as viable as the other possible choices.

Question 3

> If you include a Help button in a group of buttons, which one should it be?
>
> ○ a. The first button in the group
>
> ○ b. The last button in the group
>
> ○ c. The next-to-last button in the group
>
> ○ d. Help should be supplied from a menu rather than from a button

Answer b is correct. The convention is to make the Help button the last button in the group.

Question 4

> What's the recommended way of presenting read-only data in a user interface?
>
> ○ a. In a label
>
> ○ b. In a disabled text box
>
> ○ c. In a normal text box
>
> ○ d. In a normal text box that's labeled "Read Only"

Answer c is correct. Read-only text should be displayed in a normal text box . The background of the text box should match the secondary window background.

Question 5

> Which of the following items are characteristics of a wizard? [Check all correct answers]
>
> ❑ a. Displayed in a primary window
>
> ❑ b. Displayed in a secondary window
>
> ❑ c. Includes a Quit button
>
> ❑ d. Usually consists of multiple pages

Answers b and d are correct. Wizards are displayed in a series of multiple pages displayed in a secondary window. Wizards display a Cancel button rather than a Quit button.

Question 6

What are the two categories of online user assistance?

○ a. Context oriented and task oriented

○ b. Help files and wizards

○ c. Online and offline

○ d. Help files and ToolTips

Answer a is correct. Online user assistance is either context oriented or task oriented. Help files and wizards are types of task-oriented assistance. ToolTips are context-oriented assistance.

Need To Know More?

 Kano, Nadine. *Developing International Software for Windows 95 and Windows NT*. Redmond, WA: Microsoft Press, 1996. ISBN 1-57231-311-0. This book presents a very thorough description of the issues related to developing and distributing software applications for international use. Chapter 4, "Preparing the User Interface for Localization," provides detailed information on the steps for preparing an application for internationalization. This documentation is also available on the Microsoft Developer Network Library.

 Microsoft Professional Reference. *The Windows Interface Guidelines for Software Design*. Redmond, WA: Microsoft Press, 1995. ISBN 1-55615-679-0. This book is the bible for designing Windows user interfaces. This online documentation is also available on the Microsoft Developer Network Library.

 Trower, Tandy. "The Human Factor: The Top 10 Windows 95 User Interface Design Errors." *Microsoft Developer Network News*, September 1995. This article discusses user interface design and identifies the ten most common errors that constitute poor design. This article is also available on the Microsoft Developer Network Library.

Deriving The Physical Design

Terms you'll need to understand:

- √ Physical design
- √ Encapsulation
- √ In-process component
- √ Out-of-process component
- √ Interface
- √ Class
- √ Collection
- √ Native database interface
- √ ODBC
- √ DAO
- √ RDO
- √ OLE DB
- √ ADO
- √ Universal storage
- √ Universal Data Access (UDA)
- √ Microsoft Data Access Components (MDAC)

Techniques you'll need to master:

- √ Evaluating how different physical designs impact performance, maintainability, extensibility, availability, scalability, and security
- √ Describing a methodology for performance tuning
- √ Describing the steps for designing a component
- √ Describing the difference between an in-process component and an out-of-process component
- √ Describing the different data access technologies
- √ Describing how to encapsulate access to a database within an object

235

After a solution architecture has been determined and the logical design is complete, the physical design process begins. The physical design identifies the physical pieces that will be implemented to support the logical design. The physical design also finalizes the deployment topology by identifying the systems that will provide the execution environment for the different pieces. The physical design will affect many important aspects of the application—especially performance.

CASE STUDY: Sizzling Semiconductors

Company Background

Sizzling Semiconductors is a medium-size company that produces specialized microprocessors. The company started only five years ago, but it has rapidly grown. It now has three different facilities where semiconductors are manufactured and two more are being planned. The company is continually in the process of expanding.

However, like all growing businesses, the company has a few problems. One of these problems is that the marketing and sales groups have come under fire recently because the company has been unable to fulfill many of the orders according to schedule.

The Situation

Bob, a senior marketing person explains, "We never seem to know what the real status is with the current bookings and order backlog. We also never quite know what the manufacturing schedule is, so we end up accepting new orders, which we can't fill by the promised date.

"You would think there would be a simple way to get this kind of information, but there isn't. We have two different systems to deal with. One is the order system and one is the manufacturing system. We have to check both systems to get the data we need. And it gets even worse. Because manufacturing is done at three different locations, each location maintains its own manufacturing database. The data doesn't get rolled into the corporate manufacturing system until the end of the day."

Larry, the Software Development Manager, explains, "All the software we use has been developed in-house. When the company was small, this was a very practical way to go. But as we started to grow, it has been difficult to keep up with all the user requirements. We're currently evaluating a major change in all our software, but in the meantime, there are a number of critical issues that must be addressed."

In order to provide the marketing and sales groups with the data they need to make more informed decisions, the information technology group has developed an application for them to use. This is the BacklogAndBookings application.

The BacklogAndBookings Application: Version 1

The BacklogAndBookings application is written in Microsoft Access. Version 1 of the application imports data from the production systems and creates local tables. This has all been automated within the application, so it's a relatively easy operation for the end users. With all the relevant data stored in local tables, there's no longer a need to go out to different systems to look up information.

The application consists of a simple menu as well as several reports that display the most useful data on a single page. Because some of the marketing reps were already familiar with Access, it was an assumption from the start that some of the power users would develop their own queries. Figure 9.1 shows version 1 of the application.

Until recently, only two users have been working with the application. Each keeps a copy of the application on his laptop computer. The laptops are connected to the local area network. Although it takes several minutes to download the data and import it into the Access database tables, the solution has worked adequately. Because of the initial favorable response to the BacklogAndBookings application, more users are starting to try it out.

User Problems

As more users began to use the application, several problems surfaced. Each user starts the day by downloading the necessary data files. This occurs every morning when network traffic is already heavy. The system administrator has

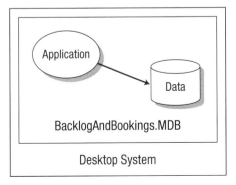

Figure 9.1   Version 1 of BacklogAndBookings.

noticed the additional network load and discussed the situation with the developers to see what, if anything, could be done. Other network users who are printing reports and accessing mail have complained that the system is slow.

Network traffic is not the only area that has been affected. With additional users accessing the production files to download data, performance on the production system has suffered.

A third consequence is that because each user maintains his own snapshot of the production data, identical reports may not produce the same results. Recently at a meeting, there was great confusion over what the actual backlog was for a certain product because two different salespeople had produced reports with conflicting data. It turned out that the two different reports were based on different snapshots, taken 30 minutes apart. A substantial order had not been included in the first snapshot.

Finally, some of the traveling sales force have started to use the application. On Monday, these sales folks download the data to their laptops at the home office. Then they hit the road for a week. Each night they dial into the local network using a Remote Access Service (RAS) line planning to download a new set of data. Unfortunately, the results have been disastrous. Gary, one of the salesmen who actually got a download to complete, remarked, "It took me at least three hours to download the new data. If I had been in my office, that operation would have only taken a few minutes."

The BacklogAndBookings Application: Version 2

To address some of these problems, the IT group proposed a modification to the existing application that could be implemented rather quickly. The version 1 application, which is based on local tables, would be split into a client side and a server side. The client side would contain all the queries, forms, and reports as well as some local data. The server side would be another Access database containing just the data tables that are populated from the production system. Each client will link to these tables rather than maintaining a local copy.

This is a configuration that Access supports, and the conversion should be rather simple. Also, there are several advantages to this solution:

➤ Only one snapshot of the production data would be taken to populate the data tables rather than each user taking his or her own snapshot.

➤ Taking only one snapshot would reduce the network traffic and ease the burden on the production system.

➤ Preparing the snapshot could be included as part of the standard operational procedures and would not be a task that each user has to perform.

➤ All the reports would be consistent because they're based on the same data.

➤ Considerably less data would be loaded on each laptop.

Figure 9.2 shows version 2 of the application.

For the users on the local network, the version 2 solution worked reasonably well. However, all of them complained that it took a lot longer to create reports, but they all agreed it was preferable to dealing with reloading the data every day.

For the remote users accessing the system over the RAS lines, the situation was quite different. They could certainly access the data and view it directly from the tables, but it was impossible to create a report. The system would begin working on the report and never complete.

Some simple queries would work, but they took a very long time. What's more, none of the queries created by two of the power users worked.

The developer who created the solution was rather puzzled, because he had not anticipated these kinds of problems with a client/server configuration. The IT manager has called you in for some expert advice on what's causing these problems.

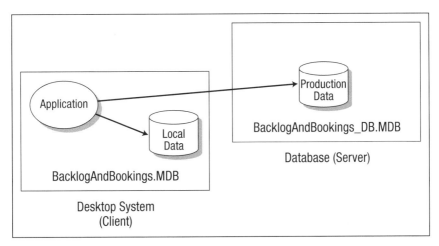

Figure 9.2   Version 2 of BacklogAndBookings.

Your Analysis

Although the version 2 configuration works reasonably well over the local network, it's virtually unusable over a dial-up line. Your analysis of the application soon revealed what's wrong.

The reports used in the BacklogAndBookings application were driven by some rather complex queries. The queries were based on multiple table joins. Although the final result set usually consisted of only several hundred rows, the join operations required that all the rows in two of the tables be accessed. This required accessing several hundred thousand rows of data.

Because of the physical configuration of the application, all this processing must occur on the client system. Although the Access application has been split into two pieces, the server piece is really no more than a shared file. No computational processing takes place on the server. As a result, all the records must be transferred across the network to the client where they can be processed. Although this is slow on the local area network, it does work. However, on the dial-up connections using RAS, the data rates are considerably slower than the LAN. Transferring the volume of data required by the queries is simply not feasible.

You set up a meeting to present your findings and discuss some alternatives that might be considered. Your alternatives will retain some of the strengths of version 2—namely, the concept of a single shared database. However, the new version must limit the amount of network traffic so that the system can be used via a dial-up line.

The BacklogAndBookings Application: Version 3

At your meeting you discuss what the major requirements are for version 3 of the BacklogAndBookings application. In particular, you want to:

➤ Minimize network traffic

➤ Shift processing from the client application to the server

There are several ways of accomplishing this, but your suggestion is to retain the client application as is. However, you will replace the server side, currently an MDB file containing database tables, with Microsoft SQL Server. Rather than linking to an Access database, the client application will now link to tables in a SQL Server database.

The major reason for doing this is to shift the processing of the queries from the client application to the database server. You explain your reasoning.

"What happens now is that when a query is executed, all the processing takes place on the client system. This is because the Access database on the server is really only a shared file. No processing can take place on the server. In order to execute a query, all the data must be transferred across the network to the client system.

"SQL Server, on the other hand, is capable of processing data on the server system. When the client sends SQL Server a query, the query can be executed directly on the server. The result set still needs to be transferred across the network to the client, but all the table joins will take place on the server. This will eliminate 90 percent of the network traffic that is required by version 2 of the application."

There is a short discussion with the developers. Mary points out that the last place she worked had experienced similar problems. "Even after they started using a SQL Server database, the problems didn't go away. They found out that the queries were still being processed by the client application."

You explain that this can happen, and it usually occurs when the query contains items that can only be determined by the client application. For example, if the query contained an expression that called a function in the client application, it is most likely that the entire query would need to be processed on the client.

However, you point out that you have already looked at the BacklogAndBookings application, and don't anticipate such problems. "Using the Upsizing Wizard, we should be able to convert the data tables to SQL Server rather quickly, and then we can try this out."

Larry, the Software Development manager, decides to engage your services to help them create version 3 of the application. She asks if you can start immediately. As you head back to your office, you make a mental note to stop by the office supply store and purchase some blank invoice forms.

Evaluating The Physical Design

The physical design and implementation of the BacklogAndBookings application at Sizzling Semiconductors greatly affects the application performance and maintainability. Although version 2 of the application improved the maintainability by not requiring each user to download new data on a regular basis, it did nothing to improve performance.

Based on a rather simple logical design of multiple clients accessing a single back-end database, the solution showed great promise and appeared quite feasible. However, the physical design chosen to implement the logical model resulted in the failure of the application to meet expectations.

 A common performance bottleneck in many database applications occurs when the application must join multiple database tables to produce a result set, and the join requires transferring all the data across a network to the client where the join can be performed. This bottleneck can be addressed by shifting the processing from the client system to the server system and returning only the result set across the network. Using a stored procedure on the database server might optimize this even further. Processing stored procedures is more efficient than processing a SQL statement because some of the initial processing has already been completed for a stored procedure.

The physical design of your application determines the physical implementation of your logical design. For example, you'll have a logical design consisting of presentation, business, and data service layers. The physical design determines how you create these services in code modules. From the source code modules comes the physical components that make up the application.

In addition to physically organizing the source code itself, physical design also encompasses the deployment topology aspects discussed in Chapter 5. Many options are available for distributing the application components across system hardware.

Before finalizing the physical design, you'll want to assess the potential impact of the design on the major characteristics of your application. These include the following:

➤ Performance

➤ Maintainability

➤ Extensibility

➤ Availability

➤ Scalability

➤ Security

Performance

Performance is perhaps one of the most critical characteristics of an application. This is especially true for interactive applications where a user is waiting for a response. However, it's also true for batch applications—especially batch applications that are driven by a deadline. Consider, for example, an application that analyzes the daily sales data for all the regional stores. This application runs every night and determines the current inventory in stock at each store. It then submits a shipping order to the warehouse so low inventory items can be replenished with the morning shipment. If this application doesn't complete in time, the items don't get shipped, and the business faces lost sales revenue.

Many performance complaints from the user community are actually based on perceived performance. These tend to be more qualitative than quantitative and can often be addressed by giving the impression that the application is "doing something." The physical implementation of your application will need to ensure good perceived performance.

Using splash screens and progress meters are two of the techniques used to improve perceived performance. In addition, the overhead processing required by many tasks is often less noticeable when the tasks are performed during the initialization processing at application startup. For example, you may decide to open a form once and keep it hidden, rather than opening and closing it every time it is needed.

However, to accurately assess performance, you'll also need to deal with real performance as well as perceived performance issues. In order to determine real performance, you'll need some tangible metrics that can quantitatively be used to characterize performance information and compare different configurations.

Performance analysis and tuning requires a well-defined methodology as well as a consistent, repeatable workload. In order to effectively deal with performance issues, you must know the following information:

➤ What the performance goals are

➤ What metrics you can use to measure the current performance

➤ What the current performance is, based on those metrics

➤ What you specifically change to alter performance

➤ How those changes affect the performance metrics

Performance tuning is an iterative process. You'll probably only see the performance improvements over time. Also, keep in mind that the actual production workload may be changing over time. Therefore, you'll want to track and monitor performance on a regular basis.

Finally, remember that total system performance is measured end to end. To achieve optimal end-to-end performance, you may have to analyze performance characteristics of individual components to determine where the bottleneck actually is. That way, you can focus on changes that will have the most impact.

Maintainability And Extensibility

An application is rarely completed with the release of version 1. In fact, the concept of *versioned releases* means that the application will evolve and be enhanced. A well-designed application implies that changes and enhancements can be easily made.

Modularity is the key to maintainability and extensibility. By partitioning the application into distinct tiers, changes can be made to one tier without affecting the other tiers. Furthermore, by building the tiers out of components, you can change and upgrade individual components without requiring other application changes.

Finally, there's no substitute for good design. Although components can be easily changed, many applications can anticipate design changes by providing a mechanism for easily making anticipated changes. For example, rather than writing certain business rules directly in the source code, the design might be based on accessing them from a database table. The code to handle this would undoubtedly be more complex but the additional flexibility might be well worth the effort.

Rather than hard-coding parameter values into an application, it might be possible to maintain parameter settings in a database table or entries in the Registry. This simplifies the task of changing these parameters.

Availability

A key concept of availability is *redundancy*. Having a backup system ready to take over when the primary system experiences a failure is a proven strategy for improving availability. Clustered systems are often used to provide this capability.

Scalability

A key concept of scalability is *modularity*. As the processing load grows, additional systems can be deployed to handle the load. Having a modularized design provides the flexibility for deploying additional components on the new system.

Systems, Clusters, CPUs, Processes, And Threads

As you evaluate the various hardware options for your physical design, it's a good idea to review some of the key concepts you'll need to understand in order to make your decision.

A *system* refers to a particular piece of computer hardware that's capable of running an application. A system has physical memory resources as well as a central processing unit (CPU), which is used to execute the instructions of the application. Some systems have multiple CPUs. This enables them to process multiple instructions at the same time.

When you get ready to run an application, the operating system creates a *process* in which the application will execute. The process has memory associated with it as well as other resources your application will need.

When your application is going to be run, the operating system loads it into memory and a *thread* of execution is started. This thread consists of the instructions that your application will execute. Threads are important because the Windows NT operating system uses a thread as the primary unit of scheduling. At any given point in time, the CPU can be executing the instructions on only one thread. If any other threads are waiting to execute, the operating system will eventually suspend the processing of the current thread and assign the CPU to one of the waiting threads. The thread that was suspended will be rescheduled and eventually get another turn to use the CPU.

When a system has multiple CPUs, it's possible to have multiple threads executing at the same time—one for each CPU.

You can also design your application so that it supports multiple threads. For example, an application supporting many concurrent users may have a separate thread assigned to each user. That way, the processing context of each user is isolated from the other users.

Distributed applications are deployed on multiple systems. Many times the systems are connected on a local area network (LAN) or across a wide area network (WAN). It's also possible for the systems to be loosely coupled into *clusters*. Clusters are one or more systems working closely together to give the appearance of a single system.

Security

In the physical implementation, security will be determined at several different levels.

At the operating system level, the Windows NT security system is used to authenticate users and identify group and user privileges. Access control lists provide another mechanism for assigning security.

The database management system will also have its own level of security. Access to items within the database and the actions that can be performed on those items will be determined by the security of the database user.

Microsoft Transaction Server adds additional security capabilities by using the concept of a *role*. Roles are similar to groups in that individual users can be added to roles. Components use roles to grant access. Users in a role have access to the component or interface, and those outside of the role do not.

Of course, the application itself might also programmatically control security by maintaining and enforcing its own level of security.

In distributed applications, and especially distributed applications with concurrent users, it's important to know what type of security is in effect at any given time. This is especially true as application processing passes from system to system.

Component Design

The *component* is the fundamental building block of the distributed multitier applications described in this book. Components are based on the Component Object Model (COM) and provide the means for *encapsulating* a specific piece of application functionality.

Components can be used in all layers of a multitier architecture. Here are the three essential steps to designing a component:

➤ Determining what services your component will provide

➤ Identifying what objects are required to organize the functionality of the component in a logical manner

➤ Deciding whether your component should be an in-process or out-of-process component

By encapsulating a specific piece of functionality into a component, the exact details of how the component provides that functionality are known only by the component and are isolated from the application. This has the advantage of allowing you to change the internals of the component at any time without affecting the rest of the application.

You can choose to expose certain services and attributes of the component to the application. These are the methods and properties of the component.

Components are reusable; if designed properly, they can be utilized by multiple applications. Therefore, from the right set of components, a business can quickly assemble and deploy new applications as the need arises.

Anatomy Of A Component

A component is really a collection of COM *classes* that have been organized into a single executable unit of code—either a DLL or an EXE file.

DLL components are known as *in-process* components because they share the same process space (virtual memory) as the container application. The container application can be the application itself or another in-process component that the application is using. There is minimal overhead processing to call an in-process component because the component shares the same process space with the caller. Therefore, calls to in-process components are very efficient and fast. However, because the component shares the same process space with the application, if an in-process component fails, the application will be impacted, and likely fail as well. An in-process component is depicted in Figure 9.3.

EXE components are known as *out-of-process* components because they run in their own process space, separate from the container application. As a result, calls to out-of-process components are slower than calls to in-process components. However, if a failure occurs in an out-of-process component, it is not likely to bring down the application. An out-of-process component is depicted in Figure 9.4.

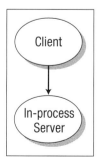

The Microsoft Transaction Server utilizes in-process components (DLLs). Therefore, if you plan to use MTS as part of your application, consider using in-process components.

Figure 9.3 An in-process component.

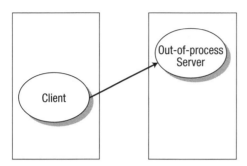

Figure 9.4 An out-of-process component.

A *class* specifies a template for an object. At runtime, you create an actual object by creating an instance of the class.

A component *interface* is a group of logically related functions that define some behavior of the component. These functions are the methods and properties available from the component. A component interface provides a standardized mechanism for accessing these methods and properties. The interface is a contract between the developer of the component and the user of the component. The contract ensures that there will be consistent access to component functionality.

The interface definition includes the names of the functions as well as the parameter types passed to each function. It also includes the return type for each function. The interface defines what behavior to expect from an object through that interface. It doesn't define any implementation. An object can implement multiple interfaces to provide access to different sets of functionality. Furthermore, it's possible to change the object behind the interface without changing the interface. Because the interface remains the same, existing applications can still use the new component.

One way to update a component is to define a new interface that supports the enhanced functionality. By maintaining the old interface, you ensure that the new component will still work with existing applications. However, new applications can access the additional functionality through the new interface.

Components are ideal for implementing business service and data service objects. Several general guidelines can be used for creating components:

➤ Base components on business entities.

➤ Plan for maintainability and reusability.

➤ Maintain a separation between presentation services, business services, and data services.

Components are language neutral. That is, the language used to implement a component or the client that uses the component is irrelevant.

Encapsulated Data Access

The data services tier of your logical design will provide access to the data your application uses. A number of different data access mechanisms are available from which to choose. In fact, many are described later in this chapter. Although some of these are already based on an object model, the objects are based on data elements and data storage.

You may consider creating a set of data service components that encapsulate the data access details for the application. You can base these components on entities that are specific to the business and thereby introduce another level of abstraction between your application and the physical data storage. Your business service components can then call these data service components to perform the actual data access operations. This approach allows you to change the physical data storage with minimal impact to your application.

Using Collection Objects To Organize Data

One way of organizing sets of objects is to use a collection. A *collection*, sometimes referred to as a *dictionary*, is a table of items in which you can look up an entry by using a key. The position of an item within the collection will change as the contents of the collection change. In addition to accessing an item by using a key, you can also access an item in a collection by using an index. Most collections are "one based," but some are "zero based." That is, the index starts at 1 in a one-based collection, and the index starts at 0 in a zero-based collection.

Because the concept of components is based on the use of objects, a collection often provides a viable means for organizing the objects and processing them. You can add and remove objects from the collection and iterate through all the objects in a collection.

 An example of the use of collections is an application that has student and teacher objects. The teachers collection would contain all the teacher objects, and the students collection would contain all the student objects.

In addition, each teacher object might have its own collection of students, which contains a student object for each pupil the teacher instructs. Likewise, each student object might have its own collection of teachers, which contains a teacher object for each of the student's teachers.

Database Access

Data is one of the key assets of every business. Rarely does a business complain that it has a lack of data. However, being able to easily access the data and derive useful information from it are often challenging operations. Here are several reasons for this:

➤ Data exists in a number of disparate formats because it's usually stored and maintained differently by each application.

➤ Data has been collected over time, and a huge volume of raw data exists.

➤ Data is often located on different systems, and it's usually not available where it needs to be processed.

The inability to access remote data from a number of heterogeneous data sources is a problem that most businesses must address.

Over the last few years, a number of different mechanisms have been proposed for providing access to data. These include the following:

➤ Universal storage

➤ Native access

➤ ODBC API

➤ ODBC

➤ Universal Data Access

➤ OLE DB

➤ ADO

➤ DAO

➤ RDO

➤ ODBCDirect

Although the relational database model is popular for new applications, a lot of businesses have not yet moved to this technology. Their data resides in some other format. Even businesses that are using relational databases are still likely to require access to legacy data created by earlier applications. Therefore, data access facilities must address all these needs.

Access to data stored in a relational database was originally accomplished by using SQL code embedded directly into the application source code. The major drawback to this method is that it usually only works for local databases. As client/server applications began to evolve, so did the strategies for data access.

Universal Storage

One approach to solving the problems associated with accessing multiple types of data sources is to put all the data into a single data store. This technique is referred to as *universal storage*. At first glance, this appears to be a viable choice. All applications would have a single place to go for data and a single means for accessing that data.

On a small scale, this might be possible. However, for most businesses, this is impractical for two reasons:

➤ There are many data types that must be stored, and this is technically difficult and could lead to inefficiencies.

➤ There's a huge amount of legacy data. This would all need to be converted to the universal storage format.

Therefore, the idea of universal storage is not widely embraced.

Native Access

All data sources provide some sort of *native access* to the data. Usually, this is provided by procedures in a support library that the application can call to access the data.

Most relational database management systems provide this support through a native (or proprietary) database application program interface (API). This API serves as the interface to the library of functions for accessing and modifying data in the database. VBSQL is an example of such an interface. VBSQL allows programs written in Visual Basic to access a SQL Server database.

The main disadvantage to a native database API is that the application is then tied to a specific database. If the application must use another database, all the code that makes calls to the proprietary API will need to be adapted to the API of the new database. In order to minimize the impact of this, a good design and development practice is to localize to a small number of procedures, all statements calling the proprietary interface. Then, if they must be modified, the locations for the changes are limited and manageable. If native database API references are spread throughout the code, making changes quickly becomes a more complex task.

On the other hand, using a native database API may be a very desirable approach if the application is going to be used with only a specific database. A native interface often provides access to unique database facilities and features that cannot be accessed through other database access mechanisms. In addition, using a native database API may optimize database access performance. Figure 9.5 depicts the use of a native database API.

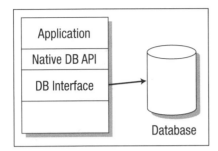

Figure 9.5 Using a native database API.

ODBC API

As relational technology became more popular, and each database vendor produced its own native access API, the problems of accessing data from multiple relational data sources became more difficult. Driven by user outcry, an industry consortium of major database vendors decided to address this problem.

The Open Database Connectivity (ODBC) API evolved from a specification developed by the SQL Access Group in 1991. Microsoft produced the first ODBC API implementation. This has gone through multiple revisions and enhancements and is currently an industry standard for database connectivity.

The ODBC API provides an interface to any data source that's ODBC compliant. The main advantage to using the ODBC API is that the application will be able to interface to multiple data sources without requiring any coding changes. Calls made to the ODBC API are first processed by the ODBC Driver Manager, which then calls the ODBC driver for the specific data source. To use the ODBC API, you write the application code necessary to call the desired ODBC procedures. Figure 9.6 depicts the use of the ODBC API.

Although early versions of ODBC were criticized for performance limitations, current ODBC performance closely matches the performance achieved using a native database API.

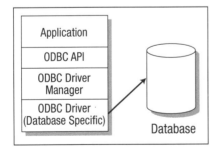

Figure 9.6 Using an ODBC API.

ODBC

Many development and end-user tools are ODBC enabled. That is, they can access ODBC data sources without requiring any user-written application code that makes calls to the ODBC API. These tools make calls to the ODBC API, but these calls are shielded from the user. This simplifies the access to ODBC-compliant data sources.

Universal Data Access (UDA)

Universal Data Access is the Microsoft strategy for providing a common method to access data. It supports access to any type of data, regardless of where the data is located, and a programming interface that's tool and language independent. The technologies that enable Universal Data Access are referred to as the *Microsoft Data Access Components* (MDAC). These components include the following:

➤ ActiveX Data Objects (ADO)

➤ Remote Data Service (RDS)

➤ OLE DB

➤ Open Database Connectivity (ODBC)

UDA is depicted in Figure 9.7.

Figure 9.7 reveals that ADO can be used to access any data source that has an ODBC driver.

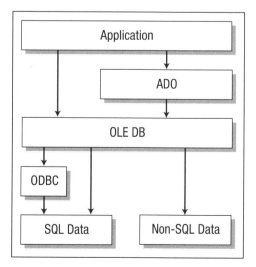

Figure 9.7   The Microsoft Universal Data Access architecture.

UDA has several important characteristics:

➤ It provides access to any type of data store, both relational and nonrelational.

➤ It's based on COM.

➤ It includes a programming-level interface that provides a single data access mechanism for all data.

OLE DB

OLE Database (OLE DB) is one of the key supporting pieces for Universal Data Access. OLE DB provides a set of OLE Component Object Model (COM) interfaces for universal data access. It defines a three-layered architecture comprising data providers, optional service providers, and data consumers. OLE DB is depicted in Figure 9.8.

Data providers are COM components responsible for providing data from data stores. OLE DB interfaces are defined so that data providers can implement different levels of support, based on the capabilities of the underlying data store. Data providers use standard APIs of the data store to access the data and expose the data in objects known as *rowsets*.

Data consumers are COM components that access data using data providers. Service providers are COM components that encapsulate specialized data management functions. Service components can be implemented independently and added as needed.

OLE DB is extensible because it's COM based. Enhancements are made by implementing new interfaces. Using the COM **QueryInterface** method, applications can determine whether a specific feature is supported.

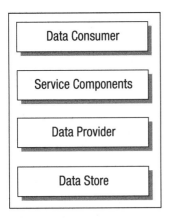

Figure 9.8 The layers in the OLE DB data access model.

OLE DB is optimized for efficient data access rather than ease of use. In particular, the OLE DB COM interfaces are not automation compatible. This means that they can't be accessed directly by some programming languages, including Visual Basic. As a result, UDA includes another layer above OLE DB to provide an easy-to-use program interface.

ActiveX Data Objects (ADO)

ActiveX Data Objects (ADO) provides an Automation wrapper for OLE DB, making OLE DB objects accessible to any programming language or tool that supports COM. This is possible because ADO supports dual interfaces. As a result, ADO provides a single data access interface that can be used to access relational and nonrelational data, regardless of where the data is located.

The ADO object model has evolved from the earlier DAO and RDO object models. Therefore, there are many similarities to the objects in these models. Some of the key objects in the ADO object model are shown in Figure 9.9.

The *Connection* object represents a unique session or connection to the underlying data store. Connection objects expose an Execute method that allows you to perform operations on the data.

The *Command* object provides a way of preparing and executing parameterized commands against the data. The Parameters collection of the Command object contains the Parameter objects needed for the command.

The *Recordset* object is used to return the results of a command. ADO Recordset objects are more powerful and flexible than their predecessors in the DAO and RDO object models. ADO recordsets are not part of a hierarchy and can be

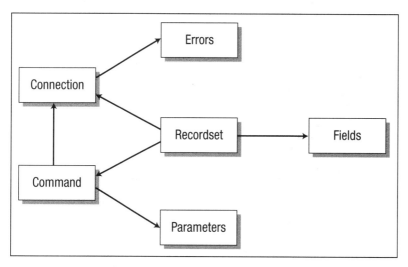

Figure 9.9 Key objects in the ADO object model.

created independently of other ADO objects. New ADO recordset properties provide mechanisms for controlling locking as well as the amount of data retrieved in the recordset.

As is the case with DAO and RDO, the *Fields* collection of the Recordset object contains Field objects for each field in the recordset.

> ADO is a good data access technology for any new applications because it uses the latest technologies and is a key part of Microsoft's data access strategy.

Data Access Objects (DAO)

Data Access Objects (DAO) is the programming interface for the Microsoft Jet database engine. DAO is based on a hierarchical object model. You can use the objects and collections in the DAO object hierarchy to manipulate your data and the structure of your Jet database.

DAO provides access to all the objects used in the Jet architecture. Because Jet allows links to ODBC-compliant data sources, it's also possible to access these ODBC data sources via DAO. The main advantage to this is that the same programming model used for Jet applies to the ODBC data source. Therefore, a developer familiar with DAO can access the ODBC data source using objects such as TableDefs and QueryDefs.

Although the DAO object model provides an object-oriented programming interface to remote ODBC databases, it does require the additional processing overhead of the Jet database engine.

> DAO is a good data access technology to use for the Jet database engine.

Remote Data Objects (RDO)

Remote Data Objects (RDO) provides an object-oriented programming interface to ODBC data sources, without requiring the Jet database engine. Therefore, any overhead processing introduced by Jet is eliminated. The RDO object model is similar to DAO but has a steeper learning curve than DAO. However, it provides a high performance interface to ODBC.

> RDO is an older technology than ADO. Although existing applications might use RDO, ADO should be the first choice for any new applications.

Practice Questions

Question 1

At Sizzling Semiconductors, the Access application was split into two separate MDB files—a client containing forms, reports, and queries and a server
containing the data tables. Where does the processing occur in this configuration?

○ a. Mostly on the client

○ b. Mostly on the server

○ c. Evenly distributed between client and server

○ d. Mostly on the network

Answer a is correct. All the processing will occur on the client. When this
particular Access configuration is used, the server data tables can be shared by
a number of users, but no processing occurs on the server. The server database
is actually just a shared file. All the data that's to be processed must be transferred across the network for processing on the client.

Question 2

Which of the following characteristics describe ActiveX Data Objects (ADO)?
[Check all correct answers]

❑ a. Has a native database interface

❑ b. Has a hierarchical data model

❑ c. Can be used to access any database having an ODBC driver

❑ d. Based on the concept of universal storage

Although this question indicates that multiple answers are correct, only answer c is correct. ADO is not a native database interface, nor is it based on the
concept of Universal Storage. Although it uses an object model, ADO is not a
strict hierarchical model like DAO.

Question 3

> Which of the following data access mechanisms is based on an architecture of data suppliers and data consumers?
>
> ○ a. VBSQL
>
> ○ b. ADO
>
> ○ c. OLE DB
>
> ○ d. ODBC

Answer c is correct. OLE DB is based on a three-tier architecture consisting of data suppliers, service components, and data consumers. None of the other choices are based on a three-tier architecture. VBSQL is a native database interface. ADO is the object model layered on top of OLE DB to provide an application level interface. ODBC is a vendor-neutral interface for data access, and is primarily used for accessing relational data.

Question 4

> You're creating a new application that will access a remote database. Currently, the only remote database the application will use is a SQL Server database. However, in the future it's possible that the application may need to access an Oracle database as well. Which of the following data access mechanisms should you use?
>
> ○ a. VBSQL
>
> ○ b. ADO
>
> ○ c. DAO
>
> ○ d. RDO

Answer b is correct. ADO is the recommended technology for data access. It's a key part of the Microsoft Universal Data Access strategy. VBSQL is a good choice if the only database to be accessed is SQL Server, but that's not the case in this situation. Therefore, answer a is incorrect. Both DAO and RDO could be used, but they are both older technologies, and ADO is the preferred choice. Therefore, answers c and d are incorrect.

Question 5

In version 2 of the BacklogAndBookings application, where was the performance bottleneck?

○ a. Mostly on the client

○ b. Mostly on the server

○ c. Evenly distributed between client and server

○ d. Mostly on the network

Answer d is correct. The performance bottleneck occurred during the transfer of all the data records across the network to the client application.

Need To Know More?

 Kirtland, Mary. *Designing Component Based Applications*. Redmond, WA: Microsoft Press, 1999. ISBN 0-73560-523-8. Chapter 3, "Data Access Fundamentals," provides a detailed description of the data access models presented in this chapter.

 McKinney, Bruce. *Hardcore Visual Basic*. Redmond, WA: Microsoft Press, 1997. ISBN 1-57231-422-2. Chapter 4, "Collecting Objects," provides a good description of collections, examples of using collections, and some of the more obscure details about collections.

 http://msdn.microsoft.com/library/backgrnd/html/ msdn_clustrwp.htm

 Microsoft Corporation. "Cluster Strategy: High Availability and Scalability with Industry-Standard Hardware." (Microsoft Corporation, Redmond, WA, 1996.) This technical paper describes what clustering is and provides several examples of cluster configurations. This paper is available on the Microsoft Developer Network Library.

 http://msdn.microsoft.com/library/sdkdoc/dasdk/ ados4t7p.htm

 Chen, Joyce and Richard Patterson. "ADO and SQL Server Developer's Guide." (Microsoft Corporation, Redmond, WA, 1998.) This technical paper describes the ADO object model and gives numerous examples of using ADO with SQL Server. It also discusses some of the more advanced topics of ADO. This paper is available on the Microsoft Developer Network Library.

 http://msdn.microsoft.com/library/sdkdoc/dasdk/ udas2xix.htm

 Lazar, David: "Microsoft Strategy for Universal Data Access." Microsoft Corporation, Redmond, WA, 1998. This technical paper provides an in-depth description of the UDA strategy as well as presenting a good overview of the design goals for MDAC. This paper is available on the Microsoft Developer Network Library.

Blakeley, Jose. "Universal Data Access Through OLE DB: A Comprehensive Introduction to OLE DB As an Enterprise Development Tool." (Microsoft Corporation, Redmond, WA, 1996.) This background paper describes the UDA strategy as well as presents a good introduction to the concepts supporting OLE DB. This paper is available on the Microsoft Developer Network Library.

Sample Test

In this chapter, we provide pointers to help you develop a successful test-taking strategy, including how to choose proper answers, how to decode ambiguity, how to work within the Microsoft testing framework, how to decide what you need to memorize, and how to prepare for the test. At the end of the chapter, we include 50 questions on subject matter pertinent to Microsoft Exam 70-100, "Analyzing Requirements and Designing Solution Architectures." Good luck!

Questions, Questions, Questions

There should be no doubt in your mind that you are facing a test full of specific and pointed questions. The Analyzing Requirements and Designing Solution Architectures exam consists of approximately 20 questions, for which you are allowed approximately 165 minutes to complete. The exam is organized into five or six timed testlets, with each testlet having between 2 and 10 questions. The instructions at the beginning of each testlet will tell you the time allowed for the testlet, the number of questions, and the types of questions.

Questions belong to one of five basic types:

➤ Multiple-choice with a single answer

➤ Multiple-choice with multiple answers

➤ Drop-and-connect question formats

➤ Build-list-and-reorder question formats

➤ Create-a-tree question formats

Always take the time to read a question at least twice before selecting an answer, and you should always look for an Exhibit button as you examine each question. Exhibits include graphics information related to a question—usually a screen capture of program output or graphical user interface (GUI) information that you must examine to analyze the question's content and formulate an answer. The Exhibit button brings up graphics and charts used to help explain a question, provide additional data, or illustrate page layout or program behavior.

Not every question has only one answer; many questions require multiple answers. Therefore, you should read each question carefully, determine how many answers are necessary or possible, and look for additional hints or instructions when selecting answers. Such instructions often occur in brackets, immediately following the question itself (multiple-answer questions).

Also keep in mind that some question types, like the create-a-tree or build-list-and-reorder, allow you to use answers more than once.

Picking Proper Answers

Obviously, the only way to pass any exam is to select enough of the right answers to obtain a passing score. However, Microsoft's exams aren't standardized like the SAT and GRE exams; they're far more diabolical and convoluted. In some cases, questions are strangely worded, and deciphering them can be a real challenge. In these cases, you may need to rely on answer-elimination skills.

Almost always, at least one answer out of the possible choices for a question can be eliminated immediately, because it matches one of these conditions:

➤ The answer does not apply to the situation.

➤ The answer describes a nonexistent issue, an invalid option, or an imaginary state.

➤ The answer may be eliminated because of information in the question itself.

After you eliminate all answers that are obviously wrong, you can apply your retained knowledge to eliminate further answers. Look for items that sound correct but refer to actions, commands, or features that aren't present or available in the situation the question describes.

If you're still faced with a blind guess among two or more potentially correct answers, reread the question. Try to picture how each of the possible remaining answers would alter the situation. Be especially sensitive to terminology; sometimes the choice of words ("remove" instead of "disable") can make the difference between a right answer and a wrong one.

Only when you've exhausted your ability to eliminate answers but remain unclear about which of the remaining possibilities is correct should you guess at an answer. An unanswered question offers you no points, but guessing gives you at least some chance of getting a question right; just don't be too hasty when making a blind guess.

Keep in mind that the 70-100 exam is presented as a series of case studies. Once you've completed a case study, you can't return to it. So if you need to guess some answers, do so before starting the next case study.

Decoding Ambiguity

Microsoft exams have a reputation for including questions that can be difficult to interpret, confusing, or ambiguous. In our experience with numerous exams, we consider this reputation to be completely justified. The Microsoft exams are tough, and they're deliberately made that way.

The only way to beat Microsoft at its own game is to be prepared. You'll discover many exam questions test your knowledge of things not directly related to the issue raised by a question. This means the answers you must choose from, even incorrect ones, are just as much a part of the skill assessment as the question itself. If you don't know something about most aspects of the question, you may not be able to eliminate obviously wrong answers, because the answer relates to an area other than the one that's addressed by the question at hand. In other words, the more you know about the subject, the easier it will be for you to tell right from wrong.

Questions often give away their answers, but you have to be Sherlock Holmes to see the clues. Often, subtle hints appear in the question text in such a way that they seem almost irrelevant to the situation. You must realize that each question is a test unto itself, and you need to inspect and successfully navigate each question to pass the exam. Look for small clues, such as the mention of times, group permissions and names, and configuration settings. Little things, such as these, can point to the right answer if properly understood; if missed, they can leave you facing a blind guess.

Vocabulary is another common difficulty in certification exams. Microsoft has an uncanny knack for naming some utilities and features entirely obviously in some cases and completely inanely in other instances. Microsoft has also changed the names of some of its technologies. Be sure to brush up on the key terms presented at the beginning of each chapter. You may also want to read through the glossary at the end of this book the day before you take the test.

Working Within The Framework

The test questions appear in random order, and many elements or issues that receive mention in one question may also crop up in other questions. It's not uncommon to find that an incorrect answer to one question is the correct answer to another question, or vice versa. Take the time to read every answer to each question, even if you recognize the correct answer to a question immediately. That extra reading may spark a memory or remind you about a feature or topic that helps you on another question elsewhere in the exam.

If you're taking a fixed-length test, you can revisit any question as many times as you like, provided you stay within the same case study. If you're uncertain of the answer to a question, check the box that's provided to mark it for easy return later on. You should also mark questions you think may offer information you can use to answer other questions. On fixed-length tests, we usually mark somewhere between 25 and 50 percent of the questions on exams we've taken. The testing software is designed to let you mark every question if you choose; use this framework to your advantage. Everything you'll want to see again should be marked; the testing software can then help you return to marked questions quickly and easily.

During exam 70-100, which is based on case studies, consider quickly reading all the questions for the case study before reading the case study itself. This will prepare you for certain areas you'll want to pay particular attention to in the case study. It will also help you to identify information in the case study irrelevant to what is covered in the questions. The key is to make a quick pass over the territory to begin with—so you know what you're up against—then to survey that territory more thoroughly after reading the case study, when you can begin to answer all questions systematically and consistently.

If you're taking an adaptive test and you see something in a question or one of the answers that jogs your memory on a topic or if you see something you feel you should record if the topic appears in another question, write it down on your piece of paper. Just because you can't go back to a question in an adaptive test doesn't mean you can't take notes on what you see early in the test in hopes that it might help you later in the test.

 In adaptive tests, don't be afraid to take notes on what you see in various questions. Sometimes, what you record from one question, especially if it's not as familiar as it should be or reminds you of the name or use of some utility or interface details, can help you on other questions later on.

Deciding What To Memorize

The amount of memorization you must undertake for an exam depends on how well you remember what you've read and on how well you know the software by heart. If you're a visual thinker and can see the drop-down menus and dialog boxes in your head, you won't need to memorize as much as someone who's less visually oriented. However, the 70-100 exam will rely more on your ability to analyze and apply your knowledge to a certain situation, rather than on your ability to recall a set of memorized facts.

At a minimum, you'll want to memorize the following kinds of information:

➤ The terms and techniques of data modeling, data normalization, and relationships in the relational data model

➤ The various solution architectures and how they relate to performance, availability, maintainability, scalability, interoperability, and security

➤ Details and standards for designing a user interface, including characteristics and types of controls

➤ Data access mechanisms and characteristics

➤ Technology details relevant to implementing the solution architectures discussed or mentioned in this book

Also, don't forget The Cram Sheet at the front of this book is designed to capture the material that's most important to memorize; use this to guide your studies as well.

Preparing For The Test

The best way to prepare for the test—after you've studied—is to take at least one practice exam. We've included one here in this chapter for that reason; the test questions are located in the pages that follow (and unlike the preceding chapters in this book, the answers don't follow the questions immediately; you'll have to flip to Chapter 11 to review the answers separately).

Give yourself about 100 minutes to take the exam, and keep yourself on the honor system—don't look at previous text in the book or jump ahead to the answer key. When your time is up or you've finished the questions, you can check your work in Chapter 11. Pay special attention to the explanations for the incorrect answers; these can also help to reinforce your knowledge of the material. Knowing how to recognize correct answers is good, but understanding why incorrect answers are wrong can be equally valuable.

Taking The Test

Relax. Once you're sitting in front of the testing computer, there's nothing more you can do to increase your knowledge or preparation. Take a deep breath, stretch, and start reading that first question.

You don't need to rush, either. You have plenty of time to complete each question and to return to those questions you skip or mark for return (if you're taking a fixed-length test). If you're taking an adaptive test, you'll have to guess and move on. Both easy and difficult questions are intermixed throughout the test in random order. If you're taking a fixed-length test, don't cheat yourself by spending too much time on a hard question early on in the test, thereby depriving yourself of the time you need to answer the questions at the end of the test. If you're taking an adaptive test, don't spend more than five minutes on any single question—if it takes you that long to get nowhere, it's time to guess and move on.

Remember the strategy of reading all the questions for the case study before reading the case study itself. That way, you'll know certain things to be on the lookout for when you read the case study.

You may also find it easier to use the All tab on the case study, which presents all the information in the study on one tab, rather than displaying different parts of the case study on individual tabs.

On an adaptive test, set a maximum time limit for questions, and watch your time on long or complex questions. If you hit your limit, it's time to guess and move on. Don't deprive yourself of the opportunity to see more questions by taking too long to puzzle over questions, unless you think you can figure out the answer. Otherwise, you're limiting your opportunities to pass.

That's it for pointers. Here are some questions for you to practice on.

Sample Test

Question 1

Which of the following are true about database stored procedures? [Check all correct answers]

- ❏ a. They can improve database performance.
- ❏ b. Although they reduce application processing, they increase network traffic, because the results must be transmitted from the database to the application over the network.
- ❏ c. They can hide data calculations from the application.
- ❏ d. Without stored procedures, you can't include business rules in the database.

Question 2

When laying out the controls for a dialog box for an application that will be used in countries where English is the primary language, where would you locate the primary field with which the user interacts?

- ○ a. In the upper-left corner of the dialog box
- ○ b. In the lower-right corner of the dialog box
- ○ c. In the center of the dialog box
- ○ d. In a location that makes the appearance of the dialog box most aesthetically pleasing

Question 3

Which of the following is true about a relational database system compared to a file system for storing data?

- ○ a. A relational database will be smaller than the corresponding file structure.
- ○ b. Indexes can only be used with a relational database.
- ○ c. The relational database management system can enforce data integrity.
- ○ d. Once in production, it is easier to make changes to the file structure.

Question 4

Which of the following is true about data normalization?

- ○ a. A table with a single column primary key is in second normal form if it is in first normal form.
- ○ b. The design must be in third normal form before it is implemented.
- ○ c. Third normal form eliminates repeating data.
- ○ d. For data access to be as efficient as possible, data normalization rules must never be intentionally violated.

Question 5

Which of the following statements are true about transactions? [Check all correct answers]

- ❑ a. Transactions can be distributed across multiple systems.
- ❑ b. Transactions can be nested.
- ❑ c. Transactions must pass the ACID test.
- ❑ d. Transactions terminate by being either committed or rolled back.

Question 6

Which of the following would you most likely find as the interface between the two tiers of an application based on a two-tier model?

- ○ a. ODBC
- ○ b. RPC
- ○ c. Queued messages
- ○ d. DCOM

Question 7

Which of the following technologies is most likely supported by the largest number of browsers?

- ○ a. A Java applet
- ○ b. A VB client-side script
- ○ c. An ActiveX control
- ○ d. An Active Server Page

Question 8

Where could you find code that validated data? [Check all correct answers]

❑ a. In the user interface

❑ b. In the business rules of the application

❑ c. In a database stored procedure

❑ d. In a database constraint

Question 9

You are designing an application that will process class assignments for the local school district. Which of the following objects will you likely use?

○ a. Student, teacher

○ b. Students, teachers

○ c. Students, student, teachers, teacher

○ d. Teacher, students

Question 10

Another developer brings you a Visual Basic application to help her analyze. You discover that the tables for the database are being created directly by the programming object model. What programming object model is being used?

○ a. DAO

○ b. ADO

○ c. ODBC

○ d. OLE DB

Question 11

A GUID is:

○ a. A 128-character string

○ b. A 128-bit integer

○ c. A 128-byte string

○ d. None of the above

Question 12

To enhance the functions of a component you previously created and distributed, you redefine the interface, changing the declaration of one of its methods. Specifically, you change the data type of one of the parameters from string to variant. The two versions are:

○ a. Version identical

○ b. Version compatible

○ c. Version incompatible

○ d. Version dependent

Question 13

On which of the following are you are likely to find an Apply button? [Check all correct answers]

❑ a. Common Dialog for Fonts

❑ b. Wizard

❑ c. Property sheet

❑ d. ImageList control

Question 14

Which of the following items are used to enforce referential integrity? [Check two answers]

❑ a. Primary key

❑ b. Foreign key

❑ c. Index

❑ d. Stored procedure

Question 15

Which of the following is used to guarantee uniqueness of a row in a relational database table?

○ a. Primary key

○ b. Foreign key

○ c. Index

○ d. Stored procedure

Question 16

Which of the following is used to improve access performance in a relational database table?

○ a. Primary key

○ b. Foreign key

○ c. Index

○ d. Constraint

Question 17

Which of the following facilities support database replication with Microsoft Access? [Check all correct answers]

❏ a. Briefcase

❏ b. ADO programming

❏ c. Replication manager

❏ d. DAO programming

Question 18

Which of the following technologies would require a browser-enhanced application? [Check all correct answers]

❏ a. DHTML

❏ b. ISAPI

❏ c. Java applet

❏ d. ActiveX control

Question 19

You are designing a new application that will access a relational database. Initially, MS SQL Server will be used as the relational database management system. However, in the future you may also need to support an Oracle relational database. Which data access technology should you use?

○ a. VBSQL

○ b. DAO

○ c. ADO

○ d. RDO

Question 20

You have designed a distributed application using COM components. You plan to deploy this application using two systems—one running NT Server and one running NT Workstation. Which technology will you use to enable communication between the components?

○ a. MSMQ

○ b. DCOM

○ c. Connection pooling

○ d. Remote Automation

Question 21

Which of the following is the most critical success factor for building a business application?

○ a. It is built using COM.

○ b. It includes access to legacy systems.

○ c. It includes an interface to the Internet.

○ d. It solves the business problem.

Question 22

The MSF Team Model has six roles. They are:

Product management

Program management

Development

Testing

User education

Logistics management

Each role has a goal. Identify the following goals with the appropriate Team role:

Smooth product deployment

Satisfied customers

Release after addressing all issues

Delivery within project constraints

Improved user performance

Delivery to product specifications

Question 23

Which of the following statements is true about the MSF Team Model?

- ○ a. There will always be at least six people on the team, one for each role.
- ○ b. It consists of the managers of all groups involved in the project.
- ○ c. It consists of the managers of all groups involved in the project, as well as an end user representative.
- ○ d. For small projects, the team might consist of fewer than six people.

Question 24

From the following list of activities, arrange the list in the order the activities would be performed to develop a new application.

Deploy components on target computers

Define data objects and business objects

Interview users to find out how they do their job

Create components for business and data services

Prepare a functional specification

Question 25

The MSF process model defines four project phases. These are:

Envisioning

Planning

Development

Stabilization

Identify the appropriate project phase that is terminated by each of the following major project milestones:

Release

Vision/scope approved

Project plan approved

Code complete

Question 26

Which of the following statements are true about TCP/IP? [Check all correct answers]

❑ a. It is a nonroutable protocol.

❑ b. It is used to support Web-based applications.

❑ c. It is supported by the Winsock control.

❑ d. It is intended only for local area networks.

Question 27

Where would a stored database procedure be executed?

- ○ a. On the client system that called the procedure
- ○ b. Within the same process as Microsoft Transaction Server
- ○ c. On the database server
- ○ d. Within the same process as Internet Information Server

Question 28

You have written a single threaded component and have discovered that it consumes most of the CPU resources of the server. You have even dedicated the server to running only this component. To increase performance, you deploy the component on another system with two CPUs. What type of performance improvement should you expect?

- ○ a. No change from the performance on the single CPU system
- ○ b. Almost twice as fast as the performance on the single CPU system
- ○ c. Twice as fast as the performance on the single CPU system
- ○ d. More than twice as fast as the performance on the single CPU system

Question 29

When designing a user interface, you decide to include a menu bar with drop-down menus. You will need File, View, and Help menus. How should you place these on the menu bar?

- ○ a. They should be arranged left to right in the order of anticipated usage.
- ○ b. There is no convention; arrange them so they are aesthetically pleasing
- ○ c. File, Help, View
- ○ d. File, View, and Help

Question 30

Which of the following items are appropriate for displaying as static text? [Check all correct answers]

- ❑ a. Labels
- ❑ b. Descriptive text
- ❑ c. Read-only text
- ❑ d. Disabled text

Questions 31 through 35 refer to information provided in the case study, Action Aerospace, in Chapters 4 and 5. You may find it helpful to review the case study before answering these questions.

Question 31

Action Aerospace implemented a pilot version of the online time card application using terminal emulation. Where did the majority of the processing occur with this application?

- ○ a. On the desktop computer
- ○ b. On the mainframe computer
- ○ c. On the network
- ○ d. Evenly distributed between desktop and mainframe

Question 32

At one time, Action Aerospace considered using a two-tier application model to implement the online time card application. A desktop application written in Visual Basic would access the DB2 database using ODBC. Why do you think they chose not to do this?

- ○ a. It would provide no real advantage over the terminal emulation prototype they already had working.
- ○ b. Retrieving data over an ODBC connection would be too slow.
- ○ c. It probably would not be scalable enough to handle the anticipated workload.
- ○ d. This solution was not possible because DB2 does not have an ODBC driver.

Question 33

Action Aerospace implemented a pilot version of the online time card application using terminal emulation. Which of the following statements best characterizes the use of terminal emulation at Action Aerospace?

○ a. It required few changes to the mainframe application.

○ b. It exemplifies the logical three-tier model.

○ c. It shifts processing from the mainframe system to the client system.

○ d. It is suitable for enterprise rollout.

Question 34

Which of the following technologies would likely be used by some of the data objects in the Employee Time Card System to access the mainframe applications?

○ a. IIS

○ b. MTS

○ c. MSMQ

○ d. COMTI

Question 35

The Employee Time Card Application uses a relational database that contains the following tables:

Employees

Timecards

TimecardEntries

Identify which tables will contain the following columns:

TimecardID

EmployeeID

ProjectCode

WeekEndingDate

Shift

ActivityCode

Hours

Name

Questions 36 through 40 refer to information provided in the case study, Southwestern Specialties, in Chapter 6. You may find it helpful to review the case study before answering these questions.

Question 36

In the Southwestern Specialties database, no order details are allowed unless there is a matching order. This is an example of:

○ a. A one-to-one relationship

○ b. A zero-to-many relationship

○ c. Referential integrity

○ d. A many-to-many relationship

Question 37

In the Southwestern Specialties database, a one-to-zero or -many relationship exists between the Orders table and the Order Details table. Which of the following conditions are possible? [Check all correct answers]

❑ a. A single order with no corresponding order detail entries

❑ b. A single order with one corresponding order detail entry

❑ c. A single order detail referenced by multiple order entries

❑ d. Multiple order details referenced by multiple order entries

Question 38

The Order Details table contains a field called ProductID. What is this field?

○ a. A primary key

○ b. A foreign key

○ c. A parent link

○ d. A child link

Question 39

In the Southwestern Specialties database, what type of relationship exists between the Customers table and the Employees table?

○ a. A one-to-one relationship

○ b. A one-to-many relationship

○ c. A many-to-many relationship

○ d. No relationship

Question 40

Which of the following situations might motivate Southwestern Specialties to denormalize their database design?

○ a. Poor database performance

○ b. Incorporation of additional suppliers

○ c. Use of a nine-character ZIP code rather than a five-character ZIP code

○ d. Ease of maintenance

Questions 41 through 45 refer to information provided in the case study, Power Patterns, in Chapters 7 and 8. You may find it helpful to review the case study before answering these questions.

Question 41

Which of the following are you not likely to find in the EnergyReporter application?

○ a. A data object

○ b. An ActiveX object

○ c. A data bound control

○ d. A stored database procedure

Question 42

The DataLoader application requires the user to identify the file that contains the input data supplied by the energy service provider. What do you think the application uses to do this?

- ○ a. A custom ActiveX control
- ○ b. A Winsock control
- ○ c. An ImageList control
- ○ d. A common dialog box

Question 43

In summary, Power Patterns obtains energy usage data from energy service providers and prepares energy usage reports for its customers. Arrange the following activities in the order that they occur.

Obtain energy usage data from energy service provider

Load energy usage data into Energy Usage database

Retrieve data from Energy Usage database

Validate energy usage data

Convert energy usage data to a common format

Create error reports

Read energy usage data in different formats

Retrieve valid data from Staging database

Load energy usage data into Staging database

Create customer reports

Question 44

When Power Patterns created their Web application, they wanted to support the largest number of browsers. Which of the following technologies might they have chosen? [Check all correct answers]

- ❏ a. DHTML
- ❏ b. ASP
- ❏ c. CGI
- ❏ d. ISAPI

Question 45

Which of the following characteristics are true of the presentation services tier implemented using Active Server Pages? [Check all correct answers]

❑ a. It works with multiple browsers.

❑ b. The system at the customer site uses the Internet to access the business services tier and get data needed for reports.

❑ c. Other than rendering performed by the browser, no other processing takes place on the client.

❑ d. Once the data is retrieved, reports are generated on the client.

Questions 46 through 50 refer to information provided in the case study, Sizzling Semiconductors, in Chapter 9. You may find it helpful to review the case study before answering these questions.

Question 46

After reviewing the problems with Version 2 of the BacklogAndBookings application, which of the following alternatives would you propose, given that you want to improve performance?

○ a. Keep the database in Microsoft Access but rewrite the client front end using Visual Basic.

○ b. Keep the present application configuration but upgrade the database system with a more powerful processor and more memory.

○ c. Upgrade the laptop systems with more memory and faster processors.

○ d. Convert the Access database to a more powerful relational database management system.

Question 47

Version 1 of the BacklogAndBookings application included a module written in Visual Basic for Applications. This module created and manipulated a recordset. What technology did Sizzling Semiconductors probably utilize to do this?

○ a. UDA

○ b. ADO

○ c. DAO

○ d. RDO

Question 48

The BacklogAndBookings application has evolved over three versions:

Version 1

Version 2

Version 3

Identify the version for each of the following application characteristics:

Could utilize stored database procedures

Uses local tables

Uses linked tables

Based on a file server model

Based on a client/server model

Utilizes HTTP

Based on a two-tier architecture

Based on a three-tier architecture

Uses ODBC

Question 49

Sizzling Semiconductors has been evaluating Oracle database products for the last three months. Shortly after Version 3 of the BacklogAndBillings application became operational, the software development manager was asked if an Oracle database could be used instead of a SQL Server database. Which of the following statements best describes the impact on the client application to support an Oracle database?

○ a. Client application changes would be minimal.

○ b. Client application changes would be moderate.

○ c. Client application changes would be substantial.

○ d. An application written in Microsoft Access can't access an Oracle database.

Question 50

Which of the following terms describe Version 3 of the BacklogAndBookings application? [Check all correct answers]

❏ a. Desktop

❏ b. Web based

❏ c. Fat client

❏ d. Thin client

Answer Key

For asterisked items, please see textual representation of answer on the appropriate page within this chapter.

1. a, c	18. a, c, d	35. *
2. a	19. c	36. c
3. c	20. b	37. a, b
4. a	21. d	38. b
5. a, b, c, d	22. *	39. c
6. a	23. d	40. a
7. d	24. *	41. c
8. a, b, c, d	25. *	42. d
9. c	26. b, c	43. *
10. a	27. c	44. b, c, d
11. b	28. a	45. a, c
12. c	29. d	46. d
13. c	30. a, b	47. c
14. a, b	31. b	48. *
15. a	32. c	49. a
16. c	33. a	50. a, c
17. a, c, d	34. d	

Question 1

Answers a and c are correct. Answer b is incorrect, because the result set must be transferred from the database to the application, whether the query originated from a stored procedure or from the application. Stored procedures don't increase network traffic. Answer d is not correct because there are other ways, such as constraints, that allow you to include business rules in the database.

Question 2

Answer a is correct. This is also consistent with the general design guidelines for control placement in a dialog box, which says that controls should be oriented in the way people read information.

Question 3

Answer c is correct. Answer a is incorrect, because relational databases usually require more storage than a corresponding file structure. This is because the relational database also contains metadata, the data about the data. Answer b is incorrect, because a relational database and a file system both support the use of indexes. Answer d is incorrect, because relational databases are usually easier to change than a file structure.

Question 4

Answer a is correct. Second normal form eliminates partial dependencies. It is possible to have partial dependencies in a table only when the primary key consists of more than one column. Therefore, if a table consists of a single column primary key, once it is in first normal form, it is automatically in second normal form as well. Answers b and d are incorrect, because normalization rules are sometimes intentionally violated in the implementation to enable better performance. Answer c is incorrect, because first normal form eliminates repeating data.

Question 5

Answers a, b, c, and d are correct. Transactions can be distributed across multiple systems; however, a resource manager, such as the Distributed Transaction Coordinator, is also required. Transactions can also be nested, but not all database management systems support this. By definition, transactions must pass the ACID test for atomicity, consistency, isolation, and durability. And, finally, transactions terminate by either committing or rolling back. Commit means that all the operations complete successfully; rollback means that none of the operations complete, and any changes already made during the transaction are undone.

Question 6

Answer a is correct. In the two-tier application model, the tiers are usually connected with an application-to-database connection, such as open database connectivity (ODBC). Remote procedure call (RPCs), queued messages, and Distributed Component Object Model (DCOM) are all application-to-application connections.

Question 7

Answer d is correct. An Active Server Page is processed on the server, so it supports the largest number of browsers. The technologies listed in the other answers all require processing by the client; therefore, they are dependent on browser support.

Question 8

Answers a, b, c, and d are all correct. Generally, you want to validate input data as early as possible, so this is usually done in the user interface. However, sometimes more complex processing is required. All of the choices identify places where validation can be performed.

Question 9

Answer c is correct. You will likely use a student object and a teacher object and create collections of these objects as well. The collection objects would be students and teachers.

Question 10

Answer a is correct. The Data Access Object (DAO) model supports Data Definition Language (DDL) directly through objects—for example, tables, fields, and indexes. Active X Data Object (ADO) does not support DDL directly through objects; therefore, answer b is incorrect. ADO supports DDL through Structured Query Language (SQL) statements. ODBC does not have a programming object model; therefore, answer c is incorrect. And although OLE Database (OLE DB) does have a programming object model, the interfaces can't be used directly by Visual Basic; therefore, answer d is also incorrect.

Question 11

Answer b is correct. A Globally Unique Identifier (GUID) is a 128-bit integer (16-byte value) that is guaranteed to be unique.

Question 12

Answer c is correct. Version incompatible means at least one property or method that existed in the old component type library has been changed or removed. Existing client applications that have references to the component cannot use the new version. Answer a, version identical, means that the interfaces are all the same, so the new version of the component type library is exactly the same as the old one. The code inside methods or Property procedures may have been changed or enhanced, but this is transparent to client applications. Answer b, version compatible, means that objects and/or methods have been added to the type library, but no changes were made to existing properties or methods. Both old and new client applications can use the component. Answer d, version dependent, is not appropriate.

Question 13

Answer c is correct. Of the choices given, only a property sheet would have an Apply button.

Question 14

Answers a and b are correct. The primary key and the foreign key are used to enforce referential integrity. An index is used to improve performance for accessing data in a table. A stored procedure is a precompiled unit of code stored in a database. The stored procedure is executed on the database server and usually provides better performance than a query submitted from the client.

Question 15

Answer a is correct. The primary key is used to identify the column or group of columns that have a unique value in a table.

Question 16

Answer c is correct. An index is used to improve performance for accessing data in a table.

Question 17

Answers a, c, and d are correct. The briefcase, replication manager, and DAO programming all support database replication for Microsoft Access. The ADO object model does not support replication.

Question 18

Answers a, c, and d are correct. Dynamic Hypertext Markup Language (DHTML), Java applets, and ActiveX controls all require browser support; therefore, these technologies require browser-enhanced applications. Internet Server Application Programming Interface (ISAPI), a technology that performs processing in the server environment, is browser neutral.

Question 19

Answer c is correct. ActiveX Data Objects (ADO) is the recommended technology for new applications requiring access to a variety of data sources. Visual Basic library for SQL Server (VBSQL), a native interface to SQL Server, would not be appropriate, because it would not work with an Oracle database. DAO and Remote Data Objects (RDO) could be used; however, ADO is preferable to both DAO and RDO.

Question 20

Answer b is correct. Distributed COM (DCOM) is used to provide communication between Component Object Model (COM) components in a distributed application. Microsoft Message Queue Server (MSMQ), answer a, provides message queuing services. Connection pooling, answer c, is a strategy for efficiently sharing resources, and Remote Automation, answer d, is a technology that enables Automation across distributed systems. Remote Automation does provide communication between COM components, but it is an earlier technology used primarily for 16-bit platforms or 32-bit platforms that do not support DCOM. Both NT Server and NT Workstation support DCOM.

Question 21

Answer d is correct. The application will not be successful unless it solves the business problem.

Question 22

The correct answer is:

Product management

Satisfied customers

Program management

Delivery within project constraints

Development

Delivery to product specifications

Testing

Release after addressing all issues

User education

Improved user performance

Logistics management

Smooth product deployment

Question 23

Answer d is correct. Although the MSF Team Model defines six different roles, the same person can perform some of these roles, provided there is no conflict of interest. The team is independent of the organizational reporting structure; therefore, answers b and c are incorrect.

Question 24

The correct answer is:

Interview users to find out how they do their job

Prepare a functional specification

Define data objects and business objects

Create components for business and data services

Deploy components on target computers

Question 25

The correct answers are:

Envisioning

Vision/scope approved

Planning

Project plan approved

Development

Code complete

Stabilization

Release

Question 26

Answers b and c are correct.

Question 27

Answer c is correct. Stored database procedures execute on the server system running the database management system.

Question 28

Answer a is correct. You will see little or no change in performance. This is because the component is single threaded and it is CPU bound. Having another CPU available will be of no use for this component, because only one thread is available for execution. The additional CPU might handle some of the operating system overhead processing, but it is not possible to execute a single thread of execution simultaneously on multiple CPUs.

Question 29

Answer d is correct. There is a convention; File should appear first and Help should appear last.

Question 30

Answers a and b are correct. Static text is intended for labels and descriptive text in a window. The text appears on the surface of a window. Disabled (engraved or grayed) appearance is intended only to represent items not currently accessible or available. Read-only text should be displayed in a normal text box.

Question 31

Answer b is correct. Using terminal emulation, the legacy application runs in the mainframe environment where all the real application processing occurs. The terminal emulation software on the desktop computer displays a window showing the command interface of the mainframe application.

Question 32

Answer c is correct. The two-tier architecture does not scale well. Using ODBC, every client would require at least one connection to the database. It would be difficult to support the load at peak times. Answer a is incorrect, because the Visual Basic application could provide a Windows-style GUI, which was not available in the terminal emulation prototype. Answer b is incorrect, because retrieving the small amount of data required for this application can be very efficient using ODBC. And answer d is not true.

Question 33

Answer a is correct. Few changes were required to the mainframe application. In general, terminal emulation software requires no changes to existing applications. Action Aerospace modified their existing applications for the pilot, because they needed new capabilities that supported individual user access. Answer b is incorrect, because terminal emulation software does not exemplify the logical three-tier model. Answer c is incorrect, because no processing is off-loaded to the client system. Answer d is incorrect, because Action Aerospace determined the pilot was not suitable for enterprise deployment because of the user interface and scalability issues.

Question 34

Answer d is correct. The COM Transaction Integrator could be used to provide direct access to the Customer Information Control System (CICS) transactions in the legacy system. Based on what we know about Action Aerospace, answers a, b, and c are incorrect because these technologies are not being used by the Employee Time Card System to access mainframe data. However, these technologies could be used in another application design.

Question 35

The correct answer is:

Employees

Employee ID

Name

Shift

Timecards

TimecardID

EmployeeID

WeekEndingDate

TimecardEntries

TimecardID

ProjectCode

ActivityCode

Hours

Question 36

Answer c is correct. Referential integrity is used to enforce a relationship be-tween two tables. A one-to-many relationship exists between the Orders and Order Details tables. There is no such thing as a zero-to-many relationship.

Question 37

Answers a and b are correct. A one-to-zero or -many relationship supports a single order having zero, one, or many order detail entries. A one-to-many relationship is the same as a one-to-zero or one-to-many relationship.

Question 38

Answer b is correct. The ProductID field in the Order Details table is a foreign key to the ProductID field in the Products table. ProductID is the primary key in the Products Table. Together, OrderID and ProductID are the primary key for the Order Details table. Parent link and child link are bogus relational database terms.

Question 39

Answer c is correct. A many-to-many relationship exists between the two tables. When two tables have a many-to-many relationship, an intermediate table is used to link the two tables.

Question 40

Answer a is correct. Poor database performance is the primary reason for intentionally violating normalization rules and denormalizing a database design. Answer b is incorrect. The current design handles adding additional suppliers to the database. Answer c is incorrect, because changing the field definition has nothing to do with denormalization. And answer d is incorrect, because a denormalized database could be more difficult to maintain than a fully normalized database.

Question 41

Answer c is correct. The EnergyReporter application is based on the logical three-tier model. As such, access to all data is through data objects. A data bound control, typically found in the presentation services, would not be permitted in this application model. The presentation services tier requests all data through the business services tier, which then makes requests to the data services tier. In some cases, the presentation services may request data directly from the data services tier.

Question 42

Answer d is correct. Common dialog boxes are useful for providing common facilities, such as opening and saving files, printing files, choosing colors, and changing fonts. Answer a is not the best choice, because it is unlikely that a custom control would need to be written to provide this facility. Answers b and c are incorrect, because these controls are not appropriate for this purpose. The Winsock control allows you to easily access Transfer Control Protocol (TCP) and the User Datagram Protocol (UDP) network services. The ImageList control is used to store a collection of images you can then use on an associated control. For example, it can store the images that appear on a Toolbar control's buttons.

Question 43

The correct answer is:

> Obtain energy usage data from energy service provider
>
> Read energy usage data in different formats
>
> Convert energy usage data to a common format
>
> Load energy usage data into Staging database
>
> Validate energy usage data
>
> Create error reports
>
> Retrieve valid data from Staging database
>
> Load energy usage data into Energy Usage database
>
> Retrieve data from Energy Usage database
>
> Create customer reports

Question 44

The correct answers are b, c, and d. Active Server Pages (ASP), Common Gateway Interface (CGI), and Internet Services Application Program Interface (ISAPI) are all technologies that perform processing on the server. Therefore, they support the largest number of browsers. Dynamic HTML (DHTML) requires script processing on the client, which not all browsers support.

Question 45

Answers a and c are correct. The ASPs implemented by Power Patterns uses server-side scripting, so all the processing occurs on the server before the HTML is generated and sent to the clients. In particular, all of the report generation processing occurs on the server. The browser does the only processing that occurs on the client when it renders the HTML. This solution works with almost all browsers, because it requires no special browser features, other than supporting HTML. It is also possible to include client-side scripting in an ASP, but Power Patterns did not do this.

Question 46

Answer d is correct. Using a more powerful database management system will directly address the problem by processing the queries (in particular, the table joins) on the server, eliminating the need to transfer all the data across the network for processing by the client application. The result set of the query, several hundred rows of data, will still need to be transferred across the network, but this is manageable. Answers a, b, and c will do little to change the performance. The main performance bottleneck occurs because of the network traffic generated when all the table rows are accessed across the network. Because no processing occurs on the server with the current configuration, upgrading the server system with a more powerful processor and additional memory will do nothing. Upgrading everyone's laptop, not an attractive solution to present to management, will provide increased processing capabilities but will do little to reduce the network bottleneck. Rewriting the user interface in Visual Basic does nothing to alleviate the performance bottleneck.

Question 47

Answer c is correct. Version 1 of the application was written in Microsoft Access and stored the data in local tables. Data Access Objects (DAO) is the database object model used for the Jet database engine, which is the native database engine used by Microsoft Access. Therefore, answer c, DAO, is the best choice for accessing data in the local tables. Universal Data Access (UDA) is the name given to the Microsoft strategy for providing a common data access method. ActiveX Data Objects (ADO) and Remote Data Objects (RDO) are both data access object models, but neither is the first choice for accessing data in a local Access database table.

Question 48

The correct answer is:

Version 1

Uses local tables

Version 2

Uses local tables

Uses linked tables

Based on a file server model

Version 3

> Could utilize stored database procedures
>
> Uses local tables
>
> Uses linked tables
>
> Based on a client/server model
>
> Based on a two-tier architecture
>
> Uses ODBC

Note: Remember, in these types of questions, you may not use all the choices listed, and some of the choices may be used more than once. Looking at the choices:

Could utilize stored database procedures

> Only Version 3, which uses SQL Server as the relational database management system (RDBMS), could use stored database procedures.

Uses local tables

> All three versions use local tables to store local data. However, Version 1 also uses local tables to store the data imported from the production system.

Uses linked tables

> Versions 2 and 3 use linked tables to store the data imported from the production system.

Based on a file server model

> Version 2 is based on a file server model.

Based on a client/server model

> Version 3 is based on a client/server model.

Utilizes HTTP

> None of the versions use HTTP.

Based on a two-tier architecture

> Version 3 is based on a two-tier architecture.

Based on a three-tier architecture

None of the versions are based on a three-tier architecture.

Uses ODBC

Version 3 uses ODBC.

Question 49

Answer a is correct. Because the application is based on linked tables and uses ODBC, few application changes should be required. New ODBC drivers supporting the Oracle database would need to be installed on each client workstation, and each client would need a Data Source Name (DSN) that identifies the Oracle database. Most of the conversion effort would be focused on the server where the SQL Server database tables would need to be converted to Oracle database tables. If stored procedures have been utilized, they will also need to be converted from SQL Server to Oracle.

Question 50

Answers a and c are correct. Version 3 of the BacklogAndBookings application is a desktop application, even though it accesses a back-end database. It is also a fat client, as opposed to a thin client, because most of the application logic is found in the client. It is not a Web-based application.

Glossary

. . . .

Access SQL—The version of Structured Query Language (SQL) used in Microsoft Access. Access SQL supports extensions and enhancements to the standard SQL language.

accessibility—Accessibility refers to the characteristic of making computers and computer applications accessible to a wider range of users than would otherwise be the case. The Windows operating system supports features an application can utilize to compensate for many types of disabilities.

ACID—An acronym for the basic transaction properties of Atomicity, Consistency, Isolation, and Durability.

ActiveX—A set of language-independent interoperability technologies that enable software components written in different languages to work together in networked environments. The core technology elements of ActiveX are Component Object Model (COM) and Distributed COM (DCOM).

ActiveX component—*See* component.

ActiveX control—A COM object you place on a form or Web page to enable or enhance a user's interaction with an application. ActiveX controls have events and can be incorporated into other controls. The controls have an .OCX filename extension. Previously referred to as custom controls and object linking and embedding (OLE) controls.

ActiveX Document—A Windows-based, non-HTML application embedded in a browser, providing a way for the functionality of that application to be accessible from within the browser interface.

ADO (ActiveX Data Objects)—A programming-level interface for data access based on a set of easy-to-use objects, properties, and methods. ADO exposes an object model incorporating data connection objects, data command objects, Recordset objects, and collections within these objects. ADO is the Automation wrapper for OLE DB and can be used with any database having an ODBC driver.

ANSI (American National Standards Institute)—The ANSI character set is an 8-bit character set used by Microsoft Windows that allows you to represent up to 256 characters (0 through 255) using your keyboard. The American Standard Code for Information Interchange (ASCII) character set is a subset of the ANSI set.

API (application programming interface)—A set of calling conventions in programming that define how a service is invoked through the application. Often API refers to a set of routines an application program uses to request and carry out lower-level services performed by a computer's operating system.

application model—As defined by the Microsoft Solution Framework, the application model provides a blueprint for designing modular applications in order to include the flexibility needed for scaling, performance, enhancement, and distribution.

ASCII (American Standard Code for Information Interchange)— The most popular coding method used by small computers for converting letters, numbers, punctuation, and control codes into digital form. The ASCII character set is a 7-bit character set and is the same as the first 128 characters (0 through 127) in the ANSI character set. In general, ASCII text contains no formatting characters enabling multiple programs to share data and documents.

ASP (Active Server Pages)—ASP is a language-neutral, server-side scripting environment used to create and run Web server applications. An Active Server Page is a mix of executable script and HTML. Internet Information Server (IIS) supports the processing environment for executing the scripts in ASP.

atomicity—The "all or nothing" characteristic of a transaction ensuring that either all actions of the transaction complete or none complete.

attributes—*See* columns.

Automation—Sometimes referred to as ActiveX Automation or OLE Automation. A language-neutral way to manipulate a COM component's methods from outside an application. Automation is typically used to create components that expose methods to programming tools and macro languages.

Automation object—An object exposed to other applications or programming tools through automation interfaces.

availability—Availability is a measurement specifying how much uptime the system must provide and how much downtime can be tolerated. Reliability of the system depends on the system meeting the availability requirements.

bandwidth—Bandwidth is the difference between the highest and lowest frequency a particular line can carry. For example, a telephone line accommodates a bandwidth of 3,000 Hz, the difference between the lowest (300 Hz) and highest (3,300 Hz) frequencies it can carry. In networking environments, a higher bandwidth, expressed in bits per second (bps), indicates faster data transfer rates.

business logic—*See* business rules.

business needs—Also known as business requirements, business needs are the critical requirements necessary for the business to operate and remain solvent. Software applications utilized by a business must satisfy actual business needs.

business process—A business process refers to a specific task or method that is part of the overall operation of the business. Business processes are usually implemented in the business services of an application.

business requirements—*See* business needs.

business rule—An algorithm that defines specific steps required for performing a process essential to the operation of a business. Business rules may involve a combination of validation edits, logon verifications, database lookups, policies, and computational transformations. Business rules define an organization's way of doing business. They are also known as business logic.

business services—In a three-tier architecture, business services apply business rules and perform the logic to complete a business task. Each business will have a unique set of business services depending on the tasks necessary to do business.

by reference—A way of passing the address, rather than the value, of an argument to a procedure. This allows the procedure to access the actual variable. As a result, the variable's value can be changed by the procedure to which it is passed. This is the default mechanism for passing arguments in Visual Basic.

by value—A way of passing the value, rather than the address, of an argument to a procedure. This allows the procedure to access a copy of the variable. As a result, the variable's actual value cannot be changed by the procedure to which it is passed. This is the default mechanism for passing arguments in C++.

capacity—In network communications, capacity is a metric for measuring the ability of the communication link to carry network traffic and support multiple resources. The capacity metric usually includes the server and is measured, in part, by the number of connections established and maintained by the server.

CGI (Common Gateway Interface)—A set of interfaces describing how a Web server communicates with software on the same computer. Any software can be a CGI program if it handles input and output according to the CGI standard.

class—The formal definition of an object. The class acts as the template from which an instance of an object is created at runtime. The class defines the properties of the object and the methods used to control the object's behavior.

class module—In Visual Basic, a source code module containing the definition of a class. The module defines the properties and methods for the class.

client-side scripting—A script executed on the client system, usually by the browser. *See also* scripting.

client/server—A model of computing whereby a client requests services from another entity, the server. The server responds to the client. This model is popular for creating client/server applications in which a client running on a desktop or personal computer accesses information on remote servers or host computers. The client portion of the application is typically optimized for user interaction, whereas the server portion provides the centralized, multiuser functionality. In a client-server environment, application processing is performed by components on both the client and the server. This can be differentiated from a file server environment in which no application components run on the file server.

CLSID (class identifier)—A unique identification tag (UUID) associated with a class object. A class object intended to create more than one object registers its CLSID in the system registration database to enable clients to locate and load the executable code associated with the object.

collection—An object containing a set of related objects. A collection is sometimes referred to as a dictionary, because you can look up an item in the collection using a key. An object's position in the collection can change whenever a change occurs in the collection; therefore, the position of any specific object in the collection may vary. All collections have a **Count** property.

columns—In a relational database table, columns store the characteristics or attributes about the table. That is, they store the facts about the items stored in the table. Each table has a fixed number of columns.

COM (Component Object Model)—The object-oriented programming model that defines how objects interact within a single application or between applications. In COM, client software accesses an object through interfaces implemented on the object. COM provides a standard model for building reusable binary components and creating objects from those components, building components independent of source language, enabling components that interact with one another independent of location, and creating new versions of components.

component—A compiled, discrete unit of code based on the Component Object Model (COM) that encapsulates a set of functionality. Earlier versions of components were referred to as OLE Automation servers, OLE Automation controllers, and ActiveX components. The functionality in a component is accessed through well-specified interfaces. A component can execute either on a client computer or on a server computer, transparent to the calling application, through DCOM. Components running within the calling application process use the file extensions .DLL or .OCX. These are known as in-process servers. Components running outside of the calling application process use the file extension .EXE. These are known as out-of-process servers.

COMTI (COM Transaction Integrator)—A Microsoft enabling technology that allows interoperability with IBM transaction-oriented mainframe applications. COMTI encapsulates Customer Information Control System (CICS) and Information Management Systems (IMS) applications behind Automation objects.

conceptual design—Conceptual design is the process of acquiring, documenting, and validating user and business perspectives of a problem and its solution. The goal of conceptual design is to understand what users do and to identify business needs. The output is scenarios.

consistency—One of the basic characteristics of a transaction ensuring that at the end of the transaction data updates have not violated any of the constraints on the data and that all of the data integrity rules are still enforced.

console application—Console-based applications are text based and don't require any graphical user interface. Although console-based applications are contained within a window on the screen, the window contains only text characters.

constraints—Constraints are rules the relational database management system automatically enforces for you. Constraints limit the possible values you can enter into a column or columns. Constraints are used to supply default values, validate data values, enforce the relationships between tables, and ensure unique values.

contextual help—Contextual help, also referred to as context-sensitive help, provides information about the object with which the user is interacting. Contextual help takes into consideration the context of the activity the user is currently performing and tries to answer questions like "What is this?" and "Why should I use this?".

controls—Controls are graphic objects representing the properties or operations of other objects. Some controls are used to initiate an operation, while others are used to enter, view, and edit data values.

DAO (Data Access Objects)—The programming interface for the Microsoft Jet database engine. DAO is based on a hierarchical object model and provides access to all the objects used in the Jet architecture. Because Jet allows links to ODBC-compliant data sources, it is also possible to access these ODBC data sources using DAO.

data model—A representation of real-world objects using entities in a database.

data normalization—A systematic process to minimize the duplication of information in a relational database through effective table design.

data services—In a three-tier architecture, data services manage the storage of persistent data.

DBCS (Double Byte Characters Set)—A character set that uses one or two bytes to represent a character, allowing more than 256 characters to be represented.

DCOM (Distributed Component Object Model)—Additions to the Component Object Model (COM) that facilitate the transparent distribution of objects over networks and over the Internet. When a client and component reside on different machines, DCOM simply replaces the local interprocess communication with a network protocol. Neither the client nor the component is aware that the communication link spans multiple computers. DCOM is part of the specification managed by The Open Group for deployment across heterogeneous platforms.

DDE (Dynamic Data Exchange)—An established interprocess communications protocol for exchanging data between Windows-based applications in a variety of formats.

DDL (Data Definition Language)—SQL statements used to create and manage database entities in a relational database. **CREATE TABLE...** and **DROP INDEX...** are examples of DDL statements.

denormalization—Intentionally modifying the design of a relational database and violating the normalization rules. The major reason for doing this is to improve database performance.

DHTML (Dynamic Hypertext Markup Language)—A feature included in Microsoft Internet Explorer 4.0 and later that gives Web developers the ability to create interactive Web pages that can feature multimedia effects. Using the scripting language of your choice, you can create, move, and modify all the elements of a Web page—tags, attributes, images, objects, text, and CSS. Dynamic HTML also provides full support for keyboard, mouse, and focus events on all page elements.

dialog box—A dialog box provides a mechanism for the exchange of information between the user and the application. Dialog boxes are often used to obtain additional information from the user to complete an operation. A dialog box usually contains an OK command button as well as a Cancel command button.

distributed application—An application model in which a problem is solved, or a task is accomplished, by multiple applications running separately and working together. The different applications may be distributed on one system or across multiple systems.

DLL (Dynamic Link Library)—A Windows term for a set of routines that can be called from procedures and are loaded and linked into your application at runtime.

DML (Data Manipulation Language)—SQL statements used to manage the data in a relational database. **SELECT, INSERT, UPDATE,** and **DELETE** are examples of DML statements.

drop-down menu—A list of menu items displayed after a user chooses a menu title from the menu bar.

durability—One of the basic characteristics of a transaction ensuring that committed updates made during the transaction, such as a change to a database, remain permanent even if the system experiences a failure, including communication failures, process failures, and disk-system failures.

EBCDIC (Extended Binary Coded Decimal Interchange Code)—A coding scheme developed by IBM for use with its computers as a standard method of assigning binary (numeric) values to alphabetic, numeric, punctuation, and transmission-control characters. Each EBCDIC character is based on an eight-bit value, which allows you to represent up to 256 characters (0 through 255).

Empty—A value indicating that no beginning value has been assigned to a variable. Empty variables are 0 in a numeric context, or zero-length in a string context.

encapsulation—A technique in which a component implements a specific piece of application functionality and exposes a set of methods and properties that can be used by other applications and components to access that functionality. Encapsulation isolates the implementation details to a single component. If the functionality needs to be updated, changes are confined to a single part of the application.

entities—*See* tables.

ERA (Entity Relationship Analysis)—The data modeling process of identifying the entities, their attributes, and the relationships between them.

extensibility—The capacity to extend or enhance a solution beyond its original capabilities.

fault tolerant—Fault-tolerant systems represent systems with the highest level of availability. One of the criteria for these systems is that there is no single point for failure within the system. To accomplish this, a true fault-tolerant system will usually have total redundancy of hardware and software components as well as data.

first normal form—The first level of data normalization implying no repeating groups. For a table to be in first normal form, the table can contain no repeating groups.

foreign key—A foreign key is a column, or group of columns, in one table that references the primary key in another table. Foreign keys allow the enforcement of referential integrity by requiring that a primary key exists in a "master" table before related entries can be created in a "detail" table.

FTP (File Transfer Protocol)—The Internet standard high-speed protocol for downloading or transferring files across the network.

GUID (Globally Unique Identifier)—A 16-byte value (128-bit integer) guaranteed to be unique. GUIDs are generated using the unique identifier on a network adapter, the current date and time, and a sequence number. GUIDs allow any party to create unique identifiers that are statistically guaranteed not to overlap with other similarly created identifiers.

HTML (Hypertext Markup Language)—HTML is a system of marking up or tagging a document so that it can be published on the World Wide Web. Documents prepared in HTML include reference graphics and formatting tags. You use a Web browser (such as Microsoft Internet Explorer) to view these documents.

HTTP (Hypertext Transfer Protocol)—The Internet standard protocol for Web server file input and output and for transferring Web pages across the network.

human factors—Application characteristics addressing the aspects of who the end users will be, how they will use the system, and what special requirements they have.

IIS (Internet Information Server)—The Microsoft Internet Information Server, included with Microsoft Windows NT Server, provides facilities for Web publishing and file transfer and enables intranet- and Internet-based applications. In addition to standard HTML pages, IIS supports Active Server Pages (ASP), a language-neutral, server-side scripting environment used to create and run Web server applications.

index—A database object that provides access to data in the rows of a table, based on key values. Indexes provide quick access to data and can enforce uniqueness on the rows in a table.

in-process component—Also known as an in-process server, an in-process component is a COM component that runs within the calling application process. Thus, the component shares the same address space as the client that calls it. In-process components use the file extensions .DLL or .OCX.

in-process server—*See* in-process component.

interface—The point at which a connection is made between two elements so they can work with one another. In the Component Object Model, an interface refers to a group of related functions providing access to COM objects. The set of interfaces defines a contract that allows objects to interact according to the COM specification.

Internet—A collection of dissimilar computer networks joined together by gateways that handle data transfer and the conversion of messages from the sending network to the protocols used by the receiving networks. These networks and gateways use the TCP/IP suite of protocols. The Internet evolved from the ARPA network, a project sponsored by the Department of Defense's Advanced Research Project Administration (DARPA).

intranet—An internal corporate network implemented by using Internet standards, technologies, and products.

IP (Internet Protocol)—The packet-switching protocol for network communications between Internet host computers. IP is not a fail-proof delivery system and cannot guarantee the arrival or accuracy of packets.

IPC (interprocess communication)—IPC refers to the mechanisms for facilitating communications and data sharing between applications. IPC is central to distributed applications because distributed applications are spread across multiple processes and often multiple systems.

ISAPI (Internet Server API)—An application programming interface for interfacing an application with an Internet Server such as IIS. Because ISAPI programs execute on the server, the technology can be used with a large number of Web browsers.

isolation—One of the basic characteristics of a transaction ensuring that concurrent transactions do not interfere with each other. One transaction cannot read the partial and uncommitted results of another transaction, which might create inconsistencies.

Java—A derivative of the C++ language, Java is SunSoft's distributed programming language, offered as an open standard.

Jet—A Microsoft desktop database engine available in most of Microsoft's development tools and office products, including Microsoft Access, Microsoft Office, and Microsoft Visual Basic.

latency—A measure of the time taken to retrieve data through a network.

legacy system—A term used when referring to existing applications that still perform functions critical to the operation of a business. Although legacy systems are usually deployed on a mainframe computer system, they also exist in the minicomputer and desktop environment.

localization—A set of information corresponding to a given language and country. Localization affects the language of predefined programming terms and locale-specific settings.

logical design—Logical design is a view of the solution from the project team's perspective that defines the solution as a set of cooperating objects and their services. These services are often grouped into the categories of user, business, and data services. The goal of a logical design is to describe the structure of the solution and the communication among its elements.

logical three-tier model—*See* three-tier logical model.

mainframe—Mainframes are the large, older computer systems still in use at many businesses. Mainframe systems are often associated with batch processing, although many mainframe systems also run critical online transaction processing applications.

maintainability—Maintainability is the capability of being able to keep the application in working order.

many-to-many relationship—Two tables have a many-to-many relationship when for every row in the first tables there can be many corresponding rows in the second table, and for every row in the second table, there can be many corresponding rows in the first table. A many-to-many relationship is modeled by breaking it into multiple one-to-many relationships.

master-detail relationship—*See* one-to-many relationship.

MDAC (Microsoft Data Access Components)—The technologies enabling Universal Data Access. These components include ActiveX Data Objects (ADOs), Remote Data Service (RDS), OLE DB, and open database connectivity (ODBC).

MDI (multiple-document interface)—An application using a single primary window, called a parent window, to visually contain a set of related child windows. Each child window is essentially a primary window but is constrained to appear within the parent window.

menu bar—The menu bar is the most common type of menu. It is displayed across the top of a window beneath the title bar and provides a set of menu titles, each of which produces a drop-down menu of menu items or choices.

Microsoft SQL Server—The Microsoft relational database management system (RDBMS) used for deploying robust, scalable database applications on a Windows NT platform.

modal—A state of a secondary window. A secondary window in the modal state requires the user to complete all activity within the window and close it before switching to another window. A secondary window can be modal with respect to the application, or it can be modal with respect to the system.

modeless—A state of a secondary window. A secondary window in the modeless state allows the user to switch between it and other windows, including other secondary windows or primary windows.

moniker—A name uniquely identifying a COM object similar to a directory path name. Monikers support an operation known as binding, which is the process of locating the object named by the moniker, activating it or loading it in memory (if it isn't already there), and returning an interface pointer to it.

MSF (Microsoft Solution Framework)—The Microsoft Solution Framework provides a set of models and measurable milestones that can provide essential guidelines as well as a roadmap for planning, building, and managing Information Technology projects.

MSMQ (Microsoft Message Queue Server)—MSMQ provides services that allow you to manage queues of messages and route messages between queues. It provides a technology for interoperability between two different applications. One application creates a message and sends it to a queue. Another application, or another part of the same application, retrieves the message from the queue and processes it.

MTS (Microsoft Transaction Server)—Software development software providing component-based transaction middleware and access to distributed transaction services. MTS combines features of a transaction processing monitor and an object-request broker. In addition, MTS automatically manages security and threading on the system.

multitier architecture—A multitier architecture is a software design based on splitting the application into separate functional components. Generally, the application is designed around three tiers: presentation (user), business, and data services. Multitier applications, also known as three-tier applications, are often implemented with component services based on the COM Object Model.

n-tier application—A logical extension of the three-tier application is the n-tier application. An n-tier application is a distributed application in which one or more of the three original tiers have been separated into additional tiers. This provides another level of abstraction for describing the model.

named pipes—An interprocess communication mechanism allowing one process to communicate with another local or remote process.

native database interface—A native database interface is the native facility provided to access the data in the database. Usually, this is provided by procedures in a support library. This type of interface is also referred to as a proprietary interface. A native interface often provides access to unique database facilities and features not accessible through other database access mechanisms. In addition, using a native database interface may optimize database access performance. The main disadvantage to a native database interface is that the application is then tied to a specific database.

normalization—*See* data normalization.

Nothing—The special value indicating an object variable is no longer associated with any actual object.

Null—A value indicating a variable contains no valid data. Null is the result of an explicit assignment of Null to a variable or any operation between expressions containing Null.

ODBC (Open Database Connectivity)—A vendor-neutral interface, based on the SQL Access Group specifications. Using ODBC, an application can access data in a heterogeneous environment of relational and nonrelational databases. ODBC drivers are typically used to provide access to SQL databases such as Microsoft SQL Server and Oracle.

ODBC API—The Application Programming Interface that allows an application to directly call procedures in the ODBC library.

ODBC data source—An ODBC data source definition must be created for each database to be accessed using ODBC. This information includes the database name, the server on which the database resides, and the network information required to access the server. The specific information required to define an ODBC data source varies depending on the requirements of its ODBC driver.

ODBC driver manager—In the ODBC architecture, this is the component providing the interface between the application and the ODBC driver for the target data source. The ODBC driver manager, named ODBC.DLL, loads the ODBC driver for the data source, passes requests to the driver from the application, and returns results to the application from the driver.

OLE (object linking and embedding)—A protocol based on the Component Object Model (COM) that enables the creation of compound documents. With OLE, an object, such as a spreadsheet, can be linked or embedded into an OLE container such as a Microsoft Access form.

OLE DB (OLE Database)—OLE DB is one of the key supporting pieces for Universal Data Access. OLE DB provides a set of COM interfaces and is based on a three-layered architecture of data providers, optional service providers, and data consumers.

one-to-many relationship—Two tables have a one-to-many relationship if for every row in the first table, there can be zero, one, or many rows in the second table. However, for every row in the second table, there is only one row in the first table. One-to-many relationships are the most common type of relationship found in the relational data model. Sometimes the tables in a one-to-many relationship are referred to as a parent/child or master/detail relationship.

one-to-one relationship—Two tables have a one-to-one relationship if for every row in the first table there is at most one row in the second table, and if for every row in the second table, there is at most one row in the first table. The two tables in a one-to-one relationship will most likely have the same primary key.

one-to-zero-or-many relationship—*See* one-to-many relationship.

out-of-process component—Also known as an out-of-process server, an out-of-process component is a COM component running outside the calling application process. Thus, the component and the container application run in separate memory spaces. Out-of-process servers use the file extension .EXE.

out-of-process server—*See* out-of-process component.

parent-child relationship—*See* one-to-many relationship.

performance—Performance is how fast the system runs and how quickly it can complete a requested task. Many different metrics are used to measure performance. A number of factors also determine performance, including workload, hardware configuration, and database activity. The solution design plays a major factor in the system performance.

physical design—Physical design is a view of the solution from the developer's perspective. It defines the components, services, and technologies for the solution. The goal of physical design is to apply real-world technology constraints to the logical model, including implementation and performance considerations. The outputs are components, a specific user interface design for a particular platform, and a physical database design.

pop-up menu—Pop-up menus display a list of menu items appropriate for an object in its current context. Pop-up menus are displayed at the location of the object.

presentation services—In a three-tier architecture, presentation services, sometimes referred to as user services, establish the user interface and provide the facility for interacting with the users.

primary key—The column, or group of columns, providing a unique value for each row in a relational database table.

primary window—The primary window is the main window in which most viewing and editing activity takes place.

procedure—A named sequence of statements executed as a unit. For example, **Function** and **Sub** are types of Visual Basic procedures. Procedures are grouped together into modules.

process—The address space where application code resides. Each process is allocated a unique virtual address space, which is a set of addresses available for the process's threads to use. Virtual address space appears to be four gigabytes (GBs) in size. The lower two GBs are reserved for system storage; the upper two GBs are reserved for program storage. A process does not execute code.

Process Model—As defined by the Microsoft Solution Framework, the Process Model shows how to organize project activities in order to make better development tradeoffs. The Process Model is one of the core MSF models.

project scope—Project scope maps the project vision against the reality of what can actually be done toward achieving this vision. In particular, a number of constraints including technology, resources, budget, and schedule will all influence the actual project scope.

property—A named attribute of an object. Properties define object characteristics such as size, color, and screen location, or the state of an object, such as enabled or disabled.

RDBMS (relational database management system)—The engine managing a data store based on the relational data model.

RDOs (Remote Data Objects)—A high-level object interface that directly calls ODBC for optimal speed, control, and ease of programming.

referential integrity—Referential integrity is a set of rules to ensure that the relationships between two related tables are valid. In particular, referential integrity ensures that the relationship between the tables is preserved when you enter new rows or delete existing rows from the tables.

registry—The database repository for information about the computer's configuration, including hardware, installed software, environment settings, and other information. Both Windows 95 and Windows NT operating systems utilize a registry.

relational database—A database based on the relational model in which data is organized into a series of tables. Mathematical operations can be performed on these tables to produce new tables.

rows—Each unique set of data values in a relational database table is stored in a row of the table. A row is analogous to a record in a sequential file structure. The number of rows a table contains varies and is determined by the number of data items for the particular table.

RPC (Remote Procedure Call)—A standard allowing one process to make calls to functions executed in another process. The process can be on the same computer or on a different computer in the network.

scalability—Scalability is the ability of the system to respond to growth. As with many other system characteristics, alternative architectures can be utilized to handle different scaling requirements.

scope—*See* project scope.

scripting—Scripting is the use of a scripting language to provide programmatic capabilities. Scripting is made possible by plugging a scripting engine into a host application. A scripting engine enables the processing of a specific scripting language such as VBScript or JScript. Examples of host applications containing scripting engines are Microsoft Internet Explorer and Internet Information Server with Active Server Pages.

SDI (single document interface)—An application using a single primary window with a set of supplemental secondary windows. SDI is a single instance model. If a user reopens an object, you activate the existing window.

second normal form—The second level of data normalization implying no partial dependencies. For a table to be in second normal form, it must be in first normal form and each nonkey column in the table must be fully dependent on the entire primary key.

secondary window—Secondary windows supplement the primary window by allowing users to specify parameters or options or provide more specific details about the objects in the primary window. Secondary windows are often used for validation of input, displaying property sheets, displaying dialog boxes, displaying message boxes, and displaying wizards.

server-side scripting—A script executed on the server system, usually by the Web server. Active Server Pages are an example of server-side scripting. *See also* scripting.

services model—A logical model based on the concept of modularizing an application into components where each module provides a specific service. These are usually grouped into three categories of service: presentation services, business services, and data services.

shortcut key—Shortcut keys, also known as accelerator keys, provide a convenient way to invoke a task with a single keystroke. Shortcut keys are usually a combination of the CTRL key with a letter or one of the function keys (F1 through F12).

single-tier application—An implementation of the logical three-tier model where all tiers are physically implemented within a single tier.

SMS (Microsoft System Management Server)—Part of the Microsoft Windows NT BackOffice Suite used to automate the tracking and upgrading of software on client computers. SMS includes desktop management and software distribution.

SNA (Systems Network Architecture)—A widely used communications framework developed by IBM to define network functions and to establish standards for enabling its different models of computers to exchange and process data.

sockets—Sockets are interfaces between programs and transport protocols controlling the flow of data. The Microsoft Windows Sockets interface is used by numerous protocols, including TCP/IP, NWLink, and AppleTalk. Using the TCP/IP protocol, Windows Sockets can be used to facilitate Internet communications.

Solutions Design Model—As defined by the Microsoft Solution Framework, the Solutions Design Model shows how to design applications from a user and business perspective in order to anticipate user needs.

SQL (Structured Query Language)—A language used in querying, updating, and managing relational databases.

SQL Access Group—An industry consortium composed of representatives from a number of different database vendors. The SQL Access Group developed the original Open Database Connectivity (ODBC) Specification describing an open architecture for data access.

SQL Server—*See* Microsoft SQL Server.

status bar—The status bar, located on the bottom edge of the window, can be used for displaying messages, progress indicators, and state information.

stored procedures—Precompiled software procedures managed and run within a relational database management system (RDBMS). Stored procedures provide a reusable service that can be shared by multiple applications and users. They typically contain business processes and data manipulation functions. In a client/server application the procedures execute on the server.

tables—Tables in a relational database are used to store data about the objects being modeled in the database. Sometimes referred to as entities, tables are made up of rows and columns.

task help—Task help provides explanations to the user on how to accomplish specific tasks or activities. It can involve a number of procedures presented in task Help topic windows.

TCP (Transmission Control Protocol)—A protocol that breaks data into packets for transmission over a network. TCP is a reliable, sequenced network communication method.

TCP/IP (Transmission Control Protocol/Internet Protocol)—Networking protocols enabling communication across networks despite diverse hardware architectures and multiple operating systems. Internet communications is based on TCP/IP.

Team Model—As defined by the Microsoft Solution Framework, the Team Model shows how to organize people to build high-performance teams. The Team Model is one of the core MSF models.

third normal form—The third level of data normalization implying no transitive dependencies. For a table to be in third normal form, it must be in second normal form, and all nonkey columns in the table must be mutually independent.

thread—Code contained in the address space of a process is executed by threads. A thread is the entity that the operating system schedules for using the CPU; they are often referred to as threads of execution. The first thread in a process, called the primary thread, is created by the operating system. The primary thread can then create other process threads. In Windows NT, a process terminates when all the threads contained in the process have ended.

three-tier logical model—A model that groups the functions of an application into three logical categories of service: presentation services, business services, and data services.

tooltips—Tooltips are small pop-up windows displaying the name of a control when the control has no text label. They are activated automatically when the pointing device is moved over the control.

Transact SQL—The version of Structured Query Language (SQL) used in Microsoft SQL Server. Transact SQL provides extensions and enhancements to the standard SQL language unique to Microsoft SQL Server.

transaction—A unit of work performed as an atomic operation. That is, all the operations within a transaction succeed or fail as a whole.

two-tier application—An implementation of the logical three-tier model in which the tiers are physically implemented in two separate tiers. This is the model used for the classic client/server application.

type library—A file or component within another file containing standard descriptions of exposed objects, properties, and methods.

UDA (Universal Data Access)—The Microsoft strategy for providing a common method to access data. It supports access to any type of data, regardless of where the data is located, and a programming interface that is tool-and-language independent.

Unicode—A fixed-width, 16-bit, worldwide character encoding standard. Unicode can represent all the world's characters in modern computer use, including technical and other special symbols. Windows NT processes characters internally in Unicode.

universal storage—A technique for solving the problems associated with accessing multiple types of data sources by putting all the data into a single data store. Universal storage is usually not practical because of the large number of data types involved and the volume of existing data that must be converted.

user interface—The graphical user interface (GUI) and logic allowing the user to interact with an application.

user services—*See* presentation services.

VBA (Visual Basic for Applications)—The development environment and language found in Visual Basic that can be hosted by applications. Office 97 components including Microsoft Word, Microsoft Excel, and Microsoft Access host VBA.

VBSQL—The Visual Basic library for SQL Server.

Visual Basic Script—A subset of the Visual Basic language used as a scripting language for Web pages. Scripts can be either server-sided, which execute on the server, or client-sided, which execute on the client.

Windows Sockets—*See* sockets.

wizard—A wizard is a series of pages displayed in a secondary window that helps a user complete a task. The pages may request the user to supply data that is then used to complete the task.

WWW (World Wide Web)—A set of services running on top of the Internet providing a cost-effective way of publishing information, the Web is a collection of Internet host systems making these services available on the Internet using the Hypertext Transfer Protocol (HTTP) protocol. Web-based information is usually delivered in the form of hypertext and hypermedia using Hypertext Markup Language (HTML). WWW services enable delivering business applications to any connected user in the world.

Index

CERTIFIED CRAMMER SOCIETY

A breed apart, a cut above the rest—a true professional. Highly skilled and superbly trained, certified IT professionals are unquestionably the world's most elite computer experts. In an effort to appropriately recognize this privileged crowd, The Coriolis Group is proud to introduce the Certified Crammer Society. If you are a certified IT professional, it is our pleasure to invite you to become a Certified Crammer Society member.

Membership is free to all certified professionals and benefits include a membership kit that contains your official membership card and official Certified Crammer Society blue denim ball cap emblazoned with the Certified Crammer Society crest— proudly displaying the Crammer motto "Phi Slamma Cramma"—and featuring a genuine leather bill. The kit also includes your password to the Certified Crammers-Only Web site containing monthly discreet messages designed to provide you with advance notification about certification testing information, special book excerpts, and inside industry news not found anywhere else; monthly Crammers-Only discounts on selected Coriolis titles; *Ask the Series Editor* Q and A column; cool contests with great prizes; and more.

GUIDELINES FOR MEMBERSHIP

Registration is free to professionals certified in Microsoft, A+, or Oracle DBA.
Coming soon: Sun Java, Novell, and Cisco. Send or email your contact information and
proof of your certification (test scores, membership card, or official letter) to:

Certified Crammer Society Membership Chairperson
THE CORIOLIS GROUP, LLC
14455 North Hayden Road, Suite 220, Scottsdale, Arizona 85260-6949
Fax: 480.483.0193 • Email: ccs@coriolis.com

APPLICATION

Name:

Address:

Society Alias:

Choose a secret code name to correspond with us
and other Crammer Society members.
Please use no more than eight characters.

Email: